# Youth's Introduction to Trade and Business ... 9Th Ed., Rev. and Improved, with the Addition of an Appendix, Containing the Methods of Solving All the Intricate Questions

## Benjamin Webb, Martin Clare

# T O

## Mafter GEORGE ONSLOW,

ONLY SON OF

### The Right Hon. ARTHUR ONSLOW, Efq;

SPEAKER of the Honourable HOUSE of COMMONS.

DEAR SIR!

FROM the large Experience I have had of your excellent Capacity, and your amiable Difpofition, I have pregnant Hopes of your becoming one Day a confiderable, that is, a wife, a good, and a ufeful Man.

FROM this Expectation it is, that I am ambitious of prefenting you this Edition of a fmall Work, which I have the Pleafure to imagine will be of Service to You, Sir, when you come to dip into NUMBERS; a Qualification equal, if not fuperior in Value, to moft we learn befides.

YOUR Worthy Father fits, where he has been long a Witnefs of the Advantage, with which the Calculift and Accomptant are always heard. And no Wonder; fince Arguments, drawn from Arithmetical Computations, carry with them uncommon Weight, having their Foundation in Reafon and in Truth.

I am, DEAR SIR,
Your moft Affectionate, and
Moft Obliged, Humble Servant,

SOHO-SQUARE,
Jan. 1, 1739.

Martin Clare.

# THE
# PREFACE.

IN the Commerce of the World, Difpatch in Bufinefs is no ordinary Accomplifhment; which being the Refult of a well-directed Education, it cannot be amifs in a Treatife of this Nature, to touch on thofe Parts of it, which are more immediately neceffary for forming the Man of Bufinefs.

After the Youth's firft Years have been employed in READ- ING his native Language, and proper Care has been taken to explain and inform him of the Meaning and Force of Words as they prefent; the next Step is to initiate him in the Rudi- ments of GRAMMAR : In which, at firft, nothing is more material, than to be very particular in the regular Divifion and Formation of Syllables. While this is doing, it is necffary for him to learn to WRITE; in which, the Teacher will find fufficient Reafon to exercife his Vigilance, and to guard againft the ill Habits his Charge will be apt to contract, both in Pofture and Performance.

It is not my Defign to defcribe at large what Part of Grammar-learning is moft neceffary for this End, nor to trace out the Methods by which it is to be effected; thofe muft be left to the Skill and Difcretion of his Inftructor: I fhall, there- fore, only recommend two Things, not generally made ufe of.

I. If the Scholar be enjoined to copy all his Exercifes, after Correction, into a fair Book, it will not only point out to him his Miftakes, and inform him how to mend them, but will even infenfibly improve his Hand, and fix it in a bold and manly Character.

II. As the principal End of inftructing a Youth, defigned for Bufinefs, in the Latin Tongue, is to make him a greater Mafter of his own; the Way to apply, and render it moft effectual to that End, is to ufe him frequently to Englifh Tranflations. The Meaning and Senfe of his Authors will thereby be impreffed on his Mind, with greater Advantage, and in Time, he will acquire a clear, juft and natural Man- ner of expreffing his Thoughts, on all Occafions; to which, if the Reading of good Authors in our own Language be added, a due Proficiency may be expected, not only in Spelling and
Propriety

Propriety of Stile, but also in that Elegance and good Sense, which distinguish one Man from another, and are absolutely requisite for all, that hope to be considerable in the World.

As the FRENCH TONGUE is, at present, the general Language of Europe, and consequently most proper for Correspondence, it ought to be recommended to the Learner, among his Grammar Studies, when his Parts will admit of so great a Variety; but not before he is sufficiently grounded in the Latin, from whence the French is chiefly derived.

WRITING must always be regarded as an essential Part of every Day's Employment; because the free and Clerk-like Manner of Writing, fit for the dextrous Dispatch of Business, is not attainable by speculative Notions, or on a sudden, but by Practice gradually, under the Direction of an able Master; nor can any other Means be depended on, to make the Hand easy, bold, and masterly.

ARITHMETIC now must be entered upon; in teaching which Art, the ensuing Treatise will be of some Advantage: The Bills of Parcels and those on Book-Debts, are such Examples of Computation, as daily occur in Commerce, and which are of use to illustrate the practical Rules, and apply them to Business. The Variety of Promissory Notes, Acquittances, Bills of Exchange, with Directions relating to them, and Things of like Nature, are all intended to give the young Clerk a Taste and Idea of the Customs and Usages of Dealers, and to obviate the Difficulties he would otherwise meet with, through his not being acquainted with Things of that general Concern in Traffic.

Transcribing and computing the Invoyces and other mercantile Precedents, will yield him a no less profitable Exercise, and conduce in some Measure, to the Understanding the Practice of BOOK-KEEPING; a Science so universally useful, that, without keeping regular Accompts, the Trader risks the sacrificing an improvable Fortune, to Negligence and Chance; the Man of Estate is thereby made subject to frequent Impositions, always to Uncertainties; and the Man in Office is likewise exposed to numberless Perplexities; and, indeed, none can properly be said to be a Judge of Business, whose Abilities, how considerable soever, are not assisted by some Insight and Skill therein.

The

The Collections of Questions interspersed, all of them solvable by the Rules of common Arithmetic, are subjoined, to exercise the Pupil in Numbers, to accustom him to Calculation, and with a Design to excite his Curiosity to look farther into their Properties and Use, not only as they regard themselves, but also as they respect Lines, Surfaces, and solid Bodies.

DRAWING is an Attainment worth every Man's Pursuit; but it is indispensibly necessary for the Mechanic: Since, among its many other Advantages, he is thereby able to convey his Designs to the Apprehensions of others, by a Sketch off-hand, with much Clearness and Certainty.

GEOGRAPHY, as it informs us of the Situation of the several Parts of the Earth, the Distance and Bearing of Places, the Extent, Language, Religion, and Products of different Countries; as it is the Key to History and the public News, and needful to the forming a right Judgment of our Country, its Interest and Concerns; is of too great Importance to be neglected.

To these more necessary Qualifications of the Man of Business, the practical parts of the Mathematics, as MEASURING, GAUGING, SURVEYING, NAVIGATION, are to be considered as very advantageous and useful Additions: The more speculative Parts, as GEOMETRY, ASTRONOMY, with EXPERIMENTAL and NATURAL PHILOSOPHY, and ALGEBRA, are also Informations that give a sublime and noble Turn of Thought; and which, though they may not seem Occurrences in immediate Business or Commerce, yet do they frequently conduce to the Improvement of both, and are always Amusements highly proper for the virtuous and intelligent Mind.

I have supposed the Learner of a promising Genius, and teachable Disposition; happy in Parents able and willing to allow him an handsome and proper Education; and happy in Teachers, who want neither Capacity nor Integrity in their Calling. Where all those do not concur, the Misfortune is not easily retrieved. When once the Time of Youth is lost, the Cares of Life are so great and many, that few or none are ever able to recover themselves from the low Condition always attending the Want of a proper and early Education.

SOHO-SQUARE,
 Dec. 30, 1719.

M. Clare.

# THE
# CONTENTS.

*An*

# viii The CONTENTS.

# YOUTH'S
# INTRODUCTION
## TO
# TRADE and BUSINESS, &c.

IT is a common Thing with young People, even thofe who muft be allowed to underftand the Principles of *Arithmetic* very well, to be often at a Lofs, when but a fimple Propofition is made them, a little out of the cuftomary Form or common Road. In order to remedy this, it cannot be improper, in a Treatife of this Nature, here and there, at proper Stages, to interfperfe little Exercifes, partly in the Way of Bufinefs, partly of Amufement and Information, to exemplify and apply what they more methodically learn. In doing which, it will not be amifs to fet them down as it were promifcuoufly, that their Genius and Judgment may the better appear in the Solution of them; and to thofe Queftions which may feem a little too intricate, for the Learner's Encouragement are given the Methods of folving them.

### RECREATION I.

I. WRITE down the Value of the following Numbers in Words at length, *viz:* 370087. 418427900. 6210003745. 45027308751. 293417604712. 618002030694713. 4703806625043325188941I.

*Ufually a lefs literal Number placed after a greater, augments its Value; before, diminifhes it.*

*The chief Roman Numbers are*, I, 1. V, 5. X, 10. L, 50. C, 100. D or IƆ, 500. M or CIƆ, 1000. CCIƆ, is 5000. IƆƆƆ, is 50000, &c. *Tenfold when repeated: So* CCIƆƆ, is 10,000.

*A Line drawn over any Number lefs than a Thoufand intimates fo many Thoufands; as* $\overline{\text{LXX}}$, is 70,000. $\overline{\text{C}}$, is 100,000. and $\overline{\text{M}}$, a Million.

II. Decypher the following Numbers, and find their Sum, IV. VI. IX. IIX. XIII. XLV. LXXXI. XCVI. CXC. CD. DCC. MCL. MDCXLVIII. $\overline{\text{M}}$CCM. IƆƆIƆCCCLVII. $\overline{\text{VICC}}$LXXXX. *Anfwer,* 1017297.

B

III. In

III. In Figures expreſs: A Million and a half in *South-Sea Bonds*. Ninescore and fourteen Thouſand, eight Hundred *Sheep*. Threescore and twelve Thouſand, thirteen Hundred *Weight of Lead*. Fifteen Thouſand and fourscore Million of *Styvers*. One Hundred and two Thouſand, two Hundred and ſix Million, ſeventy Thouſand ſeven Hundred and ſeven *Ryals of Plate*. Three Million and thirty three Thouſand and thirty *Pieces of Eight*. Four thouſand and forty Hundred Pounds, thirty four Shillings, and fourteen Pence, five Farthings.

IV. For the Practice of Figure-making, in even Ranks, ſet down all the Numbers in the State-Lottery, as they riſe ſucceſſively, between 7500 excluſive, and 8000 incluſive; and find their Sum.            *Anſwer*, 3875250.

Find the Number of Chapters contained in the New Teſtament, after that the Number of Verſes, and give their joint Sum.            *Anſwer*, together 8217.

Do the ſame by the five firſt Books of Moſes.
            *Anſwer*, together 6039.

✦✦✦✦✦✦✦✦✦✦✦✦✦✦✦✦✦✦✦✦✦✦✦✦✦✦✦✦✦✦✦✦✦✦✦

## A TABLE of the Clerk-like Contractions of Words, for Diſpatch of Buſineſs.

*A.* Anſwer.

*A. B.* Batchelor of Arts; *Artium Baccalaureus*.

*A. Bp.* Archbiſhop.

*Abr.* Abraham.

*A. D.* In the Year of our Lord; *Anno Domini*.

*Accs.* Accompt.

*Adml.* Admiral.

*Admr.* Adminiſtrator.

*agſt.* againſt.

*Alexr.* Alexander.

*a. m.* before Noon; *ante meridiem*.

*A. M.* Maſter of Arts; *Artium Magiſter*.

*A. M.* In the Year of the World; *Anno Mundi*.

*Amt.* Amount.

*Amſt.* Amſterdam.

*And.* Andrew.

*Anth.* Anthony.

*Arth.* Arthur.

*Aſſ.* Aſſigns.

*Aſſeſſr.* Aſſeſſor.

*Atto.* Attorney.

*Aug.* Auguſtine.

*B. D.* Batchelor of Divinity; *Baccalaureus Divinitatis*.

*Barth.* Bartholomew.

*Bart.* Baronet.

*Benj.* Benjamin.

*Bp.* Biſhop.

*Britn.* Britain.

*Bur.* Burlace.

*Buſhl.* Buſhel.

*B. V.* Bleſſed Virgin.

*Bucks.* Buckinghamſhire.

C. is

C. in Number 100, *Centum.*
C.C.C. Corpus Christi College.
☉. a Hundred Weight.
*Capt.* Captain.
*Cent.* or *Centum,* an Hundred.
*Chap.* Chapter.
*Cha.* Charles.
*Ch.* Church.
*Chanc.* Chancellor.
*Chr.* Christopher.
*Cit.* City, Citizen, Citadel.
*Clem.* Clement.
*Cl.* Clerk, Clergyman.
C. P. S. Keeper of the Privy-
    Seal; *Custos Privati Sigilli.*
*Co.* County.
*Col.* Colonel.
*Collr.* Collector.
*Comp.* or *Co.* Company.
*Comrs.* Commissioners.
*Const.* Constable.
*Conts.* Contents.
*Corresp.* Correspondent.
*Counselr.* Counsellor.
C. S. Keeper of the Seal;
    *Custos Sigilli.*
*Cr.* Creditor.
*Cust.* Custom.
*Curt.* Current.
D. in Number 500.
*D.* Duke, or Duchess.
D. D. Doctor of Divinity;
    *Doctor Divinitatis.*
*d.* a Peny; *denarius.*
*Dan.* Daniel.
*Dav.* David.
*dld.* delivered.
*Den.* Denis.
*Dep.* Deputy.
*Devon.* Devonshire.
*Do.* Ditto, the same.
*Dr.* Debtor, Doctor.

*Dor.* Dorothy.
*Dorset.* Dorsetshire.
*db.* day.
*E.* Earl, Evening, or East.
E. A. P. Priest of the Church
    of England; *Ecclesiæ Angli-*
    *canæ Presbyter.*
*Edm.* Edmund.
*Edw.* Edward.
*e. g.* for Example; *exempli*
    *gratiâ.*
*Elea.* Eleanor.
*Eliz.* Elizabeth.
*Esqr.* Esquire.
*Engd.* England.
*Excellt.* Excellent.
*Exa.* Example.
*Exo.* Exchange.
*Exr.* Executor.
*Exon.* Exeter.
*ft.* the Ending *ful.*
*Ft.* Fort, Foot, and Feet.
*Frd.* Friend.
*Fr.* French.
*Fra.* France.
*Factr.* Factor.
*fd.* the Ending *ford.*
F. R. S. or R. S. S. Fellow
    of the Royal Society; *Frater*
    *Regalis Societatis* or *Regalis*
    *Societatis Socius.*
*Fran.* Francis or Frances.
*Fred.* Frederick.
*Fre.* Freight.
*Gab.* Gabriel.
*Gar.* Garrison.
*Geo.* George.
*Gent.* Gentleman.
*Genl.* General.
*Genmo.* Generalissimo.
*Ger.* Gerrard.
*Gilb.* Gilbert.

B 2                    Gov.

*Gov*. Governor.

G. R. King George; *Georgius Rex*.

*Grt*. Great.

*Greg*. Gregory.

*Gr*. Grofs.

*Han*. Hannah.

*Hants*. Hampfhire.

*Hen*. Henry.

*Honble*. Honourable.

*Hond*. Honoured.

*Honrs*. Honours.

*Holld*. Holland.

*Hum*. Humphry.

I. in Number 1.

*Jac*. Jacob.

*Ja*. James.

*Jeo*. Jeoffroy.

*Jer*. Jeremiah.

*J. D*. Doctor of Laws; *Jurium Doctor*.

*J. H. S*. Jefus the Saviour of Men; *Jefus Hominum Salvator*.

*Infta*. Inftance.

*Inft*. Inftant.

*Impl*. Imperial.

*ibid*. in the fame place; *ibidem*.

*i. e*. that is; *id eft*.

*id*. the fame; *idem*.

*Inftl*. Inftal

*Jno*. John.

*Jon*. Jonathan.

*Jof*. Joseph.

*Juft*. Juftice.

*Ingenr*. Ingineer.

*Ks*. King.

*Knt*. Knight.

*Kath*. Katherine.

L. in Number 50.

*l*. Book; *liber*.

*Lau*. Laurence.

*L. C. J*. Lord Chief Juftice.

*Dy*. Lady.

*Leo*. Leonard.

*Lew*. Lewis.

*Ld*. Lord.

*L. L. D*. Doctor of Laws; *Utriufque Legis Doctor*.

*L. S*. the Place of the Seal; *Locus Sigilli*.

*Ldp*. Lordfhip.

*Ladp*. Ladyfhip.

*Lieut*. Lieutenant.

*Lib*. Liberty.

£. a Pound Sterling.

*lb*. a Pound Weight; *Libra*.

*Lancafh*. Lancafhire.

*Londo*. London.

*Lyd*. Lydia.

M. in Number 1000; *Mille*.

*Ma*. Mary.

*M*. Monfieur, Marquis.

*Madm*. Madam.

*M. A*. Mafter of Arts; *Magifter Artium*.

*Majty*. Majefty.

*Mar*. Margaret, Martha, Margery.

*Mat*. Matthew.

*Mn*. Martin.

*M. D*. Doctor of Phyfic; *Medicinæ Doctor*.

*Mdm*. Memorandum.

*Mr*. Mafter.

*Mrs*. Mrs. Miftrefs.

*Math*. Mathematics.

*Meffrs*. Mafters.

*Mercht*. Merchant.

*Mich*. Michael.

*Michs*. Michaelmas.

*Minr*. Minifter.

*Middx*. Middlefex.

*Meafr*. Meafure.

*Mon*.

*Mon.* Month.
*Mos.* Moses.
*Monsr.* Monsieur.
*Mss.* Manuscripts; *Manuscripta.*
*M. S.* Sacred to the Memory; *Memoriæ Sacrum.*
*ment.* the Ending *ment.*
*Nat.* Nathanael.
*Neh.* Nehemiah.
*Nic.* Nicholas.
*N.* North.
*N. B.* Remark; *Nota benè.*
*Northn.* Northampton.
*No.* Number; *Numero.*
*Nt.* Neat, or Netto.
*N. S.* New Stile.
*ob.* Half-peny; *obolus.*
*Objt.* Object.
*Obedt.* Obedient.
*or.* Our.
*Ordr.* Order.
*O. S.* Old Stile.
*Oli.* Oliver.
*Omnipt.* Omnipotent.
*Ow.* Owen.
*Oxon.* Oxford.
*pd.* Paid.
℔ by; *per.*
℔ *Cent.* by the Hundred; *per Centum.*
*Pat.* Patrick.
*Partr.* Partner.
*Parlmt.* Parliament.
*Pet.* Peter.
*Philomath.* a Lover of Learning; *Philomathes.*
*Ph.* Philip.
*p. m.* Afternoon; *post meridiem.*
*Ps.* a Piece.
*Principl.* Principal.

*Proct.* Proctor.
*Prop.* Proposition.
*Prest.* Present.
*q. d.* as if he should say; *quasi dicat.*
*Q. E. D.* which was to be demonstrated; *Quod erat demonstrandum.*
*Q. E. I.* which was to be found out; *Quod erat inveniendum.*
*Q.* Question, Query.
*qrt.* Quart.
*qt.* Quantity.
*qr.* quarter or ¼ part.
*Ra.* Ralph.
*Ran.* Randal, Randulph.
*Rich.* Richard.
*R.* King or Queen; *Rex aut Regina.*
*Rt.* Right.
*Rtn.* Return.
*Rctr.* Rector.
*Revd.* Reverend.
*Regt.* Regiment.
*Royl.* Royal.
*Recd.* Received.
*Reb.* Rebecca.
*Remr.* Remainder.
*Recr.* Receiver.
*Regr.* Register.
*Rob.* Robert.
*Rog.* Roger.
*Rol.* Roland.
*Rotto.* Rotterdam.
*Salop.* Shropshire.
*Sar.* Sarah.
*S.* South.
*Sr.* Sir.
*S.* or *St.* Saint.
*stead.* the Ending *stead.*
*sd.* said.
*Sergt.* Serjeant.

Sh. Shire.
s. a Shilling; *Solidus.*
Serv*. Servant.
Secry. Secretary.
Scotld. Scotland.
Sim. Simon.
Sol. Solution.
Sp. Spanish.
Spirit*. Spiritual.
S. T. P. Doctor of Divinity;
  *Sanctæ Theologiæ Profeſſor.*
Steph. Stephen.
Templ. Temporal.
Theo. Theophilus.
Tho. Thomas.
Tim. Timothy.
Tob. Tobias.
Tot. Total.
Treaſy. Treaſury.
Tr. Tare.
Tr*. Tret.
V. in Number 5.
v*. vain.
viz. that is to ſay; *videlicet.*
v. ſee; *vide.*
v*. verſe.
Val. Valentine.
Ven. Venerable.
Vin. Vincent.
Victr. Victualler.
Vicr. Vicar.
Ult. the laſt; *ultimus.*
wk. week.
Wal. Walter.
W. Weſt.
Ward*. Warden.
Weſtm*. Weſtminſter.
W*. William.
Win. Winifred.

Wilts. Wiltſhire.
wt. weight or weighing.
wt. what.
wch. which.
wth. with.
wn. when.
Worl. Worſhipful.
Worp. Worſhip.
wondl. wonderful.
X. in Number 10.
X. Chriſt.
Xpn. Chriſtian.
Xtmas. Chriſtmas.
ye. the.
yn. then.
yor. your.
yors. yours.
ys. this.
yt. that.
&. and.
&c. and forth; *et cætera.*
Zac. Zachary.
Jan.     January.
Feb.     February.
Mar.     March.
Apr.     April.
May.     May.
Jun.     June.
Jul.     July.
Aug.     Auguſt.
Sept.  } September.
  7ber. }
Oct.  } October.
  8ber. }
Nov.  } November.
  9ber. }
Dec.  } December.
  10ber. }
  Xber. }

# RECREATION II.

(1) A Person dying, left his Widow the Use of 5000 *l*. To a Charity he bequeathed 846 *l*. 10*s*. To each of his three Nephews 1230 *l*. To each of his four Neices 1050 *l*. To twenty poor House-keepers five Guineas each, and 200 Guineas to his Executor. What must he have died possessed of?  *Answer*, 14051 *l*. 10*s*.

(2) A Nobleman, going out of Town, is informed by his Steward, that his Corn-chandler's Bill comes to 123 *l*. 19*s*. His Brewer's to 41 *l*. 10*s*. His Butcher's to 212 *l*. 6*d*. To his Lordship's Baker is owing 24 *l*. To his Tallow-chandler, 13 *l*. 8*s*. To his Taylor, 137 *l*. 9*s*. 9*d*. To his Draper, 74 *l*. 13*s*. 6*d*. His Coachmaker's Demand was 214 *l*. 16*s*. 6*d*. His Wine Merchant's 68 *l*. 12*s*. His Confectioner's, 16 *l*. 2*s*. His Rent 82 Guineas. And his Servants Wages, for half a Year, came to 46 *l*. 5*s*. What Money must he send to his Banker for, in case he would carry with him, 50 *l*. to defray his Expences on the Road?  *Answer*, 1108 *l*. 18*s*. 3*d*.

(3) A Merchant buys up six Bags of Canterbury Hops, N° 1. of which weighed, *Cwt.* 2: 2. 10. N° 2. *Cwt.* 2. 1. 16. N° 3. *Cwt.* 2. 0. 24. N° 4. *Cwt.* 2. 3. only. N° 5. *Cwt.* 2. 1. 12. N° 6. *Cwt.* 2. 1. 16. besides a couple of Pockets D° that weighed, *lb.* 58¼ each: How many Hundred-weight has he to pay Carriage for, on bringing them to Town?  *Answer*, *Cwt.* 15. 2. 27.

(4) A Corn-factor buys seventy Quarter of Oats for 46 *l*. 7*s*. 6*d*. thirty-eight Quarter of Beans, for 100 *l*. twelve Quarter of Peas, which cost 16 *l*. 16*s*. eighty-eight Quarter of Barley, for 73 *l*. 8*d*. sixteen Ditto of Wheat, for 56 *l*. 9*s*. 10*d*. and six Quarter of Rye, for 4 *l*. 1*s*. 6*d*. The Water-carriage of all comes to 13 *l*. 2*s*. 7*d*. his Riding Charges to 1 *l*. 13*s*. and if he clears eighteen Guineas by the Bargain, What do his Bills of Parcels amount to?  *Answer*, 330 *l*. 9*s*. 1*d*.

(5) The Collector of Cash has been out with Bills, and gives Account, that *A.* paid him 13 *l*. and half a Crown; *B.* 2 *l*. 13*s*. *C.* 14*s*. and a Groat; *D.* 1 *l*. 9*s*. 8*d*. ¼. *E.* 11 *l*. 6*d*. ¼. *F.* 17*s*. and a Tester; *G.* 12*s*. 2*d*. *H.* a Pound and

and half a Guinea; *J.* a Moidore and 13*s.* *K.* two Broad-pieces of 23*s.* each, a Jacobus of 25*s.* and a Shilling; *L.* nine Pound and a Mark; *M.* 12*l.* 12*s.* *N.* a Bank Note of 15*l.* and *O.* three Crown-pieces and an Angel: What Cash has he in Charge?    *Answer,* 76*l.* 2*s.* 6*d.* ¼.

(6) In a Gentleman's Service of Plate, there are fourteen Dishes, weighing *oz.* 193. 13 *dwt.* Plates thirty-six, weighing *oz.* 421. 11 *dwt.* Four Dozen of Spoons, weighing *oz.* 104. 6 *dwt.* Six Salts chased, weighing *oz.* 32. Knives and Forks, weighing *oz.* 83. 9 *dwt.* Four Presenters, weighing *oz.* 113. 4 *dwt.* In Mugs, Tumblers, Beakers, and other odd Pieces, weight *oz.* 264. 18 *dwt.* A Silver Tea-kettle and Lamp, weighing *oz.* 126. 9 *dwt.* and the rest of that Equipage, *oz.* 93. 2 *dwt.* What Quantity of Plate had the Butler under his Care?    *Answer,* *oz.* 1432. 12 *dwt.*

(7) A Horse in his Furniture is worth 35*l.* 10*s.* out of it 12*l.* 12*s.* How much does the Price of the Furniture exceed that of the Horse?    *Answer,* 10*l.* 6*s.*

(8) *A.* of Amsterdam, is Debtor to *B.* of Bristol. For Mercery Wares as ⅌ Factory, 418*l.* 2*s.* 6*d.* For forty *Cwt.* of Cheshire-Cheese, 52*l.* 18*s.*, For English Broad-Cloth, fifteen Pieces, 317*l.* 12*s.* 10*d.* For nineteen Fodder of Lead, 320*l.* For twelve Tons of Bar-Iron, 173*l.* 3*d.* For eight Tons of Copper, 1110*l.* 10*s.* 1*d.* For his Acceptance of a Bill drawn, 88*l.* 14*s.* For another paid for Honour, 50*l.* Ten Dozen Morocco Skins, 28*l.* 15*s.* 4*d.* Paid Convoys, Insurances, and Port-charges, 43*l.* Warehouse Room, Postage, Sledage, Boatage, and incidental Charges, 5*l.* 5*s.* The Factorage of all came to 112*l.* 6*s.* For what Sum must *B.* draw to clear the Accompt?    *Answer,* 2720*l.* 4*s.*

(9) Having a Piece of Ground, 127 Feet in Front, let off to *A.* 57 Feet to build on at one End, and to *B.* at first 27 Feet and ½ from the other, which he afterward by Consent extended to 42 Feet; what Ground was left me in the Center?    *Answer,* 28 Feet.

(10) How much is *A.* (born sixteen Years ago) elder than *B.* who will come into the World fourteen Years hence?    *Answer,* 30 Years.

Having

HAving obſerved the Miſtakes young Perſons are liable to, for want of an Opportunity of informing themſelves of the Stile and Titles due to Perſons in Office, and thoſe of elevated Rank and Fortune, it cannot be improper, in this Place, to ſhew the fitting Directions and Addreſs to Perſons of Diſtinction. the Chief of which being known, the reſt will be attained without much Difficulty.

*\** Note, *The Terms of Addreſs are put in a different Character.*

## To the Royal Family.

TO the King's moſt Excellent Majeſty. *Sire,* or *May it pleaſe Your Majeſty.*

To his Royal Highneſs *George* Prince of *Wales. May it pleaſe Your Royal Highneſs.*

And in like manner to any other of the Royal Family, changing what is to be changed.

## To the Nobility.

TO His Grace *L.\** Duke of *D.\* My Lord Duke, Your Grace.*

To the moſt Noble *P.* Lord Marquis of *C. My Lord Marquis, Your Lordſhip.*

> \* *The Learner is to ſubſtitute real Names and Titles in the Place of theſe initial Letters all through the following Directions.*

To the Right Honourable *J.* Earl of *B. My Lord, Your Lordſhip.*

To the Right Honourable *G.* Lord Viſcount *T. My Lord, Your Lordſhip.*

To the Right Honourable *T.* Lord *O. My Lord, Your Lordſhip.*

The Wives of Noblemen are addreſſed in Terms equal to their Huſband's Rank.

The Title of *Lord* and *Right Honourable* is given, by Courteſy, to all the Sons of *Dukes* and *Marquiſes,* and to the eldeſt Sons of *Earls;* and the Title of *Lady,* and *Right Honourable* to all their Daughters: The younger Sons of *Earls* are all *Honourable* and *Eſquires.*

C The

The Sons of *Viscounts* and *Barons* are stiled *Esquires* and
Honourable, and their Daughters are directed to, *The
Honourable* Mrs *N. N.* but without other Stile; they
have however Rank among the first Gentry without
Title.

The King's Commission confers the Title of *Honourable*
on any Gentleman in a Place of Honour or Trust.

The Stile of *Right Honourable* is due to no Commoner,
but such as are Members of his Majesty's most Honourable Privy-Council; except the three Lord Mayors,
of *London*, *York*, and *Dublin*, and the Lord Provost of
*Edinburgh*, during Office.

Every considerable Servant to the King, upon the Civil
or Military List, or to any of the Royal Family, is
stiled *Esquire*, *pro tempore*.

> P. C. *in the Margin denotes a Privy-Counsellor,*
> *and therefore* Right Honourable.

## To the Parliament.

TO the Right Honourable the Lords Spiritual and
Temporal in Parliament of *Great-Britain* assembled. *My Lords*; *May it please Your Lordships.*

To the Honourable the Knights, Citizens and Burgesses,
in Parliament of *Great-Britain* assembled. *Gentlemen,*
*May it please Your Honours.*

P. C. To the Right Honourable Sir *G. H.* Speaker of the
Honourable House of Commons, *Sir.*

## To the Clergy.

TO the Most Reverend Father in God *W.* Lord
Archbishop of *C. My Lord, Your Grace.*

To the Right Reverend Father in God *E.* Lord Bishop of
*L. My Lord, Your Lordship.*

To the Right Reverend the Lord Bishop of *G.* Lord
Almoner to his Majesty.

To the Reverend Mr (or Dr if the Degree of Doctor has
been taken) *A. B.* Dean of *C.*

To the Reverend Dr——Chancellor of *D.*

To the Reverend Dr——Archdeacon of *E.*

To the Reverend Mr——Prebendary of *F.*——Rector of
*G.*——Vicar of *H.*——Curate of *J.*——

The proper Address to these last Gentlemen is in general
only Sir; and being written to, Reverend Sir.
Deans and Archdeacons are called usually Mr Dean,
and Mr Archdeacon.

## To the Officers of His Majesty's Houshold.

THEY are generally addressed to according to their
Rank and Quality, but sometimes according to their
Office; as *My Lord Steward, My Lord Chamberlain,*
Mr *Comptroller,* Mr *Vice-Chamberlain.*

In Superscriptions of Letters, relating to Gentlemens
Employments, their Stile of Office ought never to
be omitted.

## To the Commissioners and other Officers on the Civil Lift.

TO *the Right Honourable R.* Earl of *W.*——,* Lord
Privy-Seal.
*To his Grace J.* Duke of *M.* Lord President of the Council.
*To the Right Honourable N.* Viscount *P.* Lord Great Cham-
berlain—— Earl Marshal of *England*——One of His
Majesty's Principal Secretaries of State, &c.
*To the Right Honourable the Lords Commissioners* of the
Treasury. Ditto, of Trade and Plantations. Ditto, of
the Admiralty, &c.

Note, *If there be a Nobleman, or even a Commoner
who is a Privy-Counsellor, among any Set of Commissioners, it will be proper to stile them collectively*
Right Honourable. *The usual Address then is,*
Your Lordships.

*To the Honourable the Commissioners of*—— * His Majesty's
Customs. Ditto, of the Revenue of Excise. Ditto, for
the Duty on Salt. Ditto, for His Majesty's Stamp-
Duties. Ditto, for Victualling His Majesty's Navy, &c.

* These Blanks are also to be filled up as before with Names and Dignities, and
made so many several Directions, repeating always the general Stile preceeding the
Blank; for Distinction here put in the Italick Character.

To -

## To the Soldiery.

TO the Honourable *A. B.* Efq; Lieutenant General of His Majefty's Forces. Ditto, Major General. Ditto, Brigadier General *of His Majefty's Forces. Sir; Your Honour,*

To the Right Honourable *J. Earl of S. Captain of His Majefty's* Firft Troop of Horfe Guards. Ditto, Band of Gentlemen Penfioners. Ditto, Band of Yeomen of the Guard, &c.

To the Honourable Colonel *Thomas Pitt.* To Major *Foubert.* To Captain *Audley,* &c. Sir.

To the Principal Officers of His Majefty's Ordnance, *Your Honours,*

To *A. B.* Efq; Lieutenant General *of the Ordnance.* Ditto, Surveyor General *of the Ordnance,* &c.

## To the Officers of the Navy.

TO His Grace *C.* Duke of *D.* Lord High Admiral of *Great Britain. Your Grace.*

To the Right Honourable *G.* Lord Vifcount *T.* Vice or Rear Admiral of *Great Britain.*

To the Honourable Sir *P. Q.* Admiral of the *Blue.* Ditto, Vice Admiral of the *Red.* Ditto, Rear Admiral of the *White. Sir; Your Honour.*

To Captain *R. L.* Commander of His Majefty's Ship the *Shoreham,* riding at *Spithead.*

---

## RECREATION III.

(11) A Perfon was 17 Years of Age 29 Years fince, and he will be drowned 23 Years hence: Pray in what Year of his Age will this happen?    *Anfwer, Ætat.* 69.

(12) A Trader failing, was indebted to *A.* 71 *l.* 12 *s.* 6 *d.* To *B.* 34 *l.* 9 *s.* 9 *d.* To *C.* 16 *l.* 8 *s.* 8 *d.* To *D.* 44 *l.* To *E.* 66 *l.* 7 *s.* 6 *d.* To *F.* 11 *l.* 2 *s.* 3 *d.* To *G.* 19 *l.* 19 *s.* And to *H.* a Fine of thirty Marks. At the Time of this Difafter, he had by him in Cafh, 3 *l.* 13 *s.* 6 *d.* in Commodities, 23 *l.* 10 *s.* in Houfhold Furniture, 13 *l.* 8 *s.* 6 *d.* in Plate, 7 *l.* 18 *s.* 5 *d.* in a Tenement, 56 *l.* 15 *s.* in reeoverable Book-Debts, 87 *l.* 13 *s.* 10 *d* Suppofing thefe Things faithfully furrendered to his Creditors, what will they then lofe by him?    *Anfwer,* 91 *l.* 5 *d.*

(13) In

(13) In the City of Pekin in China is a Bell weighing, it is said, 120000 Pounds; at Nankin, in the same Country, is another weighing 50000 Pounds. The first exceeds the great Bell at Erfurt, in Upper Saxony, by 94600 Pounds: How much then is the German Bell inferior in Weight to the Second?  *Answer*, Near one Half.

(14) Your Grandfather, if living, is 119 Years of Age; your Father actually 63; you are not so old as your Grandfire by 83 Years: What is the Difference in Years between your Father and you?  *Answer*, 27 Years.

(15) A Robbery being committed on the Highway, there was assessed on a certain Hundred, in the County of S. the Sum of 373*l.* 14*s.* 8*d.* of which the four Parishes paid 37*l.* 16*s.* 4*d.* apiece, the four Hamlets 28*l.* 3*s.* 10*d.* each, the four Townships 19*l.* 19*s.* each; what was the Deficiency?  *Answer*, 30*l.* wanting 2*s.*

(16) Received in lieu of two Gold Repeaters, sent to Jamaica in 1730, the five Chests of Indigo following; and on a like Adventure, in 1732, the subsequent five Chests: The Question is, how much Indigo I had less the second Time than the first?

| *Anno* 1730. Cwt. qr. lb. | lb. | *Anno* 1732. Cwt. qr. lb. | lb. |
|---|---|---|---|
| No 1.   2—1—16 | Tare 43. | No 1.   1—3—07 | Tare 32. |
| 2.   2—2—11 | — 47. | 2.   1—3—17 | — 32. |
| 3.   2—0—12 | — 41. | 3.   1—2—10 | — 30. |
| 4.   2—0—19 | — 42. | 4.   1—0—13 | — 27. |
| 5.   2—3—17 | — 49. | 5.   2—0—11 | — 34. |

*Answer*, 342. lb.

(17) A. made a Bond for 114*l.* 10*s.* the Interest came to 19*l.* He then paid off forty Guineas, and gave a fresh Bond for what was behind. By the time there was 13*l.* 4*s.* 8*d.* due on the second, for Interest, he paid off 37*l.* 14*s.* 2*d.* more, took up the old Bond, and signed a new one still for the Residue. The Principal again ran on till there was 9*l.* 11*s.* 3*d.* more due, and then he determined to take it up. Pray what Money had his Creditor to receive?

*Answer*, 76*l.* 11*s.* 9*d.*

(18) Received from my Factor at Alicant, on Account of Sales of Tin, to the Value of 197*l.* 12*s.* Sterling; of Bees-Wax, to 71*l.* 7*s.* 6*d.* of Stockings, to 47*l.* 3*s.* 6*d.* of Tobacco, the Net proceeds whereof were 943*l.* 15*s.* 10*d.* of Cotton, 123*l.* 3*s.* 7*d.* and of Wheat, to the Amount of 116*l.* 5*s.* 6*d.* He at the same time advises, that he has,

Order, shipped for my Account and Risk, Alicant Wines, to the Value of 226 *l.* 16*s.* 6*d.* Figs of 157*l.* 11*s.* 3*d.* Fruit, ninety Chests. cost 104 *l.* 6*s.* Olives, 136*l.* 10*s.* Oil, 193 *l.* 17*s.* Raisins, 143*l.* 4*d.* and Spanish Wool, to the Value of 73 *l.* 13*s.* 8*d.* the Commission of the whole Consignment came to 71 *l.* 18*s.* 11*d.* The Question is, which of us is to draw for the Difference, and how much?

*Answer,* 391 *l.* 14*s.* 3*d.* is to be remitted by him.

(19) *A. B.* and *C.* open an Account with a Banker, Jan. 11. 1739. and put into his Hands, *viz. A.* 17*l.* 17*s.* *B.* 34*l.* 11*s.* 6*d.* *C.* 28*l.* 18*s.* 10*d.* On the 21st *A.* withdrew 9*l.* 10*s.* and *C.* advanced 12 *l.* and a Crown. The 24th *B.* called for 6 *l.* 10*s.* The 30th *C.* wanted 19 *l.* 8*s.* 4*d.* On the 12th of Feb. *B.* deposited with him eleven Carolus's and three Moidores. On the 19th *A.* sent for 5*l.* and a Noble more; but on the 24th, returned him 42*l.* On the 2d of March, *C.* paid in twenty Guineas, and *B.* drew for six. The 14th *B.* sent in 17 *l.* 8*s.* 8*d.* and the 17th *A.* had back 12 *l.* 2*s.* 6*d.* On the 19th, they sent for five Guineas a Man, and on the 24th they returned that Sum, and ten Marks a piece more: How much did their said Banker owe them jointly and separately at *Lady-Day?*

*Answer,* to *A.* 39*l.* 11*s.* 2*d.* *B.* 62*l.* 11*s.* 6*d.* *C.* 49*l.* 8*s.* 10*d.*

(20) *W. X. Y. Z.* send in their Money to the Bank, and draw upon it in the following Manner, *viz.* June 4, 1748. *Z.* sent in 70 *l.* 8*s.* *Y.* had 116*l.* 14*s.* 10*d.* remaining on Balance, and the 14th sent in 120 *l.* more. *W.* paid in 47 *l.* 18*s.* 2*d.* in Cash, and delivered a Bank Note for 200 *l.* *X.* paid in a Bill of Exchange, on a good Man, for 33 *l.* 14*s.* 9*d.* and in Cash made it up 100 *l.* *Y.* on the 16th drew for 43 *l.* 12*s.* 6*d.* and on the 20th *Z.* for eleven Guineas. *W.* on the 24th added 14 *l.* 12*s.* 10*d.* and *X.* withdrew 47 *l.* 10*s.* 8*d.* *Y.* on the 28th paid in 18 *l.* 5*s.* and two Days after drew for 88 *l.* 13*s.* 4*d.* *W.* sent for sixty-three Guineas on the 30th, and in five Days after for 15 *l.* 10*s.* 9*d.* more. *Z.* on the 7th of July, demanded 12 *l.* 8*s.* 3*d.* and *X.* 7 *l.* 3*s.* 1*d.* *Z.* on the 15th remitted them 31 *l.* 12*s.* 4*d.* and Assignment, they received for him at the same time double that Sum. *Y.* required 81 *l.* 19*s.* 8*d.* on the 12th, and *W.* 10*l.* 10*s.*

*Y.* Three

*Y.* three Days after that sent in 42 *l.* and *W.* 52 *l.* On the 19th *X.* sent for 38 *l.* 18 *s.* 10 *d.* and the 24th paid in 19 *l.* 19 *s.* The Question is, how stood these Gentlemens Cash severally, and what Money can they jointly raise?

*Answer,* *W.* 222 *l.* 7 *s.* 3 *d.* *X.* 33 *l.* 6 *s.* 5 *d.* *Y.* 82 *l.* 14 *s.* 4 *d.* *Z.* 141 *l.* 5 *s.* 9 *d.*

(21) A Merchant at his Out-setting in Trade owed 280 *l.* He had in Cash, Commodities, the Stocks, and good Debts, 11505 *l.* 10 *s.* He cleared the first Year by Commerce 393 *l.* 13 *s.* 1 *d.* What at the Year's end was his neat Balance?

*Answer,* 11619 *l.* 3 *s.* 1 *d.*

(22) Miss Kitty told her Sister Charlotte, whose Father had before left them Twelve thousand twelve hundred Pounds apiece, that their Grandmother by Will had raised her Fortune to fifteen thousand Pounds, and had made her own twenty thousand: Pray what did the old Lady leave between them? *Answer,* 8600 *l.*

(23) A Merchant taking an Inventory of his Capital, finds in his Vaults 28 Pieces of Brandy, which cost him 874 *l.* 10 *s.* 6 *d.* Bourdeaux Claret 40 Tuns, which stood him in 754 *l.* 4 *s.* 22 Lasts, 4 Bushels of Corn in his Granary, worth 675 *l.* 17 *s.* 3 *d.* with 2 Lasts of Canary Seed, worth 113 *l.* In his Warehouse were 10 Casks of Indigo, worth 632 *l.* 12 *s.* A Parcel of Saffron, worth 253 *l.* 5 *s.* *W. P.* of Stafford, owed him 384 *l.* 10 *s.* In the Hands of *F. G.* at Lynn, he had Wines to the Amount of 1011 *l.* 10 *s.* Pepper, in the keeping of *S. Q.* of the Custom-house, Value 1552 *l.* 16 *s.* 8 *d.* besides which *R. O.* owes him on Bond, 300 *l.* and *T. M.* on Note, 260 *l.* 14 *s.* He has in India Bonds to the Value of 459 *l.* and the Interest of those Securities made 25 *l.* 14 *s.* 6 *d.* He had Bank-Stock to the Value of 2134 *l.* 4 *s.* 6 *d.* There lay in his Banker's Hands 1892 *l.* 17 *s.* 6 *d.* He was at this Time indebted to *D. E.* 713 *l.* 13 *s.* To *M. F.* 352 *l.* 10 *s.* 8 *d.* To *L. P.* the Foot of his Account, one hundred and seventy two Guineas. To *J. B.* on Balance 57 *l.* 12 *s.* 10 *d.* To an Insurance, 190 *l.* The present State of this Person's Fortune is required?

*Answer,* 9830 *l.* 7 *s.* 5 *d.*

The

## The Superscriptions and Terms of Address continued.

### To the Ambassadry.

TO His Excellency Sir *A. B.* Bart. His Britannic Majesty's Envoy Extraordinary, and Plenipotentiary to the Ottoman Porte. *Your Excellency.*

To His Excellency *C. D.* Esq; Ambassador to His most Christian Majesty, *Your Excellency.*

To His Excellency the Baron de *E.* His Prussian Majesty's Resident at the Court of Great Britain. *Your Excellency.*

To Seignior *F. G.* Secretary from the Republick of Venice, at London. *Sir.*

To Seignior *H. J.* Secretary from the Great Duke of Tuscany, at London.

To *K. L.* Esq; His Britannic Majesty's Consul at Smyrna.

### To the Judges and Lawyers.

TO the Right Honourable *M.* Baron of *N.* Lord High Chancellor of Great Britain. *My Lord, Your Lordship.*

P. C. To the Right Honourable Sir *O. P.* Knight, Master of the Rolls. *Sir, Your Honour.*

P. C. To the Right Honourable Sir *R. S.* Bart. Lord Chief Justice of the King's-Bench. Ditto, of the Common Pleas. *My Lord, Your Lordship.*

To the Honourable Sir *W. W.* Knight, Lord Chief Baron of the Exchequer.

To the Honourable *G. S.* Esq; one of the Justices of the Court of Common-Pleas. Or, to Judge *S. Sir*, or *May it please you, Sir.*

To Sir *S. M.* His Majesty's Attorney General. Ditto, Solicitor. Ditto, Advocate-General. *Sir.*

To *Y. Z.* Esq; Serjeant——Barrister, or Counsellor at Law. *Sir.*

To Mr *Edward Bustle,* Attorney at Law. *Sir.*

⁎⁎⁎ N. B. *Upon the Circuits, and when they sit singly, every one of the Judges are addressed to and treated with the same Respect and Ceremony as the Chief Justices.*

To

## To the Lieutenancy and Magistracy.

TO the Right Honourable *S.* Earl of *B.* Lord Lieutenant and Custos Rotulorum of the County of *H.*

To *P. E.* Esq; High Sheriff for the County of *C.* *Mr High Sheriff; Sir.*

To the Right Honourable Sir *A. B.* Knight, Lord Mayor of the City of London. *My Lord, Your Lordship.*

To the Right Worshipful *C. D.* Esq; Alderman of Tower Ward, London.

To the Right Worshipful Sir *E. F.* Recorder of the City of London.

To the Worshipful *G. H.* Esq; Mayor of *C.* *Mr Mayor, Sir; Your Worship.*

To the Worshipful *J. K.* Esq; one of his Majesty's Justices of the Peace for the County of *S.* *Your Worship.*

To *L. M.* Esq; Deputy Steward of the City and Liberty of *W.* *Mr Deputy; Sir.*

## To the Governors under the Crown.

TO His Excellency *J.* Lord *C.* Lord Lieutenant of the Kingdom of Ireland. *My Lord Lieutenant; Your Excellency.*

To their Excellencies the Lords Justices of the Kingdom of Ireland. *Your Excellencies.*

To the Right Honourable *J.* Earl of *L.* Governor of Dover Castle, and Lord-Warden of the Cinque-Ports. *My Lord, Your Lordship.*

To the Right Honourable *C.* Lord Viscount *D.* Constable of the Tower.

To His Excellency *J. H.* Esq; Captain General and Governor in Chief of the Leeward Caribbee Islands, America. *Governor; Your Excellency.*

To the Honourable *F. N.* Esq; Lieutenant-Governor of South Carolina.

To the Honourable *J. G.* Deputy-Governor of Portsmouth.

To the Honourable *G. P.* Esq; Governor of Fort St George, Madras, in East-India.

D          To

To the Worshipful the President and Governors of Christ's Hospital, London.

> *The Second Governors of Colonies, appointed by the King, are stiled* Lieutenant-Governors: *Those appointed by Proprietors, as the East-India Company, &c. are called* Deputy-Governors.

## To Incorporate Bodies.

TO the Honourable the Court of Directors of the United Company of Merchants of England, trading to the East-Indies.

To the Honourable the Sub-Governor, Deputy-Governor, and Directors of the South-Sea Company.

To the Honourable the Governor, Deputy-Governor, and Directors of the Bank of England.

To the Master and Wardens of the Worshipful Company of Drapers.

## To the Gentry.

TO the Honourable Sir *C. W.* Bart. at *B.* near *L.*
To the Honourable Sir *W. S.* Knight, at *G.* in Suffolk.

To *R. Y.* Esq; at *M.* in Cheshire: Or to Mr *Y.* &c.

> *,\* The Wives of Knights and Baronets, are called* Lady *W.* or Lady *S. But the Wives of Esquires and other Gentlewomen, only* Mistress, *&c.*

## To Men of Trade and Professions.

TO Mr *G. F.* Merchant in Austin-Friars, London.

To Dr *R. M.* in Bloomsbury-Square, London.

To Mr *D. S.* Surgeon, in Covent-Garden, London.

To Mr *X. Y.* Pewterer, in Friday-Street, London.

To Mr *J. D.* Writing-Master, at Rotherhith, near London.

> *,\* It will be proper to mention the Designations of the Abodes of less eminent Traders, as well as their Professions.*

To

To the Honourable the Court of Directors of the United Company of Merchants of England, trading to the East-Indies.

*The Humble Petition of* HAMPDEN HARDY,

SHEWETH,

THAT your Petitioner, having been bred to Writing and Merchants-Accompts, humbly presumes himself qualified to serve your Honours in the East-Indies.

Your Petitioner therefore humbly prays, Your Honours will please to entertain him as a Writer for one of your Factories in India; wherein he will demean himself with the utmost Diligence and Faithfulness, and give such Security as your Honours shall require.

*And your Petitioner shall ever pray,* &c.

---

## RECREATION IV.

(24) A Chaise, Horse, and Harness, were together valued at 50 *l.* the Horse in Harness was worth 38 *l.* 16 *s.* 6 *d.* the Chaise and Harness were estimated at 13 *l.* 13 *s.* Their several Valuations are required?

*Answer,* Harness 2 *l.* 9 *s.* 6 *d.*

(25) Supposing that for a Quarter's Rent I paid in Money 7 *l.* 7 *s.* 6 *d.* and was allowed for a small Repair 18 *s.* 9 *d.* and for the King's Tax 8 *s.* 9 *d.* What did my Tenement go at a Year?

*Answer,* 35 *l.*

(26) At Leicester and several other Places they weigh their Coals by a Machine, in the Nature of a Steelyard, Waggon and all; three of these Draughts together amount to Cwt. 137. 2 *qrs.* 10 *lb.* and the Tare of the Waggon was Cwt. 13 ¼: How many Coals had the Customer to pay for?

*Answer,* Cwt. 97. 3 *qr.* 10 *lb.*

Seth

(27) Seth was born when Adam was 130 Years of Age, and 800 Years before our said Grandsire's Death: Seth at the Age of 105 Years, had Enos: He, at 90, was Father to Cainan, who at 70 had Mahalaleel. This Man at 65 begat Jared, who, having lived 162 Years, was Father to Enoch: This Patriarch at 65 Years of Age had Methuselah: And by the Time he was 187 Years of Age, his Son Lamech came into the World, who at 182 Years old was Father to Noah; and when Noah was 600 Years old, the Flood swept away the Bulk of Mankind. In what Year of the World did this happen, and how long after the Death of Adam?

*Answer*, 726 Years after Adam's Decease.

(28) From the Creation to the Flood was 1656 Years; thence to the Building of Solomon's Temple, 1336 Years; thence to Mahomet, who lived 622 Years after Christ, 1630 Years: In what Year of the World was Christ then born?

*Answer*, Anno 4000.

(29) When the Air presses with its full Weight, in very fair Weather, it may be demonstrated, that there press upon a human Body about 33905 Pounds of that fluid Matter; and in very foul-Weather, when the Air is most light, but 30624 Pounds. What Difference of Weight lies on such a Body, in the two greatest Alterations of the Weather?

*Answer*, 3281 Pounds Avoirdupoiz.

(30) If the mean Distances between the Earth and Sun be 81 Millions of Miles, and between the Earth and Moon 240 Thousands: How far are these two Luminaries asunder in an Eclipse of the Sun, when the Moon is lineally between the Earth and Sun? and in another of the Moon, when the Earth is in a Line between Her and Him?

*Answer*, Of the Sun 80760000 Miles; the Moon 81240000.

(31) Hipparchus and Archimedes of Syracuse, about 200 Years before Christ; Possidonius 50 Years before the said grand Period, and Ptolomy 140 Years after it, all advanced the Science of Astronomy. How long did each of these Persons flourish before the Year of Christ 1750?

*Answer*, Possidonius 1800. Ptolomy 1610 Years.

(32) What Difference is there between the Ages of *A.* born in the Year 1693, and *B.* that will be born 13 Years hence; The Question being put Anno 1750?

*Answer*, 70 Years.

*Various*

*Various Forms of* ACQUITTANCES, *when an Apprentice or Servant receives Money for the Use of his Master or Employer,* &c.

REceived May 13, 1764. of Mr Adam Brown, Nine Pounds twelve Shillings, for my Master Daniel Cole, on Accompt,

9*l.* 12*s.*                              ♰ *Timothy Telmoney.*

Received the 24th of June, 1764. of Clement Dandridge, Forty-five Pounds eight Shillings six Pence, in full for my Master Edward Ford,

45*l.* 8*s.* 6*d.* -                      ♰ *George Harmless.*

Received the              of              of Mr Philip Quiney and Company One hundred Pounds, for Mr Jonathan Gosling and Partners,

100*l.*                                    ♰ *Richard Smithers.*

Received the              of              of the Honourable East-India Company, by the Hands of Richard Blount Esq; Two thousand Pounds ten Shillings, for Mr Durant and Company,

2000*l.* 10*s.*                           ♰ *Titus Valuable.*

Received the                         of the Governor and Company of the Bank of England, by the Hands of Mr Abraham Gualtier, Seven thousand forty-one Pounds eleven Shillings, for Mr Zeuxy and Company,

7041*l.* 11*s.*                           ♰ *Young Zanthy.*

Received                         of the Worshipful Company of Mercers, by the Hands of Mr George Clerk, Ninety-two Pounds, for my Father Edward Yates.

92*l.*                                     ♰ *James Yates.*

\*\*\* *Date each Transaction in Business according to the precise Time when it happened.*

Received

Received                    of the Right Honourable Sir John Eyles, Baronet and Lord Mayor of London, Thirty Pounds, for the Use of the Artillery Company, London.

30 *l.*                    ⅌ *John Blackwell,* Clerk.

Received Nov. 17. 1764. of Mr Edward Froward, Ten Pounds for a Quarter's Rent due at Michaelmas laſt, for my Maſter Geo. Truſtnone.

10 *l.*                    ⅌ *Clement Dealwell.*

Received the          of                    of Mr Lawrence Shifter, Twenty-nine Pounds ſix Shillings, in Part of a Bill of ninety Pounds, due the third Inſtant to Mr Simon Dealwell.

29 *l.* 6 *s.*                    ⅌ *Phineas Quiet.*

Received of Mr Andrew Allpaid, by Order and on Account of Mr Humphry Hoardmoney, One hundred Pounds for Mr John Graham and Company, this 14th of March, 1764.

100 *l.*                    ⅌ *Thomas Truſty.*

Received the          of                    of Mr Benjamin Banker, by Order of Mr Nicolas Factor, the Sum of One hundred Pounds ſix Shillings eight Pence, on Accouut of Mr Thomas Truſtall of Colcheſter. I ſay, Received for my Maſter Edm. Goodman and Partner,

100 *l.* 6 *s.* 8 *d.*                    ⅌ *Jonas Diligent.*

Received this 2d of October, 1764. of *P. D.* Eſq; the Sum of Ninety-four Pounds in Caſh, and an Aſſignment on Meſſrs *R. S.* and *S. T.* for One hundred Pounds more, which when diſcharged, will be in full for Meſſrs *T. B.* and *S. N.*

  ⅌ Caſh, 94 *l.*
  ⅌ Aſſign. 100 *l.*
                    ⅌ *Jonas Competent.*

    In all——194 *l.*

                    *R E C R E*

# RECREATION V.

(33) A Gentleman at his Death left his eldeft Son once and a half what he allotted his Daughter, and to the young Lady 1383 *l*. lefs than her Mother; to whom he bequeathed four Times what he left towards the Endowment of Hertford College, Oxon, *viz.* 1640 Guineas. I require what he intended for his younger Son, who claimed under the Will, half as much as his Mother and Sifter? How much lefs than 30,600 *l*. did the Teftator die worth his Debts and Funeral Expences being 988 *l*. 10 *s*.?

*Anfwer*, 4426 10*s*.

(34) A Grant was made by the Crown, Anno 1239, which was forfeited 237 Years before the Revolution in 1688: How long did the fame fubfift?

*Anfwer*, 312 Years.

(35) Mofes was born Anno Mundi 2433; Homer 832 Years after him, Julius Cæfar lived 40 Years before our Saviour, and Alexander 312 Years before Cefar: Now as Chrift was incarnate 4000 Years after the Creation, the Sum of the Intervals between Homer and the three great Per- fonages laft mentioned is required?

*Anfwer*, 1813 Years.

(36) The Semidiameter of the Earth's Orbit, or annual Path round the Sun, in the Center of the Syftem, is about 81,000,000 of Miles; that of Venus 59,000,000; when they are both on the fame Side the Sun they are *in Perigæo*; when on different Sides, *in Apogæo*: What is the Difference of their Diftances in both thofe Circumftances?

*Anfwer*, 118 Millions of Miles.

(37) A young Fellow owed his Guardian 74 *l*. 18 *s*. 2 *d*. on Balance. He paid off 41 *l*. 14 *s*. 8 *d*. and then declared his Sifter owed the Gentleman half as much again as him- felf: On hearing this, fhe pays off in a Pet 13 *l*. 12 *s*. 10 *d*. and gives out that her Uncle William was not then lefs in Arrear than her Brother and fhe together. The Uncle here- upon pays in 24 *l*. 7 *s*. 3 *d*. and then the Uncle's Brother, who, by the By, was not the Uncle of thofe Children, for 150 *l*. undertakes to fet them all clear, and has 35 *l*. 15 *s*. 5 *d*. he fays, to fpare: Can that be true?

*Anfwer*, The Father was no doubt an Accomptant.

(38) A

(38) *A.* was born when *B.* was 18 Years of Age: How old shall *A.* be when *B.* is 41? And what will be the Age of *B.* when *A.* is 72?

*Answer,* A. 23. B. 90.

(39) In a Company *S.* had 3 *l.* 17 *s.* 2 *d.* more than *T.* who had six Guineas less than *R.* who had within 16 *s.* 8 *d.* as much as *W.* who was known to have 100 Guineas wanting ten Marks of 13 *s.* 4 *d.* each. Pray what Money had they among them?

*Answer,* 382 *l.* 1 *s.* 10 *d.*

(40) The Building of Solomon's Temple was in the Year of the World 3000; Troy was by Computation, built 443 Years before the Temple, and 260 before London: Now Carthage was built 113 Years before Rome, founded 744 Years before Christ, born Anno Mundi 4000; is London or Carthage the ancienter City, and how much?

*Answer,* London by 326 Years.

(41) You were born 34 Years after me; how old shall I be when you are 17? and how old will you be when I am 70 Years of Age?

*Answer,* I 51. You 36.

(42) *A.* is 17, *B.* 7. what will their Ages severally be when the Elder is double the Age of the Younger?

*Answer,* A. 20. B. 10.

(43) Five notable Discoveries were made in 215 Years Time, *viz.* 1. The Invention of the Compass. 2. Gun-Powder. 3. Printing. 4. The Discovery of America. 5. Truth, in the Reformation. The last was brought about Anno 1517: The third 77 Years before: The second 42 Years after the first; and the fourth 148 Years after the second. The Question is, In what Year of Christ did each of these happen to be found?

*Answer,* Compass, Anno 1302. Fire-Arms, 1344. Printing, 1440. America, 1492.

(44) Three and thirty Years before the Restoration in 1660, the Crown granted Demesnes to certain Uses for 210 Years then to come. The Proprietor in 1715, procured a reversionary Grant for 99 Years, to commence after the Expiration of the first: In what Year of Christ will the second Term end?    *Answer,* Anno 1936.

Trajan's

(45) Trajan's Bridge over the Danube is said to have had 20 Piers to support the Arches, every Pier being 60 Feet thick, and some of them were 150 Feet above the Bed of the River; they were also 170 Feet asunder: Pray what was the Width of the River in that Place; and how much did it exceed the Length of Westminster Bridge, which is about 1200 Feet from Shore to Shore, and is supported by 11 Piers, making the Number of Arches 12?

*Answer,* The Danube in that Place was 3570 Feet broader than the Thames at Westminster.

(46) A public Edifice was finished toward the Close of the 10th of King John, who began his Reign 134 Years after the Conquest in 1066; and it stood till within 70 Years of the Peace of Utrecht, in 1713: Of what Duration was it?

*Answer,* 433 Years.

(47) The Powder-plot was discovered 88 Years after the Reformation in 1517: The Murder of King Charles the First was committed 43 Years after that Discovery: The Accession of the Brunswic Family to the Crown was in 1714; just 54 Years after the Return of King Charles the Second, who had lived in Exile ever since the Death of his Father Charles the First: How long was that?

*Answer,* 12 Years.

(48) A. is 13 Years younger than B. and 17 Years older than C. who in the Year 1711, was known to be 24 Years of Age: How old was each of these Persons in 1733?

*Answer,* A. 63. B. 76. C. 46.

(49) Arphaxad was born to Shem two Years after the Deluge, and 500 before his Father's Death; but at 35 Years of Age he had Selah, who at 30 was Father to Eber; who at 34 had Peleg; and he lived 430 Years after that: The Question is, whether Shem or Eber died the first? and at nine-score and fourteen Years after the Death of the longer Liver, what Interval might be wanting to complete the Term of 1000 Years after the Flood?

*Answer,* Eber was the Survivor by 29 Years. Interval 275 Years.

(50) B. was born 14 Years after C. who came into the World 19 Years before A. who was 23 Years of Age eight Years ago: What then is the Age of D. who is within 22 Years of being as old as those three together?

*Answer,* 95 Years.

E         Various

## Various Forms of ACQUITTANCES upon Receipt of Money by MASTERS, AGENTS, and MEN of BUSINESS.

REceived the 29th of July, 1764. of Meſſrs Samuel and Simon Surepay, Five hundred and forty Pounds on Accompt,

540 *l.*                                    ⅌ *William Percival.*

Received the                of                of the Right Honourable Arthur Onſlow Eſq; the Sum of Two hundred and fifty Pounds, in full of all Demands for Self and Company,

250 *l.*                                    ⅌ *Joſiah Milner.*

Received the                of                of Mr Clerk Powel, the Sum of Ten Pounds ten Shillings in Part of my growing Salary and Subſiſtance,

10 *l.* 10 *s.*                         ⅌ *Hamilton Horſeman.*

Received the                of                of Mr Charles Torriano, Twenty-five Pounds, in full for the Difference of two thou-ſand five hundred Pounds Bank Stock,

25 *l.*                                    ⅌ *Jacob Farmer.*

Received the 19th of June, 1764. of Mr James Shaw, Thirty Pounds, in full for ſix Months Intereſt of twelve hundred Pounds, due at Lady-Day laſt,

30 *l.*                                    ⅌ *Gabriel Growth.*

Received the        of                by the Order and for the Uſe of Mr Henry Marr, of Mr Stephen Stone, Eight Pounds ten Shillings, and allowed for Taxes and Re-pairs One Pound ten, together the Sum of Ten Pounds, in full for a Quarter's Rent due at Michaelmas laſt,

10 *l.*                                    ⅌ *Randal Rentgather.*

Received

Received             of Mr Lewis Landlove, Twenty five Pounds, in full for half a Year's Rent due at Chriſtmas laſt; out of which, deducted for Taxes Five Pounds, and for Repairs Two Pounds. I ſay, Received for and by Order of Robert Richer Eſq;

25 *l.*                   ♣ *Chriſtopher Countwell.*

Received            by the Hands of Mr Peter Prentice, by Order of Chamberlain Truſtee Eſq; Thirteen Pounds ſeven Shillings in Money, allowed for Taxes Thirty three Shillings, in all Fifteen Pounds, being for half a Year's Rent due at Lady-Day laſt, from Capt. Richard Roundears,

15 *l.*                  ♣ *Martin Moore.*

Received            of the Executors of Charles late Earl of Glendore, by the Hands of Mr Iſaac Cavendiſh, the Sum of Seventy five Pounds, in full for my half Year's Annuity due at Lady-Day laſt,

75 *l.*                  ♣ *Ann Bridgman.*

Received May 23, 1764. of the Right Reverend Edward Lord Biſhop of Durham, by the Hands of Mr Stephen Rainer, the Sum of Ninety Pounds, and is in full for three Quarterly Payments of my Annuity due at Michaelmas, Chriſtmas, and Lady-Day laſt,

90 *l.*                  ♣ *Charlot Cruſty.*

Received of Mr *A. B.* the Sum of Ten Pounds in Money, and a Note of his Hand, bearing equal Date with this, for Fourteen Pounds more; which Note, when paid, will be in full of all Demands to this        Day of
                     ♣ *Charles Cautious.*

Received            of Robert Ayliff Eſq; and Owners of the Prince Frederic, the Sum of Seventy three Pounds ten Shillings, in full for Cordage, Tackle and Trimming furniſhed the ſaid Ship,

73 *l.* 10 *s.*              ♣ *Samuel Cluely.*

## PROMISSORY NOTES by BANKERS Apprentices and Servants.

London, Jan. 27. 1764.

I Promise to pay the Honourable Charles Villiers Esq; or Bearer, on Demand, Fifty Pounds,

For Sir Richard Daventry and Partners,

*Charles Streeke.*

———

50 *l.*

London,

I promise to pay to the Honourable Directors of the English Company Trading to East - India, or Bearer, on Demand, Four hundred Pounds,

For my Father James Smith,

*Thomas Smith.*

———

400 *l.*

London,

I promise to pay the Royal African Company, or Bearer, on Demand, Three thousand six hundred and forty four Pounds thirteen Shillings and six Pence,

For my Masters Jennings and Willbraham.

*Adam Tellmoney.*

———

3644 *l.* 13 *s.* 6 *d.*

## MASTERS PROMISSORY NOTES.

I Promise to pay Mr Edward Jones, or Bearer, on Demand, Seven hundred Pounds. April 14. 1764.

*Simon Sogood.*

———

700 *l.*

I promise to pay to the Governor and Company of the Bank of England, Nine thousand Pounds,

For Self and Partners. July 6th. 1764.

*Francis Fairfax.*

———

9000 *l.*

London, 1764.

I promise to pay Joseph Pennington Esq; Cashier of His Majesty's Revenue of Excise, or Order, forty Days after Date, Four hundred and thirty Pounds, Value received,

⅌ *Conrade Collector.*

———

430 *l.*

I pro-

I promise to pay Paul Portsoken Esq; or Order, on Demand, Three hundred ninety-four Pounds two Shillings and six Pence, Value received this        of        1764.

394 *l.* 2 *s.* 6 *d.*        ℔ *Timothy Theobalds.*

I promise to pay Sir Joseph Jebb, or Order, the Sum of Thirty Pounds in Manner following; Ten Pounds, Part thereof, two Months after Date; Ten Pounds more the 17th of March next; and the remaining Ten Pounds, the 24th of June next following; Value received: Witness my Hand at London, the        of        1764.

30 *l.*        *Daniel Douglas.*

Bromley, May 10. 1764. 100 *l.*

Borrowed and received of Mr Aaron Goodfriend, the Sum of One hundred Pounds Sterling, which I promise to pay the said Aaron Goodfriend, or Order, upon Demand: Witness my Hand,

Witness { *John Brown,* *Geo. Radford.*        *Nicolas Needham.*

I promise to pay to Capt. Alexis Edgecomb, or Order, on Demand, Eighteen Pounds eight Shillings and nine Pence, furnished by my Order to Lieutenant Charles Cornwall, as appears by his Receipts delivered this 12 December, 1764. to

18 *l.* 8 *s.* 9 *d.*        *Hugh Harrold.*

London, July 5. 1764.

I promise to furnish Mr Gregory Fitz-Harding with Bills of Exchange to the Value of Five thousand Pounds Sterling, at current Exchange, payable to himself or Order in Messina the next ensuing Fair: Value of Sir John Trevor received,

5000 *l.*        ℔ *Edward Essington.*

I promise to pay to Gregory Goosequill Esq; or Order, the Sum of Fifty Pounds, on Demand, after Receipt of a Bill of Exchange drawn the 10th current by Humphry Herringbone on Henry Dashet of Southampton, Malster, for the like Sum payable to William Pierce Esq; or Order, which said Gregory Goosequill has indorsed to me this 28th of January, 1764.

*Alfred Dunning.*

50 *l.*        I pro-

I promiſe to return her Grace the Dutcheſs Dowager of Tredegar, or Order, on Demand, one Caſket of Jewels, ſealed, One hundred Ounces of Gold Plate, Three hundred and fifty of ditto Silver, Seventy Caracts of Oriental Pearl, and a Thouſand Pound Bank-Note, Received of her ſaid Grace,

For Self and Company, Nov. 19. 1764.

₱ *Trojan Truſly.*

Received of *W. L.* Eſq; nine Deeds, all relating to his Eſtate in the Pariſh of Dovebridge, near Utoxeter; which I promiſe to return the ſaid *W. L.* or Order, undamaged, on Demand. Witneſs my Hand, this      Day of

*Roger Norton.*

Obſerve, Promiſſory Notes for a valuable Conſideration ſhould always mention the *Value received,* if the Thing itſelf be not ſpecified; this gives them Validity in a Court of Judicature.

A Promiſſory Note, mentioning *Order*, is indorſible from one Perſon to another, which is done by the preſent Poſſeſſor's writing his Name on the Back of it, and delivering it up to the Party to whom he intends to aſſign over his Property therein.

It is unneceſſary to have a Promiſſory Note payable to *Bearer* indorſed, if you are ſatisfied the Note is good.

The delivering up a Promiſſory Note to the Perſon who ſigned it, is a ſufficient Voucher of its being paid; nor is there any need of writing a Receipt thereon.

Promiſſory Notes, and Book-Debts, if not legally demanded in the Space of ſix Years, cannot be recovered by Law.

If you keep a Promiſſory Note *on Demand* in your own Hands above three Days, and the Perſon it is upon ſhould fail, the Loſs will be your own; but if he fail within the three Days, it will light, in Equity, on the Perſon that paid it you.

*RECRE-*

## RECREATION VI.

(51) JACOB, by Contract, was to serve Laban for his two Daughters 14 Years; and when he had accomplished 11 Years, 11 Months, 11 Weeks, 11 Days, 11 Hours, and 11 Minutes, Pray how long had he yet to serve?

*Answ.* 1 Year, 9 Mon. 3 Wks, 2 Dys, 12 Ho. 49 Min.

(52) Of the noble Family of Cornaro, the Grandsire's Age was 134 Years, and he was 93 Years older than the Son, at the Time when the Son and Father's Age together made 112 Years: Distinguish their Ages?

*Answer,* Son 41, &c.

(53) *B.* was 14 Years old when *C.* was 25: How old shall *C.* be when *B.* comes to be 25?

*Answer,* 36.

(54) *K.* is 19 Years older than *L.* who was 27 Years of Age in the South-Sea Year, 1720: How old is *M.* in 1740, who, in the Year 1738, was within 24 Years of being as old as both of them together?

*Answer,* 87.

(55) England was conquered by William I. Oct. 4. 1066; his Son William II. came to the Crown Sept. 9. 1087, and left it Aug. 2. 1100; William III. received it Feb. 3. 1689, and died March 8. 1701: How many Days did each of these Princes govern, respect being had to the intercalary Days (added to February every Leap-Year) as they rose in the Course of Time?

*Answer, Will.* I. 7645 Days. *Will.* II. 4710 Days. *Will.* III. 4416 Days.

Note, *Every fourth Year is* Leap-Year *or* Bissextile: *To find which are such, divide the Year of our Lord by 4. and when nothing remains, those are the Leap-Years; and to such you add one Day more than 365.*

(56) *B.* Born 161 Years ago, died when *C.* was 47 Years of Age, who it seems came into the World 180 Years since, and out-lived *B.* 43 Years: The Sum of the Ages of these two Persons is required?

*Answer,* 118 Years.

If

(57) If Sampson was born 17 Years after Timothy, and Timothy 26 Years before Jacob, who 28 Years hence will be juft 50: In what Year of Chrift were they feverally born; the Queftion being propofed Anno 1750?

*Anfwer, Jacob* 1728. *Sampfon* 1719. *Timothy* 1702.

(58) Richard the Firft fucceeded his Father Henry II. July 7. 1189; John his Brother fucceeded him April 6. 1199. Richard the Second fucceeded Edward the Third on the 21ft of June 1377; and was depofed by Henry IV. on the 30th of September, 1399. The third Richard caufed his Nephew Edward V. and his Brother, to be murdered on the 18th of June, 1483; and was flain himfelf on the 22d of Auguft, 1485. How many Days was the Realm governed by the three Richards, refpect being ftill had to the intercalary Days as they happened?

*Anfwer*, 12493 Days.

(59) *B.* born Anno 1108, lived 48 Years before *C.* who was 113 Years fenior to *D.* and *X.* was 114 Years before *Y.* who was 74 Years after *Z.* born Anno 1527: In what Years of Chrift were thefe Men feverally born?

*Anfwer, C.* 1156. *D.* 1269. *X.* 1487. *Y.* 1601.

(60) *A.* Born 445 Years before the Year 1733, died Anno 1362; *B.* born 37 Years ago, will die 18 Years hence; *C.* born 256 Years ago, died 197 Years fince; *D.* born Anno 1578, lived till within 75 Years of the faid 1733: The Length of thefe Peoples Lives is feverally required?

*Anfwer, A.* 74. *B.* 55. *C.* 59. *D.* 80 Years.

(61) *A.* Born Anno Chrifti 318, lived 207 Years before *B.* who lived 104 Years after *C.* who was Succeffor to *D.* 84 Years; *E.* was alfo 112 Years after *D.* but Predeceffor to *F.* by 47 Years: In what Year of Chrift did each of thefe Gentlemen flourifh?

*Anfwer, B.* 525. *C.* 421. *D.* 337. *E.* 449. *F.* 496.

(62) If I am 42 Years older than you now, what will be the Difference of our Ages 14 Years after my Deceafe, in cafe you fhall then furvive? *Anfwer*, 28 Years.

(63) A Snail in getting up a Maypole, only 20 Feet high, was obferved to climb 8 Feet every Day, but every Night he came down again 4 Feet: In what Time by this Method did he reach the Top of the Pole? *Anfwer*, in 4 Days.

BILLS

## BILLS OF PARCELS.

The Honourable the Lady Ashley,

Bought of Lemuel Linen-Draper and Partner.

|  |  | s. | d. |  | l. |
|---|---|---|---|---|---|
| 1764. |  |  |  |  |  |
| Mar. 16 Ells of Dowlas | at | 1 | 4 | ℔ Ell. |  |
| 22½ Ells of Holland | at | 3 | 4 |  |  |
| 1 Ps. of Cambrick |  |  |  |  | 3 . 4 . 6 |
| A Ps. of Muslin |  |  |  |  | 2 . 17 . 3 |
| 8s½ Ells of Diaper | at | 1 | 10 |  |  |
| 19½ Ells of Damask | at | 4 | 3 |  |  |
|  |  |  |  |  | l. 22 . 17 . 8½ |

Madam Strawberry.

Bought of Manywords Milliner.

|  |  | s. | d. |  | l. |
|---|---|---|---|---|---|
| 1764. |  |  |  |  |  |
| Apr. 15½ Yards of flower'd Ribband | at | 2 | 3 |  |  |
| 3 Pair of Roman Gloves | at | 9 | 4 | ℔ Pair |  |
| 6 Dozen of Irish Lamb, ditto | at | 1 | 3 |  |  |
| 7 Sarcenet Hoods, white | at | 4 | 6 | each |  |
| 15 Fans, French Paper Mount | at | 3 | 3 |  |  |
| A Ps. of Mechlin Lace, 16 Yards | at | 13 | 10 | ℔ Yard |  |
|  |  |  |  |  | l. 22 . 14 5½ |

The Right Honourable the Countess of Night and Day,

Bought of Mary Tombs.

| 1764. | | | l. | s. | d. | | l. |
|---|---|---|---|---|---|---|---|
| 3 Feb. | 36 China Plates | at | 0 | 3 | 8 each | | |
| | 18 Dishes, ditto | at | 0 | 10 | 6 | | |
| | 2½ Pair of Jars, and a Pair of Beekers, allowed | | | | | | 13 . 10 . 6 |
| | A Tea-Table Set compleat | | | | | | 3 . 18 . 4 |
| | Indian Sprig'd Muslin, 1 Ps. qt. 14⅞ Yards | at | 0 | 9 | 0 | | |
| | Fine Chints, 10 Ps. | at | 3 | 3 | 6 ⅌ Ps. | | |

l. 71 . 14 . 2½

Mrs Frances Pindust,

Bought of Isaac Hosier, 10 Apr. 1764.

| | | | s. | d. | | l. |
|---|---|---|---|---|---|---|
| 15 | Pair of Womens Worsted, mixt | at | 5 | 7 ⅌ Pair | | |
| 23 | Pair of Mens Silk | at | 17 | 4 | | |
| 22 | Pair of Mens Yarn | at | 3 | 2 | | |
| 18 | Pair of Norwich Hose | at | 4 | 9 | | |
| 38 | Pair of Thread | at | 3 | 4 | | |
| 13 | Pair of Women Gloves, Silk | at | 4 | 8 | | |

l. 41 . 4 . 11

Mrs Sarah Johnson,

## Bought of Theophilus Fruiterer.

| 1764. | | | l. | s. | d. | |
|---|---|---|---|---|---|---|
| 3 Apr. | 7 Dozen of Malaga Lemons | ——— | at | 2 . | 3 | ₰ Dozen — l. |
| | 8¼ Hundred of Lisbon, ditto | ——— | at | 7 . | 2 | ₰ Hund. |
| | 9 Ropes of Spanish Onions | ——— | at | 1 . | 6 | each |
| | 1 Bushel of ditto Chesnuts | ——— | | | | 0 . 7 . 10 |
| | 43 Dozen of best China and Seville Oranges | | at | 1 . | 2 | ₰ Dozen |
| | 12 Pomegranates | ——— | at | 0 . | 4¼ | |

l 7 . 12 . 8

Mr Claude Cockson,

## Bought of Robert Fishmonger and Partner.

| 1764. | | | l. | s. | d. | |
|---|---|---|---|---|---|---|
| 27 Mar. | 3 Hundred of Haberdine | ——— | at | 7 . | 10 . 6 | each — l. |
| | 1½ Hundred of Ling | ——— | at | 8 . | 12 . 6 | |
| | 4¼ Hundred of Stockfish | ——— | at | 4 . | 10 . 6 | |
| | 4 Kegs of Sturgeon | ——— | at | 0 . | 16 . 10½ | |
| | 6¼ Barrels of Herrings | ——— | at | 3 . | 10 . 2 | |
| | 95 Dried Salmon | ——— | at | 0 . | 1 . 2 | |

l. 87 . 11 . 11

F 2

James Bateman Esq;

Bought of Clement Coffeeseller, Feb. 10. 1764.

| | | s. | d. | | |
|---|---|---|---|---|---|
| 27¼ Pound of Smyrna Coffee | at | 5 . | 8 | ℘ Pound | |
| 33 Pound of Mocha, ditto | at | 5 . | 4 | | |
| 26½ Pound of Imperial Tea | at | 25 . | 0 | | |
| 10¼ Pound of best Bohea | at | 14 . | 6 | | |
| 13 Pound of Royal Green Tea | at | 18 . | 8 | | |
| 21 Pound of Sugar double refined | at | 1 . | 0½ | | |
| | | | | | l. 70 . 13 . 4 |

The Honourable Mrs Vaughan,

Bought of Simon Salter and Partner.

| 1764. | | | s. | d. | | l. |
|---|---|---|---|---|---|---|
| 5 June. | 13½ Pound of Anchovies | at | 1 . | 4½ | ℘ Pound. | |
| | 30 Pound of Capers | at | 0 . | 10¼ | | |
| | 12¼ Pound of Saltpetre | at | 1 . | 2½ | | |
| | 2½ Gall. of pickl'd Mushrooms | at | 3 . | 7 | ℘ Quart. | |
| | 4½ Gall. of Lucca Oil | at | 12 . | 0 | ℘ Gallon. | |
| | A Westphalia Ham, wt. 20lb. | at | 0 . | 11½ | ℘ Pound. | |
| | | | | | | l. 8 . 8 . 7 |

Mr Edward Shakespear,    Bought of James Pewterer and Jonathan Brasier,

1764.
Oct. 20. Hard-metal Plates, 3 doz. wt. 50 lb. ——— at 1 . 4 ⅌ Pound. ——— l.
8 Dishes ditto, a Monteth, and Colender, wt 40 lb. at 1 . 6
A Copper, with a discharging Cock, wt. 66½ lb. at 1 . 4½
Iron-Work to ditto, and a Crane, wt. 97 lb. at 0 . 2¾
A Stove Grate, with Shovel, Tongs, Poker and Fender
A large Brass Pot and Saucepan, wt. 38 lb. ——— at 1 . 7    1 . 18 . 6

l. 16 . 19 . 0

Mr John Doyley,    Bought of Ferdinand Farrier, May 5. 1764.

s. d.
Coney Skins, 1300 ——— at 13 . 6 ⅌ Hund. ——— l.
Beaver, 180 l. at 7 . 8 ⅌ Pound.
A Sable Muff and Tippet, allowed    21 . 0 . 0
Fitch Skins, 90 at 0 . 3 ⅌ Skin.
Otter Skins, 50 at 3 . 0
Hare Skins, 14c at 9 . 6 ⅌ Hund.

l. 108 . 5 . 0½

Mr Edward Cordwainer,     Bought of Adam Leatherseller.

| | | | | s. | d. | | | l. |
|---|---|---|---|---|---|---|---|---|
| 1764. | | | | | | | | |
| Nov. 17. | Large oiled Lamb Skins, 215 | — | — | at 1 . | 3½ | ⅌ Skin. | — | — |
| | Goat Skins, 130 | — | — | at 0 . | 11¼ | | — | — |
| | Allomed Sheep Skins, 137 | — | — | at 1 . | 3 | | — | — |
| | Calves Skins, 19 | — | — | at 4 . | 3 | | — | — |
| | Oil'd Buck, 15 | — | — | at 12 . | 9 | | — | — |
| | Russia Hides, 82 | — | — | at 12 . | 9 | | — | — |

l. 94 . 8 . 4

Capt. John Elford,     Bought of Thomas Cheesemonger.

| | Cwt. | qr. | lb. | l. | s. | d. | | l. |
|---|---|---|---|---|---|---|---|---|
| 1764. | | | | | | | | |
| Dec. 21. | Old Cheshire Cheeses, 12 — 5 . | 2 . | 24 | — at 1 . | 17 . | 4 | ⅌ Hund. | — |
| | Glocestershire Cheeses, 45 — 4 . | 2 . | 20 | — at 1 . | 12 . | 6 | | — |
| | Firkins of Butter, 12 — | | | — at 1 . | 10 . | 0 | each. | — |
| | Stilton Cheeses, 93 — 2 . | 3 . | 25 | — at 2 . | 16 . | 10 | ⅌ Hund | — |
| | Fitches of Bacon, 7 — wt. 49 Stone. | | | — at 0 . | 3 . | 4 | each. | — |
| | Suffolk Butter, 12 Weys | | | — at 8 . | 3 . | 8 | | — |

l. 150 . 18 . 9

Mr Jonathan Mariot,    Bought of George Grocer and Company.

1764.
Mar. 12.

| | Cwt. | qr. | lb. | | l. | s. | d. | |
|---|---|---|---|---|---|---|---|---|
| Sugar, 2 Hhds. | 17 | 2 | 17 | at | 1 | 13 | 10 | ℔ Hund. -- £ |
| Raisins, 11 Barrels | 12 | 1 | 19 | at | 1 | 14 | 5 | - |
| Tobacco, 1 Hhd. | 4 | — | 12 | at | 4 | 19 | 4 | - |
| Rice, 1 Barrel | 1 | — | 15 | at | 2 | 16 | 4 | - |
| Pepper, 1 Bag | 1 | 3 | 19 | at | 3 | 12 | 4 | - |
| Brimstone | 2 | 1 | 19 | at | 1 | 19 | 1 | - |
| Bees-Wax, 4 Cakes | 2 | 2 | 12 | at | 1 | 18 | 4 | - |

l. 91 . 9 . 9¼

Mrs Jane Somerset,    Bought of Edmund Brisk and Oswald Obliging.

1764.
Nov. 9.

| | | s. | d. | |
|---|---|---|---|---|
| 12¼ Yards of rich Brocaded Sattin | at | 18 | 6 | ℔ Yard. -- l. |
| 6 Yards of Mohair | at | 4 | 2 | - |
| 25¼ Yards of Paduasoy | at | 11 | 8 | - |
| 15½ Yards of flower'd Damask | at | 8 | 8 | - |
| 34¼ Yards of Poplin | at | 3 | 0 | - |
| 12½ Yards of Italian Mantua | at | 7 | 6 | - |
| 30 Yards of double Taffaty | at | 2 | 9 | - |

l. 48 . 8 . 9½

When the Money is paid down, either of the Partners may write thus:

Received at the same time of Madam Somerset the Sum of Forty-eight Pounds eight Shillings six Pence, in full of all Demands, for Self and Partner.

₧ *Oswald Obliging.*

Mr. Charles Thorold,

Bought of Sir William Ashurst and Company, Feb. 8, 1764.

|  | s. | d. |  | L |
|---|---|---|---|---|
| 10½ Yards of Yorkshire Cloth ——— | at 6 . | 6 | ₧ Yard. —— | |
| 7 Yards of fine Spanish Black ——— | at 16 . | 3 | | |
| 6¾ Yards of fine Grey-Cloth ——— | at 15 . | 9 | | |
| 16¼ Yards of Frieze ——— | at 3 . | 6 | | |
| 4 Yards of second Drab ——— | at 15 . | 6 | | |
| 5½ Yards of superfine Spanish Cloth ——— | at 18 . | 6 | | |
| 31 Yards of Livery Scarlet Cloth ——— | at 13 . | 6 | | |

l. 46 . 0 . 7¼

Received at the same time the full Contents for Sir William Ashurst and Company,

₧ *Michael Medcalf.*

*RECREA.*

# RECREATION VII.

(64) THE first Queen Mary came to the Crown July 8. 1553; she reigned 5 Years, 4 Months, and 9 Days; her Sister Elizabeth succeeded, and James I. came to her Throne the 14th of March 1602; and he left it to his Son Charles I. on the 27th of March 1625, who was forced from it, Jan. 30. 1648. The Question is, how many Days did these Princes reign? and at the Death of Charles I. how long had England been under an uninterrupted Succession of Protestant Princes (Mary I. being the last profess'd Papist that enjoy'd the Crown) not neglecting the intercalary Days in February, as before?

*Answer*, Eliz. 16188. James I. 8049. Charles I. 8709 Days.

(65) A Dealer bought two Lots of Snuff, that together weighed *Cwt.* 9. 100 *lb.* for 97 *l.* 17 *s.* 6 *d.* Their Difference in Point of Weight was *Cwt.* 1. 2 *qr.* 16 *lb.* and of Price 8 *l.* 13 *s.* 3 *d.* Their respective Weights and Values are required?

*Answer*, { Lot. 1. *Cwt.* 5 .. 86 *lb.* Cost 53 *l.* 5 *s.* 4 *d.* ⅘
{ Lot. 2. *Cwt.* 4 . 14 *lb.* 44 *l.* 12 *s.* 1 *d.* ⅘

(66) My Purse and Money, quoth Dick, are worth 12 *s.* 8 *d.* but the Money is worth seven of the Purse: Pray what was there in it?

*Answer*, 11 *s.* 1 *d.*

(67) By God's Blessing upon a Merchant's Industry, in ten Years Time he found himself possessed of 13000 *l.* It appeared from his Books, that the last three Years he had cleared 875 *l.* a Year; the three preceeding but 586 *l.* a Year; and before that but 364 *l.* a Year. The Question is, What was the State of his Fortune at every Year's End that he continued in Trade? and consequently, what had he to begin with?

*Answer*, 7167 *l.* original Stock.

(68) A. Born Anno 1441, lived till B. was 7 Years of Age, which was 23 Years before the Reformation in 1517. B. survived this remarkable Æra just 49 Years; C. born 9 Years after the Death of A. lived but till B. was 36 Years of Age: The Sum of the Ages of these three Persons is required?

*Answer*, Their Sum is 152 Years.

G                                            Sam

(69) Sam was born 28 Years before Toby who died at 12, and lived 19 Years after him. Rachel came to light when Sam was 16, and died 11 Years before him. Joſhua, when Rachel was 7 Years, being himſelf then 14, went abroad, where he continued 9 Years, and returning, ſurvived Rachel four Years. How old was each of theſe, and what is the Sum of their Ages? *Anſwer*, Sum 146 Years.

(70) A Grant was made Dec. 14 in the 10th of Henry I. who began his Reign Aug. 2. 1100; it was reſumed November 19, in the 4th of Henry III. who came to the Crown Oct. 19. 1216; it was revived the 16th Day of July, in the 13th of Henry VII. who aſcended the Throne Aug. 22. 1485: But it was a ſecond Time revoked, and finally ſuppreſſed in the 16th of his Succeſſor, Henry VIII. on the 10th of May. Now as this Man's Father died July 21. 1509; the Queſtion is, How many Days was this Grant in force, and how many did it lie dormant?

*Anſw.* 49947 Days in force; ſuperſeded 101778 Days.

(71) *A.* Born Anno 1438, died at 48 Years of Age; *B.* died Anno 1502, aged threeſcore and ſeventeen; *C.* in the Year 1577, was 22 Years of Age, and ſurvived that Time 54 Years: *D.* Anno 1616, had lived juſt half his Time, and died in 1648; *E.* was 13 Years old at the Death of *D.* and 14 Years after that was Father to *F.* who was 31 when his Son *G.* was born; who at his Grandſire's Death was 7 Years of Age; the Years of Chriſt, wherein theſe Men were born, and the Years wherein the firſt five of them died, are ſeverally required?

*Anſwer,* $\begin{cases} \text{Birth,} & A.\ 1438,\ B,\ 1425,\ C.\ 1555.\ D.\ 1584. \\ \text{Demiſe,} & 1486. \quad 1592. \quad 1631. \quad 1648. \\ \text{Birth,} & E.\ 1635.\ F.\ 1662.\ G.\ 1693. \\ \text{Demiſe,} & 1700. \end{cases}$

(72) *A.* Born 17 Years after *C.* and 13 before *B.* died 42 Years before King George the Second's Inauguration in 1727, aged 47 Years; *A.* died Anno 1712, and *B.* exactly 8 Years before him: *D.* born 23 Years before *C.* died at 64; *E.* born 1 Years after *B*'s Death, will die 12 Years after the Year 1733; and *F.* born juſt in the Midway of the Interval, between the Births of *A.* and *D.* is not to reach the Time of *E*'s Death by 14 Years: What is the Sum of all their Ages, and which of them liv'd longeſt?

*Anſwer,* The Sum 398 Years. *F.* Senior by 22 Years.

A Per-

(73) A Person said he had 20 Children, and that it happened there was a Year and a half between each of their Ages; his eldest was born when he was 24 Years old, and the Age of his youngest is now one and twenty: What was the Father's Age?          *Answer,* 73½ Years.

(74) A Sheepfold was robbed three Nights succeffively; the firft Night half the Sheep were stolen, and half a Sheep more; the second Night half of the Remainder were loft, and half a Sheep more; the laft Night they took half what were left, and half a Sheep more, by which time they were reduced to twenty: How many were there at firft?
*Answer,* 167.

(75) The Silk Mill at Derby contains 26586 Wheels, and 97746 Movements, which wind off or throw 73726 Yards of Silk every time the great Water-Wheel, which gives Motion to all the reft, goes about, which is three times in a Minute. The Queftion is, How many Yards of Silk may be thrown by this Machine in a Day, reckoning ten Hours a Day's Work? and how many in the Compafs of a Year, deducting for Sundays and great Holidays 63 Days, provided no Part of it ftand ftill?
*Answer,* 40077453600.

(76) What Difference is there between twice eight and twenty, and twice twenty eight: As alfo between twice five and fifty, and twice fifty five?
*Answer,* 20.   *Answer,* 50.

(77) What is the Difference, and what the Sum of fix dozen Dozen, and half a dozen Dozen?
*Answer,* Diff. 792. Sum 936.

(78) What Number taken from the Square of 54, will leave 19 times 46?          *Answer,* 2042.

(79) Subtract 30079 out of fourfcore and thirteen Millions, as often as it can be found, and fay what the laft Remainder exceeds or falls fhort of 21180?
*Answer,* Remainder 4631 more.

(80) What Number, added to the forty third Part of 4429, will make the Sum 240?          *Answer,* 137.

(81) What Number, deducted from the 26th Part of 2262, will leave the 87th Part of the fame?
*Answer,* 61.

# BILLS on BOOK-DEBTS.

The Right Honourable the Lord Bolfover, Dr.

To Paul Purfeproud, Upholder.

| 1764. | | l. | s. | d. |
|---|---|---|---|---|
| Apr. 19. | A rich Crimfon-Damafk Bed, laced, compleat | 75 | . — . | 8 |
| May 5. | A Set of Window-Curtains, and Vallance, ditto | 16 | . 11 . | 8 |
| 7. | A fine Carpet, Counterpane, and an Otter-down Quilt | 12 | . 10 . | 6 |
| June 6. | A Crimfon Velvet Eafy Chair, and 2 Stools, ditto | 13 | . 7 . | 6 |
| 13. | A wrought Dimity Bed and Furniture, compleat | 28 | . 18 . | 4 |
| Aug. 10. | A Down Bed, Bolfter, Pillows, with a Mattrafs and Quilt | 15 | . — . | — |
| | Chairs 10, with two-arm'd ditto, Walnut-tree framed | 34 | . 12 . | 6 |
| Nov. 20. | A Fire-Screen, Bed-Table, and Dreffing-Glafs | 8 | . 14 . | 6 |
| | The Lady Wanton's Picture in a rich Frame carv'd | 21 | . — . | — |

Sum l.

If a Servant receives the Bill, let the Receipt run thus :

Received the 30th December 1764. of the Right Honourable the Lord Bolfover, by the Hands of Mr Simon Steward, the full Contents, for my Mafter P. Purfeproud.

per B. Batchelor.

Her Grace the Duchess of Plinlimon, Dr.

## To Crew Cabinetmaker.

| | | l. | s. | d. |
|---|---|---|---|---|
| 1764. | | | | |
| Octob. 3. | A Chimney Glass, and a Pair of Sconces | 5 | 18 | — |
| | A Pair of Pier Glasses 72 Inches, in gilt Frames | 60 | — | 1 |
| 10. | A Pair of Indian Cabinets, at 43 l. 10 s. each | | | |
| | A fine Indian four-leaved Screen, and a Fire-Screen | 17 | 10 | — |
| Nov. 18. | A Book-Case, with Glass Doors, and a Corner Cupboard, ditto | 21 | — | 1 |
| 30. | A Walnut-tree Table, and a Set of Dressing-Boxes, japaned | 3 | 4 | 10 |
| Dec. 7. | A Tea-Table and Stand plated, wt. 103 oz. at 8 s. 4 d. ℔ 0℥ | | | |
| 30. | A Dozen and half of fine matted Chairs, at 18 s. 6 d. each | | | |
| 31. | Twelve Elbow-Chairs stuffed with Hair, at 1 l. 15 s. 6 d. each | 6 | 16 | 6 |
| | A Dressing-Table, with Implements for Writing | | | |
| | | l. 282 | 6 | 8 |

Received the 31st of December, 1764, of Her Grace the Duchess of Plinlimon Fifty Pounds in Part, for Mr Crew Cabinetmaker.

*per* Fairspoken Fairfax.

## Mr James Shortmeasure, Dr.

### To Walstone Winecooper.

| 1764. | | | s. | d. | |
|---|---|---|---|---|---|
| Mar. 28. | Palm Sack, 18 Gallons | at | 8 . | 6 | ℔ Gall. |
| Apr. 13. | Port Red, 35 Gall. | at | 5 . | 4 | |
| May 26. | Sherry, 17 Gall. | at | 6 . | 6 | |
| 31. | Rhenish, 19 Gall. | at | 6 . | 8 | |
| July 13. | White Lisbon, 32 Gall. | at | 4 . | 10 | |
| Aug. 30. | A double Chest of Florence, agreed for | | | 4 . 6 . 0 | |
| | 10½ Dozen of best Burgundy | at 50s. | | | ℔ Doz. |

l. 66 . 16 . 6

### The Reverend Mr Euclid Peachy, Dr. To John Percival and Partners.

| 1764. | | | s. | d. | |
|---|---|---|---|---|---|
| Mar. 27. | Oats | 5 Qrs. | at | 2 . | 3 ℔ Bush. |
| Apr. 9. | Beans | 9 Bush. | at | 4 . | 10 |
| May 16. | Bran | 7 Qrs. | at | 1 . | 10 |
| June 19. | Tares | 19 Bush. | at | 1 . | 1½ |
| 24. | Peas | 16 Bush. | at | 3 . | 1-1½ |
| July 2. | Pale Malt | 28 Bush. | at | 3 . | 2 |
| 17. | Hops | 17 Pounds | at | 1 . | 4 each |

l. 22 . 7 . 3

Messrs Drake and Compton, Dr.

To Richard and Jacob Broughton, Dyers.

For Dying the Goods following, delivered ℔ Order, to Edward Evelyn, Packer.

1764.

| | | | | l. | s. | d. | |
|---|---|---|---|---|---|---|---|
| May | 7. | Exeter Stuffs, yellow | 70 Ps. | at 0 | 14 | 0 | ℔ Ps. |
| | 13. | Norwich ditto, blue | 30 | at 0 | 11 | 6 | |
| | 20. | Tamies, black | 42 | at 0 | 12 | 8 | |
| July | 1. | Colchester Bays, green | 28 | at 0 | 9 | 0 | |
| | 28. | Camlets, orange | 24 | at 0 | 15 | 0 | |

l. 121 . 4 . 0

Mr. Roland Upholder, Dr.

To William Warehouse and Company.

1764.

| | | | | l. | s. | d. | |
|---|---|---|---|---|---|---|---|
| Oct. | 7. | Superfine 10/4 Blankets | 17 Pr. | at 1 | 3 | 10 | |
| | 9. | Medium ditto | 13 | at 0 | 13 | 6 | |
| | | Harrateen blue | 31 Ps. | at 0 | 7 | 5 . 8 | |
| Nov. | 6. | Cheney ditto | 20 | at 1 | 18 | 0 | |
| | 18. | Green Lintseys | 10 | at 1 | 18 | 0 | |
| Dec. | 9. | 15 Printed Callico Quilts | 4 | at 0 | 16 | 8 | |

l. 164 . 6 . 4

The Honourable Sir Michael Newton, Knight of the Bath, Dr.

## To Thomas Goldsmiths.

| 1764. | | oz. | dwts. | gr. | | s. | d. | per oz. l. |
|---|---|---|---|---|---|---|---|---|
| May 31. | A Silver Set of Casters | wt. 25 | 10 | 18 | at | 7 | 9 | |
| July 7. | Half a Doz. Soup Plates | 85 | 14 | 14 | at | 6 | 6 | |
| 10. | A Silver Teapot and Lamp | 29 | 16 | 15 | at | 6 | 4 | |
| Aug. 9. | A large Punchbowl | 67 | | 16 | at | 6 | 10 | |
| Nov. 6. | A Dozen Silver Spoons | 33 | 11 | 10 | at | 6 | 2 | |
| 11. | A Dozen Desert Knives, Forks and Spoons, with a Shagreen Case | | | | | | | 40 . 0 . 0 |

l. 120 . 8 . 11

48

## Mrs Ann Finch, Dr.

## To Samuel Silkman and Partner.

| 1764. | | lb. | | s. | d. | per Pound l. |
|---|---|---|---|---|---|---|
| July 30. | Tripoli Belladine Silk | 44 | at | 19 | 10 | |
| Aug. 30. | Legee of Smyrna | 112 1/2 | at | 16 | 7 | |
| 14. | A Fangot of raw Silk | 130 | at | 13 | 8 | |
| Sept. 15. | Ditto of Afdas | 118 | at | 12 | 4 | |
| 30. | Gold and Silver Twist | 17 | at | 16 | 4 | per Ounce |
| 30. | Twisted Silk in Grain | 92 1/4 | at | 3 | 0 | |

l. 331 . 2 . 7

The

Mr Charles Cloudefly, Dr.

To Joseph Ironmonger.

| 1764. | | | | | s. | d. | | |
|---|---|---|---|---|---|---|---|---|
| June | 10. | Spring Door Locks with Hinges | 19 | at | 4 | 3 each | | |
| | 19. | Bolts | 42 Pounds | at | 0 | 9 | | |
| Aug. | 1. | Birmingham Brafs Locks | 30 | at | 7 | 6 | | |
| | 24. | A Caft-Iron Back, *Cwt.* 1 . 3 . 10 | | at | 14 | 8 ꝑ *Cwt.* | | |
| Sept. | 10. | Sheffield Nails 2 . 1 . 12 | | at | 0 | 4½ ꝑ *lb.* | | |
| | 21. | Plate-Iron 3 . 3 | | at | 0 | 6¼ ꝑ *lb.* | | |
| | | | | | | | | *l.* 34 . 4 . 8 |

H

Mr Humphry Virginia, Dr.

To Thomas Tobacconift.

| 1764. | | | | *Cwt.* | | s. | d. | | *l.* |
|---|---|---|---|---|---|---|---|---|---|
| Mar. | 26. | 1 Hhd. of beft bright Tobacco | qt. Nt. | 5½ | at | 0 | 10½ ꝑ *lb.* | | |
| Apr. | 15. | 1 Box of Oroonoko | qt. Nt. | 75½ *lb.* | at | 0 | 11¾ | | |
| | 19. | 5 Bags of old Spanifh | qt. Nt. | 684 *lb.* | at | 0 | 4½ | | |
| May | 25. | ½ Hhd. — qt. Gr. 335. Tr. 42 is Nt. *lb.* | | 293 | at | 0 | 5¾ | | |
| | 27. | 2 Rolls | qt. Nt. | 94 *lb.* | at | 1 | 5½ | | |
| July | 14. | A Parcel of Patomeck River | qt. Nt. | 113 *lb.* | at | 1 | 8 | | |
| | | | | | | | | | *l.* 64 . 2 . 6 |

Messrs Owen and Oswald, Dr. To Tho. Teaduft and Connade Coffeepot, Druggift.

| 1764. | | | Cwt. | lb. | lb. | | l. | s. | d. | | l. |
|---|---|---|---|---|---|---|---|---|---|---|---|
| Oct. | 13. | Galls - - wt. | 1½ | Tr. 12. | Nt. 156. | at | 0 | 0 | 9½ | ⅌ lb. | |
| | 27. | Meftica Cochineal | 18⅜ | Pounds | | at | 1 | 12 | 10 | | |
| Nov. | 16. | Scammony | 37¼ | Pounds | | at | 0 | 10 | 0 | | |
| | 19. | Gum Arabick | 127 | | | at | 0 | 0 | 8½ | | |
| Dec. | 1. | Saffafras | 3¼ | Hundred | | at | 0 | 0 | 3¾ | | |
| | 31. | Opium | 10½ | Pounds | | at | 0 | 6 | 0 | | |
| Jan. | 11. | Tea, one Canifter | 75 | | | at | 0 | 13 | 8 | | |
| | 24. | Affafoetida | 48 | | | at | 0 | 4 | 6 | | |
| Feb. | 9. | Contrayerva Root | 7½ | | | at | 0 | 18 | 6 | | |
| | | | | | | | | | | | l. 136 . 11 . 0 |

Messrs Somerfet and Draper, Dr. To Blackwell Hall and Company.

| 1764. | | | | | | s. | d. | | l. |
|---|---|---|---|---|---|---|---|---|---|
| Sept. | 3. | Serge de Nifmes | 13 Ps. | each 30 Yards | at | 3 | 10½ | ⅌ Yard | |
| | 7. | Silk Drugget | 24 | each 28½ | at | 5 | 10 | | |
| Oct. | 12. | Grograms | 30 | each 41 | at | 2 | 8 | | |
| | 19. | Silk Camblets | 11 | each 40 | at | 3 | 1½ | | |
| Nov. | 6. | Duroys | 40 | | at | 32 | 0 | ⅌ Ps. | |
| | 30. | Shalloons | 51 | | at | 50 | 0 | ⅌ Ps. | |
| | | Anterines | 10 | each 26½ | at | 2 | 2 | ⅌ Yard | |
| Dec. | 30. | Sagathy | 23 | | at | 1 | 4 | | |
| | | | | | | | | | l. 774 . 14 . 2 |

The Right Honourable Richard Earl of Castlemain, Dr.

To Benj. Builder, for Work and Materials in his House at Henly Park, Surry.

| 1764. | | | | l. | s. | d. | |
|---|---|---|---|---|---|---|---|
| Mar. 27. | Oaken Timber | — 12 Load | — at 2 | — 5:0 | | | 0. 2 Ton per — l. |
| 30. | Fir Timber | — 35 Ton | — at 1 | — 12 | | | to a Load per — l. |
| Apr. 5. | Oaken Plank | — 96 Feet | — at 0 | 0 | | 3¼ | per Foot |
| 16. | Norway Deals | — 590 | — at 6 | 15 | | 6 | per Hund. |
| | Sixpeny Nails | — 29 Thousand | — at 0 | 3 | | 10 | per Thouf. |
| May 5. | Ten Groat Nails | — 3 Hundred | — at 0 | 14 | | 10 | Ditto |
| June 28. | Work for myself | — 90 Days | — at 0 | 3 | | 4 | per Ditto |
| | Ditto for 3 Men | — 90 | — at 0 | 2 | | 6 | each |
| | Wainscot | — 73 Yards 7 Feet | — at 0 | 3 | | 2 | per Yard agreed |
| | Double Quarter | — 58 Feet | — at 0 | 0 | | 4 | per Foot |
| July 30. | Christiana Deals 135 | — at 7 | 10 | | 0 | per Hund. |
| | Riga Timber | — 180 Feet cub'd | — at 0 | 1 | | 1 | per Foot |
| | | | | l. 207 | 13 | 3¼ | |

Note. Deal and Nails are 120, or fix Score to the Hundred. 50 Feet are a Load, and 40 Feet a Ton of Timber. 100 square Feet are the Square of Carpentry, Tyling, &c.

Sir Edward Cornwall, Dr.

To Bernard Bricklayer, for Work and Materials in his House on Tower-Hill, London.

| 1764 | | | | | | s. | d. | |
|---|---|---|---|---|---|---|---|---|
| Mar. | 28. | Bricks | 25 Thousand | at | 15 | . 7 | ⅌ Thouf. l. |
| | 30. | Tiles | 11 Ditto | at | 19 | . 5 | Ditto |
| Apr. | 1. | Lime | 28 Hundred | at | 15 | . 11 | ⅌ Hund. |
| | 12. | Sand | 19 Load | at | 3 | . 10 | ⅌ Load |
| June | 28. | Work for myfelf | 90 Days | at | 3 | . 0 | ⅌ Diem |
| | | Ditto for a Labourer | 90 | at | 1 | . 8 | |
| | | Ditto for my Man | 90 | at | 2 | . 6 | |

*l.* 88 . 6 . 7½

*A Brick ought to be 9 Inches long, 4¼ broad, and 2¼ thick. 500 Bricks are a Load. 1000 Tiles (the like. 35 Buſhels are a Hundred of Lime. About 4500 Bricks will make a Rod of Brick-work, viz. 272¼ ſq. Feet, a Brick and half thick.*

The Right Honourable, Charles Lord Bruce, Dr.

For Bricklayers Work at Savernacle, Wilts, performed by Philip Piluſte.

| | | | | | *l.* | *s.* | *d.* | |
|---|---|---|---|---|---|---|---|---|
| Brick-work, 30 Rods, 68 Feet Statute Meaſure | | | | at | 5 | . 10 . 0 | ⅌ Rod — l. |
| Tyling plain, 15 Square, 75 Feet | | | | at | 2 | . 3 . 0 | ⅌ Square |
| Rubed Return, 250 Feet | | | | at | 0 | . 3 . 0 | ⅌ Foot |
| Streight Arch, 72 Feet | | | | at | 0 | . 2 . 0 | |
| Jack Arch, 36 | | | | | | | |
| Paving with 10 Inch Tile, 1769 Feet | | | | at | 0 | . 2 . 3 | |
| | | | | at | 0 | . 0 . 3½ | |

*l.* 384 . 15 . 8

Meaſured and Valued July 10, 1764.

⅌ *William Sands.*

# RECREATION VIII.

(82) WHAT Number, multiplied by 72084, will produce 5190048 exactly?

*Answer*, 72.

(83) What Number, divided by 419844, will quote 9494, and leave juſt a third Part of the Diviſor remaining?

*Answer*, 3986138884.

(84) The Sum of two Numbers is 360; the leſs is 114: What is their Difference, Product, and larger Quote?

*Answer*, 132. 28044. $2\frac{8}{15}$.

(85) I would plant 2072 Elms, in 14 Rows, 25 Feet aſunder: How long will this Grove be?

*Answer*, $616\frac{2}{3}$ Fathoms.

(86) A Brigade of Horſe, conſiſting of 384 Men, is to be formed into a ſquare Body, having 32 Men in Front: How many Ranks will there be?

*Answer*, 12.

(87) The Spectator's Club of fat People, though it conſiſted but of 15 Perſons, is ſaid, No. 9. to weigh no leſs than three Tons: How much, at an Equality, was that ꝑ Man.

*Answer*, Four Hundred Weight.

(88) The Remainder of a Diviſion Sum is 423; the Quotient 423; the Diviſor is the Sum of both and 19 more: What then was the Number to be divided?

*Answer*, 366318.

(89) What Number is that, from which if you deduct the 25th Part of 22525, and to the Remainder add the 16th Part of 9696, the Sum will be 1440?

*Answer*, 1735.

(90) A Perſon dying left his Widow 1780*l.* and 1250*l.* to each of his four Children, 30 Guineas a-piece to 15 of his poor Relations, and 150*l.* to Charities; he had been $25\frac{1}{2}$ Years in Trade, and at an Average had cleared 126*l.* a Year. What had he to begin with?

*Answer*, 4189*l.* 10*s.*

(91) The Globe of the Earth, under the Line, is 360 Degrees in Circumference, each Degree $69\frac{1}{2}$ Miles; and this Body being turned on its own Axis, in the Sydereal

Day,

Day, or 23 Hours 56 Minutes: At what Rate an Hour are the Inhabitants of Bencoolen, situate in the midst of the burning Zone, carried from West to East, by this Rotation?
*Answer*, 1045$\frac{345}{1440}$ Miles.

(92) A Fellow was saying, that when he told over his Basket of Chestnuts, two by two, three by three, four by four, five by five, or six by six, there was still an odd one; but when he told them seven by seven, they came even: How many had he?　　　　*Answer*, 721.

(93) Goliath is said to have been 6 Cubits and an half, or a Span high; this answers to 10 Feet four Inches and $\frac{102}{1000}$: Pray what was the length of the Cubit in British Measure?
*Answer*, Inches 19,168.

(94) There are 2 Numbers; the bigger of them is 73 times 109, and their Difference 17 times 28. I demand their Sum and Product?
*Answer*, 15438. and 59526317.

(95) I would put 60 Hogsheads of London Beer into 30 Wine Pipes, and would know what the Cask must hold that receives the Difference; 231 solid Inches being the Gallon of Wine, and 282 that of Beer?
*Answer*, 143$\frac{29}{47}$ Beer Gallons.

(96) The continual Multiplication of the nine Digits will give the Number of Changes that may be rung on 9 Bells, (as well as of any other Combinations) how many are there?
*Answer*, 362880.

(97) There are two Numbers, the less is 187, the Difference 343; give the Square of their Product, Ditto of their Sum and Difference, and the Sum of those Squares?
*Answer*, Sum of Sq. 1708088549.

(98) There are two Numbers, whose Product is 1610, the greater is given 46: What is their Sum, Difference, and Quotes; what the Sum of their Squares, and what the Cube of their Difference?
*Answer*, Sum of Sq. 3341. The Cube of Diff. 1331.

(99) There are other two Numbers, the greater 7050, which divided by the less, quotes 94: What is the Difference of their Squares; and what the Square of the Product of their Sum and Difference?
*Answer*, Diff. of Sq. 49696875.

There

(100) There are ftill two Numbers, 75 is the lefs, to which the greater is in Proportion as 8 to 5: What is the Sum, and the Product of their Sum and Difference; the Difference of their Squares, and the Sum of the Squares of their two Quotes, the greater divided by the lefs, and the lefs again by the greater?

*Anfwer*, Sum of Sum and Diff. 240. Product of Sum and Diff. 8775. Diff. of Sq. 8775. Sum Sq. of the two Quotes $2\frac{1521}{1600}$.

(101) There are two Numbers more, the greater 224, bearing Proportion to the other as 8 to 7: What is the Square of their Sum, Difference, and either Quote; and what is the Refult of the Square of the Sum of their Difference, added to the Product of their Sum and Difference?

*Anfwer*, Sq. of Sum 176400. Sq. Sum of Diff. and Prod. 138956944.

(102) In order to raife a Joint-Stock of 10000 *l.* L. M. and N. together fubfcribe 8500 *l.* and O. the reft; Now M. and N. are known together to have fet their Hands to 6050 *l.* and N. has been heard to fay, that he had undertaken for 420 *l.* more than M. What did each Proprietor advance?

*Anfwer*, L. 2450 *l.* M. 2815 *l.* N. 3235. O. 1500 *l.*

(103) What Number multiplied by 57 will produce juft what 134 multiplied by 71 will do?

*Anfwer*, 166$\frac{46}{57}$.

(104) A. B. and C. play in concert at Hazard; and at making up Accompt, it appears that A. and B. together brought off 13 *l.* 10 *s.* B. and C. together 12 *l.* 12 *s.* and A. and C. together won 11 *l.* 16 *s.* 6 *d.* What did they feverally get?

*Anfwer*, A. 6 *l.* 7 *s.* 3 *d.* B. 7 *l.* 2 *s.* 9 *d.* C. 5 *l.* 9 *s.* 3 *d.*

(105) Some others advance in Trade as follows, viz. W. X. and Y. raifed 350 *l.* 10 *s.* W. X. and Z. 344 *l.* 10 *s.* X. Y. and Z. made up together 400 *l.* and W. Y. and Z. contribute 378 *l.* 4 *s.* In the Conclufion, they parted with their joint Property for 450 Guineas: What did they gain or lofe by their Adventure?

*Anfwer*, They loft 18 *l.* 11 *s.* 4 *d.*

BILLS

# BILLS of PARCELS used by Merchants and Wholesale Dealers.

London, April 4, 1764.

Mr Samuel Robinson,

Bought of William Stapleton, 6 Parcels of French Cloth, to pay at 6 Months, as follows, viz.

| | | | | l. | s. | d. |
|---|---|---|---|---|---|---|
| Nº 4. | qt 3 | Ps. Dowlas | at | 3 . | 6 . | 0 |
| 7. | 4 | Ps. Ditto | at | 4 . | 10 . | 0 |
| 8. | 3 | Ps. Ditto | at | 4 . | 15 . | 0 |
| 14. | 3 | Ps. Lockrams | at | 2 . | 15 . | 6 |
| 17. | 3 | Ps. Ditto | at | 2 . | 18 . | 0 |
| 20. | 4 | Ps. Ditto | at | 2 . | 7 . | 6 |

20 Ps. in all amount to     l. 68 . 13 . 6

William Cobb Esq; Octob. 21, 1764.

Bought of James Inwyn and Partner, 8 Bags of Farnham Hops, for ready Money, viz.

| | Cwt. | qr. | lb. |
|---|---|---|---|
| Nº 1. | wt. 2 . | 2 . | 18 |
| 2. | 2 . | 3 . | 10 |
| 3. | 2 . | 2 . | 17 |
| 4. | 2 . | 1 . | 0 |
| 5. | 3 . | 0 . | 8 |
| 6. | 3 . | 1 . | 3 |
| 7. | 3 . | 0 . | 20 |
| 8. | 2 . | 2 . | 7 |

Cwt.    at 11 d. ½ ⅌ Pound    l. 116 . 15 . 3

Mr Daniel Wait, London, Jan. 7. 1764.

Bought of Patrick Jefferies, 6 Casks of Barbadoes Sugar, at a Month, *viz.*

| | Cwt. | gr. | lb. | | gr. | lb. |
|---|---|---|---|---|---|---|
| No. 81. wt. | 8 | 3 | 23 | — Tare | 3 | 7 each |
| 82. | 8 | 2 | 21 | | | |
| 83. | 8 | 0 | 12 | | | |
| 84. | 8 | 1 | 16 | | | |
| 85. | 7 | 3 | 20 | | | |
| 86. | 8 | 0 | 16 | | | |

Gr.
Tr.

Nt.    at 47 . 6 ⅌ Cwt.    *l.* 107 . 13 . 7

*s.* *d.*

Mr Richard Sands,

Bought of Anne Smart and Company, Sept. 13. 1764. 5 Butts of Rape Oil, *viz.*

| | Cwt. | gr. | lb. | | gr. | lb. |
|---|---|---|---|---|---|---|
| No. 43. wt. | 10 | 2 | 10 | — Tare | 2 | 13 |
| 48. | 11 | 2 | 18 | | 2 | 26 |
| 52. | 10 | 1 | 0 | | 2 | 13 |
| 57. | 11 | 0 | 12 | | 2 | 21 |
| 60. | 12 | 3 | 17 | | 3 | 9 |

Gr.
Tr.

Cwt.

Nt. ———— Gall.    23*l.* 16*s.* ⅌ Tun.    *l.* 79 . 2 . 1

Note, *The Tun of sweet Oil is 236 Gallons and 7 lb. ½ make a Gallon of Oil.*

Sir Andrew Gosling and Company,
Bought of the United East-India Company, &c. at four Months.     Nov. 27. 1764.

Pepper, 2 Lots, viz.
|  |  | Cwt. qr. lb. | lb. |
|---|---|---|---|
| N° 17. | 10 Bags | qt. 27. 1.18 Tr. | 150 |
| 20. | 10 Ditto | 24. 3.24 | 138 |

Gr.
Tr.
Nt. ............ at 10½ d. ℔ ℔. ——————— l.

Red-wood, 2 Lots, viz.
|  |  | Ton. Cwt. |
|---|---|---|
| N° 47. | 120 Sticks | 10. 13¾ |
| 48. | 100 Ditto | 11. 12 |

220 —— Sticks wt. ............ at 3. . 7. ℔ Ton. —————— l.

Worm-seed, 3 Bales, viz.
|  | Cwt. qr. lb. |
|---|---|
| N° 18. | wt. 3. 1. 10 |
| 24. | 4. 2. 0 |
| 37. | 2. 3. 19 |

Gr.
Tr. 1. 0. 15
Nt. Cwt. ............ at 13½ ¼ d. ℔ lb. —————— l.

l. 376 . 8 . 8

Mr. Peter Paydown and Company's.

Bought of Titus Tradewell, for ready Money, Cotton 13 Bags, viz.

London, April 24. 1764.

|        | Cwt. | qr. | lb. |
|--------|------|-----|-----|
| No 17.—— | 2 | 3 | 16 |
| 24.—— | 3 | 1 | 10 |
| 28.—— | 3 | 0 | 27 |
| 30.—— | 2 | 3 | 4 |
|        | 12 | 1 | 1 |

Total Grofs.
Tare allowed.

lb.
Sattle 2619.
Tret. 100.

Net. 2519 at 14d. ℔.

|        | Cwt. | qr. | lb. |
|--------|------|-----|-----|
| No 1.—— qt | 3 | 1 | 7 |
| 2.—— | 2 | 3 | 0 |
| 3.—— | 2 | 3 | 5 |
| 4.—— | 3 | 0 | 15 |
|      | 11 | 3 | 27 |
|      | 12 | 1 | 1 |
|      | 24 | 1 | 0 |
|      | 0 | 3 | 13 |
| Cwt. | 23 | 1 | 15 |

More, viz.

|        | Cwt. | qr. | lb. |
|--------|------|-----|-----|
| No 30.—— | 2 | 3 | 12 |
| 31.—— | 3 | 0 | 10 |
| 32.—— | 3 | 1 | 26 |
| 33.—— | 3 | 2 | 8 |
| 34.—— | 2 | 2 | 7 |

} Damaged.

Gr.
Tr. 0 . 2 . 2

lb.
Suttle . . . .
Tret. . . . .
Net. . . . .     at 4d. ℔ Pound.

l. 173 . 16 . 6

## RECREATION IX.

(106) BY felling 240 Oranges at five for 2 d. half of which coft me two a Peny, and the other half three a Peny, I evidently lofe a Groat: Pray how comes that about?

*Anfwer,* There were twenty Penyworth more of the laft Sort bought, than of the firft; the Remainder at the felling Price mentioned, will fetch but 16 d. whereas they coft me 20 d.

(107) In a Series of proportional Numbers the firft is 5, the third 8; the Product of the fecond and third is 78,4: What is the Difference of the fecond and fourth?

*Anfwer,* 5,88.

(108) What Quantity of Water will you add to a Pipe of Mountain Wine, value 33 l. to reduce the firft Coft to 4 s. 6 d. the Gallon?

*Anfwer,* 20⅔ Gallons.

(109) If the Cubick Inch of Oil Olive be ,52835 decimal Parts of an Ounce Avoirdupoiz; what Quantity of Oil, weighing 7¼ Pound ♔ Gallon, will be contained in a Cafk, allowed to hold 13⅓ Gallons of Water, each 282 folid Inches?

*Anfwer,* 16⅛ Gallons.

(110) With 13 Gallons of Canary, at 6 s. 8 d. a Gallon, I mingled 20 Gallons of White Wine, at 5 s. a Gallon; and to thefe added 10 Gallons of Cyder at 3 s. a Gallon, at what Rate muft I fell a Quart of this Mixture, fo as to clear 10 ♔ Cent?

*Anfwer,* 16 $\frac{9}{14}$ d.

(111) What Difference will there be to the Proprietors of an Aqueduct, between doubling an Expence, and halving a Profit?

*Anfwer,* 4 to 1.

(112) If 100 l. in 12 Years, be allowed to gain 39 l. 19 s. 8 d. in what Time will any other Sum of Money double itfelf by the fame Rate of Intereft?

*Anfwer,* Something more than 30 Years.

(113) What Difference is there between the Intereft of 500 l. at 5 ♔ Cent. for twelve Years, and the Difcount of the fame Sum, at the fame Rate, and for the fame Time?

*Anfwer,* 112 l. 10 s. Advantage to the Intereft.

When

(114) When the Sun is in the Meridian at Soho-Square, in what Time will it be fo at Tyburn, lying due Weft of it, at the Diftance of a meafured Mile, in the Latitude of $51\frac{1}{2}$ Degrees, where the Degree of Longitude turns out Miles $37\frac{1}{10}$, known by the diurnal Rotation of the earth to pafs in 4 Minutes time?

*Anfwer*, 6 Seconds, and 26 Thirds nearly.

(115) If 12 Apples are worth 21 Pears, and 3 Pears coft a Halfpeny; what will be the Price of fourfcore and four Apples? *Anfwer*, 2 s. 0 d. $\frac{1}{2}$

(116) Six of the Female Cricketers that play'd lately in the Artillery Ground, fetched in Company Strokes as follows, *viz.* *A. B. C. D. E.* 207, *A. C. D. E. F.* 213, *A. D. E. F. B.* 189, *A. E. B. C. F.* 234, *A. B. D. C. F.* 222, *B. F. D. C. E.* 250: How many did they fetch on the other Side, fince thefe 6 Perfons wanted but fourfcore and 13 Notches to decide the Game? *Anfwer*, 356.

(117) If a Sack of Coals be the Allowance of 7 poor People for a Week, how many Poor belonged to that Parifh, which, when Coals were 36 s. ⅌ Chaldron, had 41 l. to pay in 6 Weeks on that Account?

*Anfwer*, $318\frac{3}{5}$.

(118) It is a Rule in fome Parifhes to affefs the Inhabitants in Proportion to $\frac{3}{10}$ of their Rents: What is the yearly Rent pray of that Houfe, which pays 8 l. 10 s. to the King under this Limitation, at 4 s. in the Pound?

*Anfwer*, 42 l. 10 s. 0 d.

(119) If by felling Hops at 3 l. 10 s. ⅌ Cwt. the Planter clears 30 ⅌ Cent. what was his Gain ⅌ Cent. when the fame Goods fold at 4 l. and a Crown?

*Anfwer*, 57 l. 17 s. $1\frac{3}{4}$ d.

(120) If by remitting to Holland, at 31 s. 9 d. Flem. ⅌ Pound Sterling, 5 ⅌ Cent. is gained: How goes the Exchange, when by Remittance I clear 10 ⅌ Cent?

*Anfwer*, 33 s. $3\frac{4}{7}$ d.

(121) If, when Port Wine is 17 Guineas the Hogfhead, a Company of 45 People will fpend 20 l. therein, in a certain Time; what is Wine a fipe, when 13 Perfons more, will fpend 63 l. in twice the time, drinking with equal Moderation? *Anfwer*, 43 l. 12 s. 6 d. nearly.

I am

(122) I am difpatched on a Commiffion from London to Edinburgh, diſtant by Computation, fay 350 Miles, and my Rout is fettled at 22 Miles a Day: You, 4 Days after, are fent after me with freſh Orders, and are to travel 32 Miles a Day; whereabout on the Road fhall I be overtaken by you?

*Anfwer,* 68$\frac{4}{10}$ Miles on this Side Edinburgh.

(123) The Net Proceeds of a Hhd. of Barbadoes Sugar, were 4 *l.* 14 *s.* 6 *d.* the Cuſtom and Fees, 2 *l.* 8 *s.* 6 *d.* Freight, 22 *s.* 8 *d.* Factorage, 4 *s.* 6 *d.* The groſs Weight was, *Cwt.* 9. 94 *lb.* Tare, 1 in 10; pray then how was the Sugar rated in the Bill of Parcels?

*Anfwer,* 19 *s.* 2$\frac{478}{493}$ *Cwt.* nearly.

(124) Sold a repeating Watch for 50 Guineas, and by fo doing loft 17 ⅌ *Cent.* whereas I ought, in dealing, to have cleared 20 ⅌ *Cent.* then how much was it fold under the juft Value?

*Anfwer,* 23 *l.* 8 *s.* 0$\frac{72}{83}$ *d.*

(125) If 6 *lb.* of Pepper be worth 13 *lb.* of Ginger, and 19 *lb.* of this be worth 4$\frac{1}{4}$ *lb.* of Cloves, and 10 *lb.* of Cloves be equivalent to 63 *lb.* of Sugar, at 5 *d.* ⅌ Pound; what is the Value of an *Cwt.* of Pepper?

*Anfwer,* 7 *l.* 2 *s.* 5$\frac{27}{114}$ *d.*

(126) If by fending Pewter to Turkey, and parting with it at 25$\frac{2}{3}$ *d.* ⅌ Pound, the Merchant clears *Cent.* ⅌ *Cent.* what does he clear in Holland, where he difpoſes of the *Cwt.* for 8 *l.*? *Anfwer,* 2 *l.* 0 *s.* 2$\frac{2}{3}$ *d.*

(127) If 30 Men can perform a piece of Work in 11 Days, how many will accompliſh another, 4 times as big, in one fifth of the time?

*Anfwer,* 600.

(128) A May-Pole, 50 Feet 11 Inches long, at a certain time of Day, will caft a Shadow 98 Feet 6 Inches long: I would hereby find the Breadth of a River, that, running within 20 Feet 6 Inches of the Foot of a Steeple, 300 Feet 8 Inches high, will, at the fame Time, throw the Extremity of its Shadow 30 Feet 9 Inches beyond the Stream.

*Anfwer,* 530 Feet, 4$\frac{487}{611}$ Inches nearly.

Of

## Of BILLS of EXCHANGE.

THE *Bill of Exchange*, in Use among Perfons of Cor-respondence and Dealing, is a fhort Order for Money, to be received in *one* Place or Country, for the Value paid in *another*; to which Men of Credit, pay a very ftrict Honour and Regard. In it are fpecified: 1. *The Place of the Draw-er's Refidence.* 2. *The Time of Payment.* 3. *To whom.* 4. *The Sum.* 5. *Ufually at what Rate of Exchange.* 6. *Of whom the Value was received,* or *to whofe Accompt the Draught is to be placed.* 7. *The Drawer's Name.* 8. *By whom,* and *Where to be paid.*

In Bills of Exchange there are commonly *four* Perfons principally concerned: 1. The *Remitter,* who pays the Value to, 2. The *Drawer,* who receives it *in one Place,* and fur-nifhes him with a Bill upon, 3. The *Acceptant,* who is ex-pected to pay in due Time, to, 4. The *Poffeffor* or *Prefenter,* who is to receive the Contents *in another Place*; not but fometimes there are only *three* Perfons concerned in a *Remit-tance,* and fometimes, though but feldom, *two only.*

All *Bills of Exchange,* upon their coming to the *Prefenter's* Hands, from the *Remitter,* are immediately to be tendered to the *Perfon* on whom they are drawn for *Acceptance,* which, by legal Appointment, ought to be made in *Writing* under the Bill.

If a Bill be payable at *Ufance,* or *after Date,* the Accep-tant's fubfcribing his Name, or making any other Mark on the fame, is fufficient and valid Acceptance; but if it be pay-able *after Sight,* the *Day* on which it is tendered for Accep-tation muft be alfo mentioned upon it; becaufe, upon that depends the Time of *Payment*; by which *Acceptance,* he be-comes abfolutely and irrevokably Debtor to the Prefenter, for the Contents; or the Courfe of Exchange would, otherwife, be fubject to great Hazards and Uncertainties.

But if the Party, to whom a Bill is directed, *refufes* to accept it, after twenty four Hours Deliberation, if it be a Foreign Bill, or upon Prefentment, if an Inland Bill, *Proteft* muft be made for Non-Acceptance at the Place of his Abode, by a Notary-Public, who is to be Witnefs of that Refu-fal; which Proteft fhould, for the Security of the *Pre-fenter,* be returned the firft Poft to the *Remitter,* that he

may

may furnish a new Bill, or take his proper Measures with the Parties concerned.

The *Drawer* of a Bill should always the same Post take Care to give his *Correspondent* Notice, by Letter, that he has drawn upon him for so much, payable as in the Bill, to prevent its being *Protested*, and sent him back *Non-Accepted*, for want of due *Advice*; for in that Case, his Correspondent may refuse to accept, till Advice arrives, if the Bill mentions Advice to be expected.

To prevent Interruption of Business by Miscarriage of Letters, or other Accidents, Merchants always draw *two*, and often *three* Outland Bills, all of the same Tenor and Date, excepting in the *second* against the *first*, and if there be *three* drawn, against the *third* also, and in the *third* against the *first* and *second*, to prevent the Accepter's paying more than one of them by Mistake; which Bills, the Remitter takes Care to send his Correspondent, to whom they are made payable, by different Posts, one of which being answered, the rest are of no Force.

If an accepted Bill be not *paid upon Demand*, the very Day it falls due, it must be *Noted*, that is, put into the Hands of a *Notary-Public*, by the *Presenter*, in order to have a *Protest* drawn up, under a *Copy* of the Bill, for Non-Payment; which *Protest,* within fourteen Days at farthest, must be returned (but not the Bill itself, unless for special Reasons) to the *Remitter*, who paid the Value, and who is to give Satisfaction for his Concern therein to the *Presenter*, and who will procure Satisfaction of the *Drawer*; not only with respect to the Principal Sum, and the Interest thereof, from the Day of Protest, but also may recover the Rechange of the said Sum, with Charges of Protest, and whatever Damages shall be incurred by the Default of his Correspondent, the Acceptant; though Rechange is not always insisted on.

The *Neglect of Protest in due Time*, leaves the *Presenter* or *Possessor* of a Bill no Security but that of the *Acceptant*; whereas he has otherwise, the Drawer, and every one of the *Indorsers*, (if any) besides the *Acceptant*, to depend on for the *Principal* and *Damages*; and if but one of them prove sufficient, he will be no Loser.

No Bill *of Exchange* can be protested, unless the *Value* be mentioned therein to be *received*, and the Person named *of whom*; nor is it usual among Dealers to note an *Inland Bill* under 20 *l.* Value, such Bills are commonly returned

turned without *Charges*; not but that it may, after Acceptance, be lawfully done, if the Bill be above 5 *l.* Value.

*If you Difcompt, or pay a Debt with an Inland Bill,* payable to your *Self* or *Order,* you write your *Name* on the Backfide, and deliver it into the Poffeffion of the *Perfon* you intend to make it over to, which is called *Indorfing,* whereby you affign all your Property therein to him; and in Cafe of the *Acceptant*'s Failure before it is paid, *You* are, by Virtue thereof, as refponfible to fuch your *Affign* for the Contents and Damages, upon *Proteft* made, as the *Remitter* is to you, and the *Drawer* to him. In like Manner, let a *Bill* be indorfed by *feveral* Perfons, the *Poffeffor,* or Perfon to whom it was laft affigned, in Cafe of Non-Payment, caufes Proteft to be made, which being returned to the laft Indorfer, he is obliged to fatisfy the laft Poffeffor, as to the Contents and Charges, and returns it in the fame Manner to the fecond; he to the third, *&c.* till at laft, it recurs upon the Drawer, who is obliged to anfwer all Damages, as before. In the fame Manner ought *Promiffory Notes* to be treated, they being, in the Eye of the *Law,* of the Nature of *Inland* Bills of Exchange.

But, on an *Outland* Bill, befides the Indorfer's Name, it is ufual to fill up the Indorfement, by appointing Payment to his *Order,* naming the *Perfon* he affigns it over to; fpecifying the Conditions and Reafons that induced him to make fuch Indorfement; as, *Pay Mr R. W———,* or *Order, Value in Accompt, S. S.* And if Mr *R. W———* fhould affign it to another; *Pay* Mr *P. D———* or *Order, Value of himfelf, R. W———* remembring always, that unlefs the Word *Order* be inferted, no *Bill of Exchange,* or *Promiffory Note,* is indorfible to another.

If the Acceptant of a Bill fhould chance to fail, between the Time of Acceptance, and that of Payment, Proteft may be made in that Cafe for better Security, before the Bill becomes due; not but, by the good Underftanding among Dealers, the Damages, as *Brokerage, Intereft,* &c. that would follow Proteft, are frequently prevented, efpecially if the Drawer, or any of the Indorfers, be fufficient Perfons; for any of their Correfpondents, out of Refpect, may Re-accept the Bill, for Honour of the Drawer or Indorfer, if applyed to by the Poffeffor, after he has, for Security of

K　　　　　　　the

the Re-accepter, caufed the Bill to be protefted, with a De-
claration, that the Bill was re-accepted for Honour of the
Drawer, *&c.* underwriting it, *Accepted for Honour of the
Drawer*, ⅌ L. L. Or, if the Refpect was fhewn to an
Indorfer; Accepted for Honour of the Indorfer, *W. W.* ⅌
*L. L.* In the fame Manner are to be ferved fuch Bills as are
drawn upon a Perfon, who has not equivalent Effects of the
Drawer's in his Hands, or that has not received due Advice
of the Bill prefented to him for Acceptance; which will
entitle him to a legal Claim upon the Drawer, if he
thinks he may venture, under thofe Circumftances, to honour
his Bills.

When thefe Bills, *accepted under Proteft*, become due, it
is the Cuftom of Merchants to have a *fecond* Proteft for Non-
payment, made by the *Poffeffor*, with a Declaration, as before, that the Re-accepter did pay the fame with Charges, for
Honour, as aforefaid; which Protefts, the Re-acceptant, for
his own Security, will take Care to return, with the firft Opportunity, to his Friend and Correfpondent, in whofe Favour
he advanced the Money.

*Proteft for better Security* may alfo be made, if the Acceptant be under an ill Repute; upon which, if he give Security
for the Payment of the Bill in due Time, the Securiry
becomes refponfible, as well as the Drawer, fhould the Acceptant prove infolvent.

The *Ufance*, or *Ufage of Merchants*, with refpect to *Foreign*
Bills of Exchange, to and from London to Rotterdam, Antwerp, or any Part of the Low Countries, is one Kalendar
Month after the Date of the Bill; double Ufance two
Months, *&c.* Ufance from Hamburg, Copenhagen, Stock-
holm, Lubeck, Strafburg to London, and *Contra*, is alfo
one Month; though Bills from thofe, and other diftant Places, are commonly drawn payable *after Sight*, becaufe of the
Uncertainty of their Arrival. Ufance from London to Lifbon
or Madrid, is two Months; to Leghorn, Venice, or any
Part of the Levant, is three Months, and *Contra*.

After Bills of Exchange become due, whether *Inland* or
*Foreign*, payable at Sight or otherwife, there are, by Cuftom of Merchants, certain *Days of Grace* allowed the Accepter, over and above the Time prefcribed by the Bill,
which are more or lefs, according to the Ufage of the
Country

Country wherein they are to be paid; as in Rotterdam they allow three Days; Rouen, five; Paris, ten; Hamburg, twelve; Antwerp and Madrid, fourteen; and London always three: And on the *third* Day before Sun-set, Payment must be demanded on the Part of the Presenter; and, if not complied with, the Bill must that very Day (being the utmost Time allowed by the Law for that Purpose) be *Noted*, in order to be *Protested* for *Non-Payment*.

If a Bill fall due on a *Sunday*, or other great Holiday, it is to be demanded and paid, or protested, the Day *before*. In any other Case, no Bill of Exchange ought to be paid by the Accepter before it is *fully* due, unless the Remitter shall signify his Allowance of it in Writing. For, as the Remitter delivered his Money to the Drawer, in order to have it paid again to such Person as he shall direct, it is, and ought to be, in his Power to guide, and even divert the Payment, by altering the Bill, and making it payable to any other Person, whom he shall think fit, during the whole Interval between the Acceptance and Day of Payment. And if the Acceptant shall voluntarily pay it before to any one, and that Person should fail, before it falls due, he will be liable to pay it to the Remitter's Order a second Time.

---

## RECREATION X.

(129) BOUGHT Hose in London at 4 s. 3 d. the Pair, and Sold them afterwards in Dublin at 6 s. the Pair: Now, taking the Charges at an Average to be 2 d. the Pair, and considering that I must lose 12 ⅌ *Cent.* by remitting my Money Home again, what do I gain ⅌ *Cent.* by this Article of Trade?

*Answer,* 19 *l.* 10 *s.* 11$\frac{17}{33}$ *d.*

(130) If the Scavenger's Rate at 1 d. ½ in the Pound, comes to 6 s. 7 d. ½, where they ordinarily assess ⅖ of the Rent: What will the King's Tax for that House be, at 4 s. in the Pound, rated at the full Rent?

*Answer,* 13 *l.* 5 *s.* 0 *d.*

(131) If my Factor at Leghorn return me 800 Barrels of Anchovies, each weighing 14 *lb.* Net, worth 12 d. ¼ ⅌ Pound,

K 2

in

in lieu of 7490 Pounds of Virginia Tobacco; and if I find that I have gained after the Rate of 17 ❡ *Cent* by the said Confignment: Pray how was my said Tobacco invoyced ❡ Pound to the Factor, that is, what was the prime Coft?

*Anſwer*, 15 d $\frac{4450}{11873}$.

(132) In the Year 1582 Pope Gregory reformed the Julian Kalendar, ordaining, that as the Year is found to confift only of 365 Days, 5 Hours, and about 49 Minutes, in order to prevent the Inconvenience of carrying the Account of Time too forward, by taking the folar Year at 365 Days, and 6 Hours full, which, in a Series of Years, muft bring Lady-Day to Michaelmas, that the Chriftian States for the future fhould drop 3 Days in Account every 400 Years: that is to fay, for each of the firft three Centuries in that fpace of Time, the intercalary Day in February fhould be omitted, but retained as formerly in the laft or fourth Century, beginning with the Year 1600, when 10 whole Days were funk at once. By which Artifice, the Variation of Time will not, at leaft for a long Space, be very confiderable: According to this Regulation, it is required to know in what Year of Chrift the New Stile, as it is called, will be 20 Days, as now it is only 11, before the Old Stile, which makes no fuch Allowance?

*Anſwer*, Anno 2900.

(133) A Tradefman increafed his Eftate annually a third Part, abating 100*l.* which he ufually fpent in his Family, and at the End of 3¼ Years, found that his net Eftate amounted to 3179*l.* 11*s.* 8*d.* Pray what had he at outfetting?

*Anſwer*, 1421*l.* 7*s.* 6*d.*

(134) *A.* and *B* paid equally for a Horfe, Feb. 7. 1750. *A.* on the 10th, took him a Journey into the Weft, and returned on the 10th of June following. *B.* on the 2d of Aug. took him into Scotland, and ftayed till Nov. 13th, and this concluded his Service this Year. From Jan. 17. following *A.* ufed him ten Days, and, in fix Weeks after his Return, employed him till April 30. *B.* then rode him from May-day to Midfummer. *A.* had him from the 14th of July, to fourteen Days after St. James's-tide. *B.* on Sept. 30. took him into Norfolk, and came back Oct 19. He then was fold for 7*l.* 10*s.* and they would have the

Money

Money parted equitably between them, *viz.* in Proportion to the Use each made of their Steed?

*Answer*, A. 3 l. 9 s. 4 d $\frac{30}{331}$.    B. 4 l. 0 s. 7 d $\frac{301}{331}$.

(135) An Accomptant told a Gentleman, who had constantly eight Persons at his Table, that he would gladly make a ninth, and was willing to give 200 Guineas for his Board, so long as he could place the said Company at Dinner, differently from any one Day before; this being accepted, what did his Entertainment cost him a Year?

*Answer*, 50 d. and about ¾.

(136) Part 1500 Acres of Land, give B. 72 more than A. and C. 112 more than B.

*Answer*, A. 414 ⅔.   B. 486 ⅔.   C. 598 ⅔.

(137) Bought Comfits to the Value of 41 l. 3 s. 4 d. for 3 s. 1 d. the Pound. It happened, that so many of them were damaged in Carriage, that by selling what remained good at 4 s. 6 d. the Pound, my Returns were no more than 34 l. 2 s. 6 d. Pray how much of these Goods were spoiled, and what did this Part stand me in?

*Answer*, 17 l. 15 s. 8 d ⅔.

(138) Ten Pounds a Quarter is allowed to the five Auditors of a Fire-Office. They attend about 7 times in the Quarter; and the Absentees Money is always divided equally among such as do attend. A. and B. on these Occasions never miss. C. and D. are generally twice in a Quarter absent, and E. only once: At the Payment, what had each Man to receive?

*Answer*, A. and B. 2 l. 9 s. 0 d ½ each. C. and D. 1 l. 10 s. 0 d. and E. 2 l. 1 s. 11 d.

(139) In some Parishes in the Country, they take off 3 l. one Year in 17 from the Rents in assessing the Farms: What will the Landlord receive Net out of a Farm of 140 l. a Year in those Places, when the King's Tax is, as now, 4 s. in the Pound?    *Answer*, 116 l. 18 s. 10 d.

(140) A. can do a Piece of Work in 10 Days, B. alone in 13; set them both about it together, in what Time will it be finished?

*Answer*, 5 $\frac{15}{23}$ Days.

Inland

## Inland BILLS of EXCHANGE.

Worcefter, April 15, 1764. *l.* 64 . 0 . 0

*Payable at Sight.* AT Sight pay Mr William Nichols, or Order, the Sum of Sixty-four Pounds, the Value received of Captain John Anderfon, and place it to Accompt, as ♯ Advice from

To Mr Michael Hale,
at the Red Lion, Smith-
field, London.

*Edward Dealmuch.*

Sir, Greenwich, May 10, 1764. *l.* 13 . 10 . 0

At Sight, pay Mr Godfrey Langham, the Sum of Thirteen Pounds ten Shillings, out of my growing Subfiftance, Value of ditto, and place it, without further Advice, to Accompt of
Your Humble Servant,

To Mr Jeoffry Ransford,
Agent at the Horfe-guards,
Whitehall, London.

*Miles Cornet.*

London, June 2, 1764. *l.* 162 . 8 . 0

*Payable after Sight.* At twelve Day's Sight, pay Mr Andrew Aldridge, or Order, the Sum of One hundred Sixty two Pounds eight Shillings, for the Value received of Thomas Jones Efq; and place it to Accompt, as ♯ Advice from Yours,

To Mr Thomas Wells,
Clothier, Shrowsbury.

*Alex. Countwell.*

Sir, Norwich, June 9, 1764. *l.* 42 . 15 . 0

At fix Days Sight, pay Mr Jeremiah Snow, or Order, Forty two Pounds fifteen Shillings, Value of himfelf, and place it without farther Advice to Accompt of

To Mr John Sherman,
Cheefe-Factor, Chefter,

*Samuel Pryor.*

Sir,

Sir,      Salisbury, July 14, 1764.     *l.* 8 . . 8 . 6

*Payable*     Twenty Days after Date, pay William Crofts
*after*      Eight Pounds eight Shillings and fix Pence, Value
*Date.*    received of the Right Honourable the Lady North-
        all, and place it, as by Advice from
   To Alderman Jofeph       Yours,
   Pitts, Exon.              *Benjamin Bufy.*

           Briftol, July 31, 1764.   *l.* 300 . 0 . 0

     Two Months after Date, pay Mr Luke Loudwa-
ter, or Order, Three hundred Pounds, Value received
of George Granby Efq; and place it to Accompt, as
by Advice from

To Mr Oliver Madders,
 at the Bull, Breadftreet,          *Titus Timely.*
 London.

         Edinburgh, Octob. 4, 1764.    *l.* 50 . 0 . 0

     The firft of November next, pay Sir William
Methwold, or Order, Fifty Pounds Sterling, Value
in ourfelves, and place it, without more Advice, to
Accompt of

To Sir John Pa-
 terfon, Limeftreet,       *Jonath.* and *David Bruce.*
 London.

   N. B. *If Sir William fends his Servant Valentine*
  *Lively, to receive this Bill, after he has indorfed it,*
  *which is his Order, the Servant may write over it;*

   Received, Nov. 4, 1764. the Contents.
                   *William Methwold.*
   *l.* 50 . 0 . 0    Witnefs, *Val. Lively.*

     *Or only witneffing it will ferve; and fo of any other.*

                             *Men*

*Men of great Bufinefs feldom trouble themfelves with Receipts and Payments of Cafh, but give an Order on their Banker, thus:*

Meffrs Norman    London, Nov. 4, 1764. *l.* 50 . — . —
and Fox,

*Payable to*    Pay Sir William Methwold, or Bearer, Fifty
*Bearer.*    Pounds, on Accompt of

*John Paterfon.*

### Another.

Mr Mead,    Tunbridge, July 30, 1764.
    Pay Mr Thomas Morgan, or Bearer, One hundred
and feventeen Pounds three Shillings and three Pence,
on Demand, and place it to my Accompt.
To Mr Mead, Fleet-    *Arlington.*
ftreet, London.

Lancelot Yeoman,    Leith, Aug. 2, 1764.    *l.* 150 . 0 . 0

*A Gentleman's*    The fecond of November next, pay Her-
*Order on a*    cules Horfeman, or Bearer, One hundred and
*Tenant.*    fifty Pounds Scots, out of your Michaelmas
    half Year's Rent; make good Payment, ex-
    pecting no farther Advice, the Value received
    of him, by
To Lancelot Yeoman,    Your Friend,
    in the Lordfhip of    *Kildrummy.*
Kildrummy, Aberdeenfh.

## Of Foreign BILLS of EXCHANGE.

FOreign Cities drawing Bills of Exchange upon London, always mention the Rate of Exchange, becaufe they draw in their own Money; but when Bills are drawn by London on Foreign Cities, in their Money, the Rate of Exchange is not mentioned, that being a particular Agreement between the *Remitter* and the *Drawer*, which concerns not the Acceptant, nor the Receiver; fo that they run abfolutely for fo many Pieces, or fo much of their Current Money: except in Holland, in which Cafe the Sum is firft prefcribed in Sterling, and then at what Rate of Exchange.

London,

London, June 10, 1764. for Crowns 612, at Ufance.

*London on*     At Ufance, pay this firft of Exchange to
*Calais.*       Col. John Ward, or Order, Six hundred and
*Firft Bill.*    twelve Crowns, for the Value here received of
           the Right Honourable Charles Earl of Wrex-
           ham, and place it to Accompt, as ℔ Advice
           from
To Mr Mofes Mayhew,         *Godfrey* and *Gower.*
   Merchant in Calais.

London, June 10, 1764. for Crowns 612, at Ufance.

*Second Bill.*    At Ufance, pay this my fecond of Exchange,
           my firft not paid, to Col. John Ward, or Or-
           der, Six hundred and twelve Crowns, for the
           Value here received of the Right Honourable
           Charles Earl of Wrexham, and place it to Ac-
           compt, as by Advice from
To Mr Mofes Mayhew,         *Godfrey* and *Gower,*
   Merchant in Calais.

Paris, July 3, 1764. for Crowns 150, at 31½ *d.* 2 Ufance.

*Paris on*      At double Ufance, pay this firft of Exchange
*London.*     to Mr Richard Rich, or Order, the Sum of
*Firft Bill.*   One Hundred and fifty Crowns, at thirty one
           Pence half Peny ℔ Crown, Value of Mr David
           Le Petre, and pafs it to Accompt, as ℔ Advice.
To Mr Paul Puttoff,          *Frederic Farfetch.*
   London.

Paris, July 3, 1764. for Crowns 150, at 31½ *d.* 2 Ufance.

*Second Bill.*   At double Ufance, pay this fecond of Ex-
           change, my firft not paid, to Mr Richard Rich,
           or Order, the Sum of one hundred and fifty
           Crowns, at thirty one Pence half Peny ℔
           Crown, Value of Mr David Le Petre, and
           pafs it to Accompt, as ℔ Advice.
To Mr Paul Puttoff,          *Frederic Farfetch.*
   London.          L           The

Foreign Bills of Exchange.

## The Protest of the abovesaid Foreign Bill, for Non-Acceptance.

Paris, July 3, 1764. for Crowns 150, at 31½d. 2 Usance.

*At double Usance, pay this first of Exchange to Mr Richard Rich, or Order, the Sum of One hundred and fifty Crowns, at thirty one Pence half Peny ℣ Crown, Value of Mr David La Petre, and pass it to Accompt, as ℣ Advice.*

To Mr Paul Puttoff,
London.                                    Frederic Farfetch.

ON the second Day of August, one thousand seven hundred and sixty four, at the Instance and Request of Mr Richard Rich of London, Merchant, I Jonas Useful, Public Notary, sworn and admitted by Royal Authority, did go to the Dwelling-House of Mr Paul Puttoff, upon whom the above Bill of Exchange is drawn; and shewed the Original unto the said Paul Puttoff, demanding his Acceptance of the same, who answered me he would not accept the said Bill, for Reasons best known to himself, of which he should inform the Drawer, Mr Frederic Farfetch: Wherefore, I the said Notary did protest, and by these Presents do solemnly protest, as well against Frederic Farfetch, as against the said Paul Puttoff, as also against all other Persons, Indorsers, and all others concerned, for all Changes, Rechanges, Damages and Interests, already suffered and sustained, or to be suffered and sustained, for want of due Acceptance of the said Bill: Thus done and protested, at my Office in London aforesaid, in Presence of *A. B.* and *C. D.* Witnesses hereunto required.

*Quod attestor regatus.*

*Jonas Useful*, Notary-Public.

London,

London, Aug. 9, 1764. for 395 *l.* Sterl. at 34 *s.* 8 *d.* Flem.
⅌ *l.* Sterl. at Ufance. ————

At Ufance, pay this firft of Exchange to
Jacob Vanderladen, or Order, Three hundred
ninety-five Pounds Sterling, at thirty-four Shillings eight Pence Flem. ⅌ Pound Sterling, Value
of James Moreton Efq; and place it, as ⅌
Advice, from Yours,

To Mr Edward Towers,
Merchant, Rotterdam. ———— *Edward Eaton.*

London, Aug. 9, 1764. for 395 *l.* Sterl. at 34 *s.* 8 *d.* Flem.
⅌ *l.* Sterling, at Ufance.

*Second Bill.* At Ufance, pay this my fecond of Exchange,
my firft not paid, to Jacob Vanderladen, or Order, Three hundred ninety-five Pounds Sterling,
at thirty-four and eight Pence Flem. ⅌ Pound
Sterling, Value of James Moreton Efq; and place
it, as ⅌ Advice, from

To Mr Edward Towers, Yours,
Merchant, Rotterdam. *Edward Eaton.*

Bruxelles, Sept. 24, 1764. for 1197 *l.* 8 *s.* 6 *d.* Sterl. ½
Ufance.

At double Ufance, pay this firft of Exchange
to Mr Philip Faro, or Order, the Sum of One
thoufand one hundred ninety-feven Pounds, eight
Shillings fix Pence Sterling, the Value of ditto,
and place it to Accompt, as ⅌ Advice from

Your humble Servant,

To Mr Gafpar Elbe,
Merchant, London. *Bertrand Vanhove.*

Bruxelles, Sept. 24, 1764. for 1197 *l.* 8 *s.* 6 *d.* Sterl. ½
Ufance.

*Second Bill.* At double Ufance, pay this fecond of Exchange, my firft not paid, to Mr Philip Faro, or
Order, the Sum of One thoufand one hundred
ninety-feven Pounds, eight Shillings fix pence
Sterling, the Value of ditto, and place it to Accompt, as ⅌ Advice from

To Mr Gafpar Elbe, Your humble Servant,
Merchant, London. *Bertrand Vanhove.*

L 2 London,

London, April 19, 1764. for Dollars 1000 effective, at
3 Months.

London on
Alicant.
First Bill.
At three Months, pay this my first of Exchange to Mr Peter Peterary, or Order, Dollars One thousand effective, the Value received of Andreas Amandretia, and pass it to Accompt, as 𝑝𝑒𝑟 Advice.

To Mr Giles Good-
pay, Merchant, in
Alicant.

Pay as above,

*Edmund English.*

*Let the Scholar constantly draw second, and sometimes third
Bills, according to former Directions and Examples.*

---

# *RECREATION* XI.

(141) ONE of the Smarts in the Accomptant's Office, making his Addresses in an old Lady's Family, who had five fine Daughters, she told him their Father had made a whimsical Will, which might not soon be settled in Chancery, and till then he must refrain his Visits. The young Gentleman undertook to unravel the Will, which imported, That the first four of her Girls Fortunes were together to make 25000 *l.* The four last 33000 *l.* The three last, with the first, 30000 *l.* The three first, with the last, were to make 28000 *l.* And the two last, and two first, 32000 *l.* Now Sir, if you can make appear what each is to have, and as you like, seemingly, my third Daughter: Charlotte, I am sure, will make you a good Wife, and you are welcome: What was Miss Charlotte's Fortune? *Answer*, 5000 *l.*

(142) B. and C. together can build a Boat in 18 Days; with the Assistance of *A.* they can do it in 11 Days: In what time would *A.* do it by himself? *Answer*, 28$\frac{4}{7}$ Days.

(143) *A. B.* and *C.* are three Horses, belonging to different Men, and are employed as a Team to draw a Load of Wheat from Hertford for 30 *s.* *A.* and *B.* are deemed to do $\frac{2}{7}$ of the Work, *A.* and *C.* $\frac{3}{7}$, and *B.* and *C.* $\frac{1}{16}$ of it. They are to be paid proportionably; and do you know how to divide it as it should be?

*Answer*, *A.* 11 *s.* 3 *d.* B. 6 *s.* 6 *d.* C. 12 *s.* 1 *d.* and a Share of 2 *d.* more.

Divide

(144) Divide 1000 Crowns, give $A$. 129 more than $B$. and $B$. 178 fewer than $C$.     Answer, $A$. 360. $B$. 231. $C$. 409.

(145) Part 250 $l$. give $A$. 37 more than $B$. and let $C$. have 28 fewer?    Answer, $A$. 117 $\frac{1}{2}$. $B$. 80 $\frac{1}{2}$. $C$. 52 $\frac{1}{3}$.

(146) A Father divided his Fortune among his Sons, giving $A$. 7, as often as $B$. 4; to $C$. he gave as often 2, as $B$. 5; and yet the Dividend of $C$. came to 2166 $l$. $\frac{1}{4}$; what was the Value of the whole Legacy?

              Answer, 17060 $l$. 4 $s$. 0 $\frac{1}{4}$ $d$.

(147) A Stationer sold Quills at 11 $s$. ℔ Thousand, by which he cleared $\frac{1}{3}$ of the Money; but growing scarce, raised them to 13 $s$. 6 $d$. ℔ Thousand; what might he clear ℔ Cent. by the latter Price?    Answer, 96 $l$. 7 $s$. 3 $\frac{1}{11}$ $d$.

(148) In what Time will the Interest of 49 $l$. 3 $s$. equal the Proceed of 19 $l$. 6 $s$. at Use 47 Days, at any Rate of Interest?           Answer, 18 $\frac{45}{100}$ Days.

(149) A Person was possessed of a $\frac{1}{3}$ Share of a Copper-Mine, and sold $\frac{1}{4}$ of his Interest therein, for 1710 $l$. what was the reputed Value of the whole Property at the same Rate?

              Answer, 3800 $l$.

(150) What Money, at 3 $\frac{1}{2}$ ℔ Cent. will clear 38 $l$. 10 $s$. in a Year and Quarter's Time?    Answer, 880 $l$.

(151) $X. Y. Z$. can, working together, complete a Stair-case in 12 Days, $Z$. is Man enough to do it alone in 24 Days, and $X$. in 34: In what time then could $Y$. get it done himself?          Answer, 81 $\frac{6}{10}$.

(152) What Number is that, to which, if $\frac{3}{10}$ of $\frac{19}{7}$ of $\frac{111}{213}$ be added, the Total will be 1?    Answer, $\frac{3648}{74435}$.

(153) A Father dying, left his Son a Fortune, $\frac{3}{10}$ of which he ran through in six Months; $\frac{3}{7}$ of the Remainder held him a Twelvemonth longer, at which time he had bare 348 $l$. left: Pray what did his Father bequeath him?

            Answer, 1284 $l$. 18 $s$. 5 $\frac{1}{2}$ $d$.

(154) There is a City in a certain Island, 708 Miles more distant from the Tropic of Cancer, than another under the same Meridian is from the Arctic polar Circle: What Cities are those; what are the Distances of those Cities from the Equator, and what from each other; remembring the polar Circle is about 23 $\frac{1}{2}$ Degrees from the Pole, as is the Tropic

                                from

from the Equator, and in this please to consider 60 geographical Miles as a Degree?

*Answer*, Both stand on the same Spot, in Lat. 50° 54′, and answer pretty well to Chichester in Sussex.

(155) If $\frac{5}{7}$ of $\frac{4}{5}$ of 7 of a Ship be worth $\frac{3}{9}$ of $\frac{6}{7}$ of $\frac{12}{13}$ of the Cargo, valued at 12000 *l.* what did both Ship and Cargo stand the Owners in?

*Answer*, 15223 *l.* 8 *s.* 10 *d.* nearly.

(156) If *A.* having $\frac{7}{8}$ of $\frac{3}{5}$ of the half of a Trading Sloop and Cargo, worth 16131$\frac{7}{10}$ *l.* sells his Brother *B.* $\frac{3}{5}$ of $\frac{4}{5}$ of his Interest therein at prime Cost: What did it cost the Brother? and what did his Cousin *P.* pay at the same Time for $\frac{9}{11}$ of the Remainder?

*Answer*, 9734 *l.* $\frac{227}{1800}$ *P.* paid.

(157) A Grocer would mix a Quantity of Sugar at 10 *d.* ℔ Pound, with other Sugars at 7$\frac{1}{2}$ *d.* 5 *d.* and 4$\frac{1}{2}$ *d.* ℔ Pound, intending to make up a Commodity worth 6 *d.* ℔ Pound: In what Proportions is he to take of those Sugars?

*Answer*, When the Quantity is undetermined, as many Answers may be produced, as there are different Ways of linking together a larger Price and a less, than the middle or mean Rate proposed.

(158) A younger Brother received 2200 *l.* which was just $\frac{5}{12}$ of his elder Brother's Fortune; and 3 and $\frac{1}{8}$ times the Elder's Money was $\frac{1}{2}$ as much again as the Father was worth: What was that? *Answer*, 11000 *l.*

(159) It is proposed by an elderly Person in Trade, desirous of a little Respite, to admit a sober and industrious young Fellow to a Share in the Business; and, to encourage him, offers, that if his Circumstances will allow him to advance 100 *l.* his Pay shall be 40 *l.* a Year: If he shall be able to put 200 *l.* into the Stock, he shall have 55 *l.* a Year, and if 300 *l.* he shall receive 70 *l.* annually: In this Proposal, what was allowed for his Attendance simply?

*Answer*, 25 *l.* a Year.

(160) Agreed for Carriage of 2$\frac{1}{2}$ Tons of Goods, 3 Miles wanting $\frac{1}{10}$, for $\frac{3}{8}$ of $\frac{3}{5}$ of Guinea: What was that ℔ Hundred for a Mile?

*Answer*, nearly $\frac{2}{3}$ of 1 *d.*

A

## A FACTOR's Remittance to his Employer.

Venice, Jan. 10, 1764. for Ducats 187. 10 Banco, at 56 d. ½ at Usance.

Venice on London.

At Usance, pay this my first of Exchange to the Right Worshipful Sir William Goring, or Order, One hundred eighty-seven Ducats, ten gross Banco, at fifty-six Pence half Peny ₱ Ducat, Value in ourselves, and place it as ₱ Advice.

To Nath. Gould Esq;
London.                                   Jones and Lumley.

[A Ducat is 24 Gross Banco.]

London, Octob. 12, 1764. for 700 Ps of ⅛ Mex. at 3 Months.

London on Legborn.

Three Months after Date, pay this my first of Exchange, to Mr Andrew la Garde, or Order, Seven hundred Mexico Pieces of ⅛, for the Value received of himself, and place it to Accompt, as ₱ Advice from,

To Mr John Horsey, Merchant at Leghorn.                  Lawrence Quinto.

Sir,        Lucca, Sept. 15, 1764. for 13 l. 11 s. 8 d.

Lucca on London.

Ready changed.

At Sight, pay this my only Bill of Exchange, to Simon Tostain, Merchant, or Order, the Sum of Thirteen Pounds, eleven Shillings and eight Pence Sterling, Value of Ditto, and place it to Accompt, as ₱ Advice.

To Mr Thomas Gilder,                     Pierre de la Roche.
Banker in London.

Genoa, April 28, 1764. for Crowns 500, at 65 d. Sterl.

Genoa on London.

At thirty Days Sight pay this my first of Exchange to Signior Francisco Spavini, or Order, Five hundred Crowns, Exchange at sixty five Pence ₱ Crown, Value received of the Lords of Regency, and place it to Accompt of Mr Jacques Baudin of Lyons, as ₱ Advice from him.

To Mr Robert French, Banker               Gervasi Orbitello.
Lombard-street, London.

## Monsieur Baudin's LETTER, advising his Concurrence to the aforementioned Draught.

Sir,                                Lyons, May 3, 1764.
 Brother Orbitello of Genoa, has this Day defired
me to furnish him Five hundred Crowns, payable
to the Resident of the States at London; I have
therefore ordered him to draw for the said Sum on
you, which please to honour as usual, and put it
to the Accompt of

To Mr Robert French,   Your Friend and Servant,
Banker, London.      *Jacq. Baudin.*

---

Lisbon, Feb. 7, 1764. for 181 M. 186. Rees Exº. at 64
$\frac{1}{2}$ d. ⅌ M.

*Lisbon on London.* At Usance, pay this my first of Exchange to
Don Pedro Olivarez, or Order, the Sum of One
hundred eighty one Milrees, and one hundred
eighty six Rees, at sixty four Pence half Peny
⅌ Millree, Value in Accompt, and place it
to Messrs Boulet and Savary of Nismes, as ⅌
Advice from them.

To Mr Mark Gaspar, on
Tower-Hill, London.   *Bertrand Alberoni.*

## A DRAUGHT on the Imployer, for Value of Goods ship'd him *per* Factor.

Sir,   St Andrews, July 15, 1764. Milrees 300,
     at Usance.
*North Britain on Lisbon.* At Usance, pay this my first of Exchange,
to Mr Elias Regnaud, or Order, Three hun-
dred Milrees, the Value here ship'd for your
Use, upon the Santa Maria of Naples, and consigned, as ⅌ Advice, from

To Signior Santilena, Your very humble Servant,
at Lisbon.

       *Melvin Gordon.*

An

## An Imployer's LETTER, with REMITTANCE to his Factor, in a Bill of the said Factor's Correspondent.

Mr James Dennis,

According to your Desire, I have remitted you One-thousand Crowns for my Accompt, in your Correspondent Aubin's Bill inclosed, payable by and to yourself; for which please to give me Credit: I recommend the Contents of my last, of the 2d Current to you, and rest

Your Friend and Humble Servant,

Paris, Aug. 18, 1764.                    *Estienne Benoit.*

Paris, Aug. 18, 1764. for Crowns 1000, at 32 d. ℔ Crown.

*The Bill.*    At double Usance, pay this my only Bill of Exchange to yourself, the Sum of One thousand Crowns, Exchange at thirty-two Pence Sterling ℔ Crown, the Value received of Monsieur Estienne Benoit, and place it, as ℔ Advice, to Accompt of

To Mr James Dennis,                    *Aubin,*
Merchant in Bristol.

## The Correspondent's LETTER of Advice.

Mr James Dennis.                    Paris, Aug. 18, 1764.
Sir,

By this Post I have drawn on you for One thousand Crowns at 32 d. payable to yourself, Value of Monsieur Estienne Benoit; which, with my other Bills depending, please to honour, and the timely Remittances shall be punctually made you, by

To Mr James Dennis,                    Sir,
Merchant, Bristol.                    Your very humble Servant,

*Aubin.*

M                    The

The following B I L L is useful between two Perſons, when an Opportunity of Drawing is expected to preſent, or when a Sum of Money owing is dubious.

London, Nov. 3, 1764. for 3000 M. at 2 Uſance.

London on Oporto.
At double Uſance, pay this my firſt of Exchange to myſelf, or Order, the Sum of Three thouſand Millrees, Value in your Hands, and place it to Accompt, as ꝑ 'Advice from

To Edward Rowe Eſq; Engliſh
Conſul at Oporto.

William Eaton.

*If the firſt Bill be accepted, Eaton, upon Advice, ſends a ſecond of the ſame. Import, indorſed to his Order, which ought to be paid by Rowe, purſuant to his Acceptance of the firſt; if it is not accepted, drawing in this Manner prevents all the Damages of Proteſt, and the Inconveniencies that would follow from other Perſons being concerned therein.*

## A L E T T E R of Advice, with a B I L L, to a Factor.

Mr Richard Stewart,　　　　　Norwich, Aug. 11, 1764.
　　　　Yours of the 29th paſt received, with the incloſed Accompt; the Balance whereof riſes higher than expected. This Day have ſhiped you, by the Peterborough of Milford, James Snape Maſter, Thirteen Bales of Goods againſt the Fair, and have taken this Opportunity to encloſe you a Bill on ſelf, for my Balance; for which, on Sales of ſaid Conſignment, be pleaſed to credit

To Mr Richard
Stewart, Briſtol.

Your Friend and Servant,
Abr. Anſtruther.

Norwich

Norwich, Aug. 11, 1764.   142 *l.* 10 *s.*

*The Bill.*   At your Fair in September next, pay this my only Bill of Exchange to yourſelf, One hundred forty-two Pounds ten Shillings, out of the Proceed of Goods this Day conſigned you for my Accompt, in the Peterborough of Milford, as ꝑ Advice from

To Mr Richard                               Your Friend,
Stewart, Briſtol.                           *Abr. Anſtruther.*

# RECREATION XII.

(161) A Perſon making his Will, gave to one Child $\frac{18}{78}$ of his Eſtate, to another $\frac{14}{19}$, and when theſe Legacies came to be paid, one turned out 540 *l.* 10 *s.* more than the other: What did the Teſtator die worth?

Anſwer, 1538 *l.* 12 *s.* 11 $\frac{271}{777}$ *d.*.

(162) A Father deviſed $\frac{14}{17}$ of his Eſtate to one of his Sons, and $\frac{14}{17}$ of the Reſidue to another, and the Surplus to his Relict, for her Life; the Childrens Legacies were found to be 257 *l.* 3 *s.* 4 *d.* different: Pray what Money did he leave the Widow the Uſe of?

Anſwer, 534 *l.* 2 *s.* 8 *d.* nearly.

(163) What Number is that, from which, if you deduct the $\frac{2}{23}$ of $\frac{7}{8}$, and to the Remainder add $\frac{1}{15}$ of $\frac{47}{48}$, the Sum will be 3?

Anſwer, 2 $\frac{4681}{7055}$.

(164) A Lad having got 4000 Nuts, in his Return was met by Mad-Tom, who took from him $\frac{4}{9}$ of $\frac{5}{7}$ of his whole Stock: Raving-Ned light on him afterward, and forced $\frac{5}{9}$ of $\frac{1}{3}$ of the Remainder from him: Unluckily Poſitive-Jack found him, and required $\frac{7}{13}$ of $\frac{16}{18}$ of what he had left: Smiling-Dolly was by Promiſe to have $\frac{1}{4}$ of a Quarter of what Nuts he brought Home: How many then had the Boy left?

Anſwer, 575 $\frac{14}{21}$.

(165) Bought 100 Quarters of Malt, Meal, and Oatmeal, together, for 142 *l.* For every 5 Buſhels of Malt I had 3 of Meal, and for every 8 of Meal I had 7 of Oatmeal: Pray

what did thefe coft me feverally a Bufhel, the Malt being half as dear again as the Meal, and the Meal double the Price of the Oatmeal?

Anfwer, Malt 4 s. 9 $\frac{240}{1313}$ d. Meal 3 s. 2 $\frac{480}{1313}$ d. Oatmeal 1 s. 7 $\frac{240}{1313}$ d.

(166) There is a Number, which, if divided by $\frac{16}{17}$ of $\frac{1}{8}$, will quote $\frac{161}{17}$: Pray what is the Square of that Number?

Anfwer, 95 $\frac{266}{1389}$.

(167) There is a Number, which, if multiplied by $\frac{1}{4}$ of $\frac{4}{7}$ of 2$\frac{1}{4}$, will produce no more than 1: What is the Cube of that Number? Anfwer, $\frac{94114}{4108707}$.

(168) What Number is that, to which, if you add $\frac{3}{11}$ of 12, more $\frac{1}{13}$ of 27, and from the Total fubtract $\frac{2}{3}$ of 7$\frac{1}{2}$, lefs $\frac{28}{38}$ of 1$\frac{4}{5}$, the Remainder fhall be 8?

Anfwer, 6 $\frac{1841}{2018}$.

(169) In raifing a joint Stock of 406 l. A. advanced $\frac{4}{13}$, B. $\frac{12}{17}$ of $\frac{3}{4}$, C. $\frac{1}{7}$ more, the Difference between A's Adventure and B's, and D. the reft of the Money: What did every one fubfcribe?

Anfwer, A. 123 $\frac{141}{8864}$ l.  B. 163 $\frac{4368}{8864}$ l.  C. 107 $\frac{1112}{8864}$ l.  D. 6 $\frac{476}{8864}$ l.

(170) A Perfon dying, left his Wife with Child, and making his Will, ordered, that if fhe went with a Son, $\frac{2}{3}$ of the Eftate fhould belong to him, and the Remainder to his Mother; and if fhe went with a Daughter, he appointed the Mother $\frac{2}{3}$ and the Girl $\frac{1}{3}$: But it happened that fhe was delivered both of a Son and Daughter; by which fhe loft in Equity 2000 l. more than if it had been only a Girl: What would have been her Dowry had fhe only had a Son?

Anfwer, 1750 l.

(171) In Diftrefs at Sea, they threw out 17 Hogfheads of Sugar, worth 34 l. ℔ Hbd. the worth of which came up to but $\frac{4}{5}$ of the Indigo they caft pverboard; befides which, they threw out 13 Iron Guns, worth 18 l. 10 s. apiece; the Value of all thefe amounted to $\frac{2}{7}$ of $\frac{9}{13}$ of that of the Ship and Loading: Pray what of the Value came into Port?

Anfwer, 4337 l. 15 s. 6$\frac{2}{3}$ d.

(172) A. In a Scuffle feiz'd on $\frac{2}{3}$ of a Parcel of Sugar Plumbs, B. catched $\frac{1}{3}$ of it out of his Hands, and C. laid hold on $\frac{1}{15}$ more. D. ran off with all A. had left, except $\frac{1}{7}$ of it, which E. afterwards fecured flyly for himfelt.

Then

Then *A.* and *C.* jointly set upon *B.* who, in the Conflict, shed $\frac{1}{2}$ he had, which was equally picked up by *E.* and *D.* who lay perdue. *B.* then kicked down *C*'s Hat, and to work they all went anew for what it contained, of which *A.* got $\frac{1}{4}$; *B.* $\frac{1}{3}$, *D.* $\frac{2}{7}$, and *C.* and *E.* equal Shares of what was left of that Stock. *D.* then struck $\frac{3}{4}$ of what *A.* and *B.* last acquired, out of their Hands. They with Difficulty recovered $\frac{5}{8}$ of it in equal Shares again, but the other three carried off $\frac{1}{8}$ apiece of the same. Upon this they call a Truce, and agree, that the $\frac{1}{3}$ of the whole left by *A.* at first, should be equally divided among them: How much of the Prize, after this Distribution, remained with each of the Competitors?

The young Accomptant, in solving this Proposition, will not be sorry to see the whole Process before him, whence he may reap some Information; and receive Encouragement to carry it through.

*A.* Having laid hold on $\frac{2}{3}$ of the whole Parcel, *B.* caught $\frac{3}{8}$ of it from him, that is, $\frac{1}{4}$ of the whole. *C.* at the same Time, seized on $\frac{3}{10}$ of the same, answering also to $\frac{1}{5}$ of the whole. *D.* ran off with what *A.* had left, save $\frac{1}{7}$ of the same. *A.* originally possessed of $\frac{2}{3}$, after *B.* and *C.* had served themselves of $\frac{5}{20}$ and $\frac{4}{20}$, had only $\frac{13}{60}$ left, of which $\frac{1}{7}$ was carried off by *E.* This $\frac{1}{7}$, or $\frac{13}{420}$, taken from his $\frac{13}{60}$, leaves $\frac{78}{420}$ for *D*'s Part of the Smuss: And thus ends the first Heat.

*B.* Having gotten $\frac{1}{4}$ as before, is attacked by *A.* and *C.* together, who make him drop $\frac{1}{2}$ of them, or $\frac{1}{8}$. This was equally picked up by *E.* and *D.* that is, by each $\frac{1}{16}$. *B.* still retaining $\frac{1}{8}$ himself: And thus ended their second Heat.

*B.* Then kicked over *C*'s Hat, wherein was $\frac{1}{5}$ of the Parcel procured at first; of this *A.* got $\frac{1}{4}$, *B.* $\frac{1}{3}$, *D.* $\frac{2}{7}$, together $\frac{73}{420}$, leaving to *C.* and *E.* equal Shares of the Remainder, $\frac{11}{420}$, that is, to each $\frac{11}{840}$; and so ended their third Heat.

*D.* Then knocked down $\frac{3}{4}$ of what *A.* and *B.* had last obtained, *viz.* $\frac{7}{60}$, of which $\frac{3}{4}$ is $\frac{7}{80}$, and of which they are said to recover $\frac{5}{8}$ between them, or $\frac{7}{256}$ ℘ Man; and *C.* *D.* and *E.* got each $\frac{1}{8}$ of $\frac{7}{80}$, or $\frac{7}{640}$ apiece more. The remaining $\frac{1}{4}$ saved by *A.* and *B.* in this part of the Conflict, *viz.* $\frac{1}{4}$ of $\frac{1}{20}$, and *B.* $\frac{1}{4}$ of $\frac{1}{15}$, was severally retained by each of them; and thus concluded the fourth Heat.

The

The original $\frac{1}{7}$ at first missed of by *A.* is agreed to be equally divided among them, that is, $\frac{1}{17}$ to each Competitor. The Items, when collected, belonging to each, will assign the Part they severally had of the Prize, which will turn out as follows: *A.* $\frac{3361}{10110}$, *B.* $\frac{6313}{20110}$, *C.* $\frac{2433}{10110}$, *D.* $\frac{10131}{25110}$, *E.* $\frac{1350}{10110}$, together making the whole Quantity, or 1.

(173) A merry young Fellow, in a small Time, got the better of $\frac{3}{5}$ of his Fortune; by Advice of his Friends, he then gave 2200 *l.* for an Exempt's Place in the Guards; his Profusion continued till he had no more than 880 Guineas left, which he found by Computation was just $\frac{1}{10}$ Part of his Money, after the Commission was bought: Pray what was his Fortune at first? *Answer,* 10450 *l.*

(174) A Tobacconist has by him 120 *lb.* of fine Oroonoko Tobacco, worth 2 *s.* 6 *d.* a Pound; to this he would put as much York-River ditto, at 20 *d.* with other inferior Tobaccos at 18 *d.* and 15 *d.* a Pound, as will make up a Mixture answerable to 2 *s.* a Pound: What will this Parcel weigh? *Answer,* 231$\frac{11}{15}$ *lb.* nearly.

---

# LETTERS of CREDIT.

Sir,        London, May 11, 1764.

PLEASE to furnish the Bearer hereof, Mr Matthew Meanwell, the Sum of Twenty Pounds, as he shall require the same, and place it to my Accompt; for which, this Letter of Credit, with his Receipt, shall be your sufficient Voucher and Warrant, giving, upon Payment, a Line or two of Advice to

To Mr Nich. Neverfail,      Your real Friend,
  Merchant in Hull.       *Samuel Standfast.*

*The Receipt.* Received June 2, 1764. of Mr Nicholas Neverfail, the Sum of Twenty Pounds; by Virtue of Mr Samuel Standfast's Letter of Credit, of May 11 last for the said Sum,

20 *l.*          ℈ *Matthew Meanwell.*
                       Sir,

Sir,         London, Jan. 17, 1764.

  Please to furnish the Bearer, Mr Jacques Bernaudin, the Sum of Three hundred Pounds Sterling, Exchange at 33 *s.* 4 *d.* Flem ℔ Pound Sterling, to employ for my Accompt; for which Sum, or any Part thereof, take his Bills on me, as ℔ Advice from

To Mr Claude Crespigny,    Your humble Servant,
  Merchant in Antwerp.    *Kendrick Keeptouch.*

   Ex°. 300 *l.* Sterling, Antwerp, March 10, 1764.

*The Bill.*   At Sight, pay this my only Bill of Exchange, to Mr Claude Crespigny, or Order, the Sum of Three hundred Pounds Sterling, the Value here received of him for your Use, and place it, as ℔ Advice, to the Accompt of

To the Worshipful Kendrick
  Keeptouch, Esq; in Mark-    Your humble Servant,
  Lane, London.      *Jac. Bernaudin.*

## An Indorsement or Assignation of the said BILL to another.

Pay Israel Falgate, or Order, Value in Accompt.

          *Claude Crespigny.*

  *This Bill, drawn upon Receipt of the Sum mentioned, by the Factor Bernaudin, upon the Imployer Keeptouch, and indorsed by the Presenter Crespigny to Falgate, for Reasons between themselves, is payable, like other indorsed Notes, to any Bearer, who shall Witness the Payment, by writing his Name under that of the Indorser; Not but Merchants, to prevent Impositions by Forgeries, require Foreign Bills, in dubious Cases, to be signed by some substantial Person in London, by way of Attestation that the Bill presented is genuine; upon Credit whereof, they will venture to accept or pay it.*

           Sir,

Sir,                               Dublin, Jan. 1, 1764.

    The Bearer, Mr Richard Avery, will have Occasion for Fifty Pounds, which Sum I desire you to furnish him, and take his Bill for said Sum, or any Part thereof, on the Honourable Quintilian Quickfight Efq; I am,

To Henry Hoare Efq;                Sir,
  Fleet-ftreet, London.         Your moft humble Servant,
                                   *Roger Renolds.*

Sir,                  Ex°. 56 *l*. London, Feb. 14, 1764.

*The Bill.*    At one and twenty Days Sight, pay this my firft of Exchange to Henry Hoare Efq; or Order, the Sum of Fifty-fix Pounds, the Value received of ditto for your Ufe, as ℔ Advice from,

To the Honourable Quintilian      Sir,
  Quickfight Efq; Dublin.        Your humble Servant,
                                   *Richard Avery.*

*In the Bill the then current Exchange, fuppofe 12 l. ℔ Cent. is to be added to the Sum ordered in the Letter of Credit, which fend indorfed to Renolds with thefe Words:*

Pay Mr Roger Renolds, or Order, Value in Accompt.
                     *Henry Hoare.*

*And if Renolds fhould have Occafion to indorfe it to fome other Perfon, thus:*

Pay Thomas White Efq; or Order, Value of ditto.
                   *Roger Renolds.*

*The laft Poffeffor will be thereby intitled to the Contents from Quickfight, when due. This Affair might alfo have been tranfacted, without Indorfement, in manner following:*

Sir,                  Ex°. 56 *l*. London, Feb. 17, 1764.

At one and twenty Days Sight, pay this my fecond of Exchange, my firft not paid, to Roger Renolds Efq; or Order, the Sum of Fifty-fix Pounds, the Value received for your Ufe of Henry Hoare Efq; as ℔ Advice from
  To the Honourable Quintilian      Your humble Servant,
    Quickfight Efq; Dublin,         *Richard Avery.*
                              A Gene-

## A General LETTER of CREDIT, to furnish a Person according to his Occasions.

Sir,            Paris, March 2, 1764.

The Bearer, Mr Stephen Monteage, one of his Britannic Majesty's Messengers, being ordered to Constantinople, will have Occasion for Money to defray his Charges, &c. Please to furnish him with the Sums he shall require at said Place, taking his Receipts; and your Draughts for the Value shall receive due Honour from

A Monsieur, Monsieur       Your humble Servant,
Salonnier, Banquier
a Vienne.                *Mich. Tossier.*

*The Bill consequent to this Letter of Credit, drawn by Salonnier at Vienna, on Tossier at Paris, for the Sum furnished Monteage.*

Sir,

Vienna, April 3, 1764. for 720 Flo. at Liv. 3 . 4 . 0

At four Days Sight, pay this my only Bill of Exchange, to Sieur Louis Dugarde, or Order, the Sum of Seven hundred and twenty Florins, Exchange at three Livres four Sol. ⅌ Florin, the Value paid at Constantinople to Monsieur Stephen Monteage, pursuant to your Letter of Credit of the 2d of March last, and as by Advice from the said Monteage.

A Monsieur, Monsieur
Tossier, Banquier a         *Andrew Salonnier.*
Paris.

## *RECREATION* XIII.

(175) A Gay young Fellow, had 18200*l.* left him by an old Uncle, to whose Memory he expended 3 ⅌ *Cent.* of his whole Fortune, in a sumptuous Funeral and Monument; 9 ⅌ *Cent.* of the Remainder, he made a Present of to his Cousins, forgotten, for his sake, by the old Man; with ¾ of what was left, he bought a fine Seat; with ⅞ of the Residue, a Stud of Horses; he squandered away 550*l.* upon one Mistress; and after he had lived at the Rate of 2000*l.* a

N          Year,

Year, for 19 Months together, he hath both ruined his Health, and impaired his Fortune: Pray, at his Death, what was there left for his Sister, who was his Heir at Law?

*Answer,* 6324 *l.* 1 *s.* nearly.

(176) A Father, ignorant in Numbers, ordered 500 *l.* to be divided among his five Sons, thus: Give *A.* says he, $\frac{2}{3}$, *B.* $\frac{1}{4}$, *C.* $\frac{2}{5}$, *D.* $\frac{1}{8}$, and *E.* $\frac{2}{7}$: Part this equitably among them, according to the Father's Intention.

*Answer,* *A.* $152\frac{1392}{2754}$ *l.* *B.* $114\frac{1044}{2754}$ *l.* *C.* $\frac{1356}{2754}$ *l.* *D.* $76\frac{696}{2754}$ *l.* *E.* $65\frac{990}{2754}$ *l.*

(177) Three Persons purchase together a West-India Sloop, towards the Payment whereof, *A.* advanced $\frac{3}{4}$, *B.* $\frac{1}{7}$, and *C.* 140 *l.* How much paid *A.* and *B.* and what Part of the Vessel had *C?*

*Answer,* *A.* and *B.* together paid $572\frac{8}{11}$ *l.*

(178) *A.* and *B* clear by an Adventure at Sea 50 Guineas, with which they agreed to buy a Horse and Chaise; whereof they were to have the Use, in Proportion to the Sums adventured, which was found to be *A.* 10. to *B.* 7. they cleared 45 ⅌ *Cent.* What Money then did each send abroad?

*Answer,* *A.* 68 *l.* 12 *s.* $6\frac{10}{17}$ *d.* *B.* 48 *l.* $9\frac{7}{17}$ *d.*

(179) *A.* and *B.* join their Stocks, and vest them in Brandies. *A*'s Stock was 19 *l.* 19 *s.* 8 *d.* more than that of *B.* Now by selling out their Commodity at 55 *s.* ⅌ Anker, *A.* cleared 74 *l.* 11 *s.* and *B* just 50 Guineas. The Quantity of Brandy dealt for is required, and the Gain upon the Anker?

*Answer,* 88 Ankers, whereon cleared 1 *l.* 8 *s.* $10\frac{1}{4}$ *d.* ⅌ Anker.

(180) Suppose the Sea-Allowance for the common Men to be 5 *lb.* of Beef, and 3 *lb.* of Biscuit a Day, for a Mess of four People, and that the Price of the first, barrelled, be to the King $2\frac{1}{4}$ *d.* a *lb.* and of the second $1\frac{1}{2}$ *d.*; such was a Ship's Company, that their Flesh cost the Government 12 *l.* 12 *s.* ⅌ Day: Pray what did it pay for their Bread ⅌ Week?

*Answer,* 35 *l.* 5 *s.* $7\frac{2}{10}$ *d.*

(181) Hetty told her Brother George, that though her Fortune on her Marriage took 19312 *l.* out of the Family, it was but $\frac{3}{4}$ of two Years Rent, Heaven be praised, of his yearly Income: Pray what was that?

*Answer,* 16093 *l.* 6 *s.* 8 *d.* a Year.

In

(182) In an Article of Trade, *A.* gains 14 *s.* 6 *d.* and his Adventure was 35 *s.* more than *B*'s, whose Share of Profit is but 8 *s.* 6 *d.* What are the Particulars of their Stock?

*Answer, A.* 4 *l.* 4 *s.* 7 *d.*  *B.* 2 *l.* 9 *s.* 7 *d.*

(183) *A.* has Currans worth 4 *d.* a Pound, but in Truck charges 6 *d.* and also requires ¼ of that in ready Money. *B.* has Candles worth 6 *s.* 8 *d.* the Dozen, and he in Barter, honest Man, charges but 7 *s.* Should these Persons deal together for the Value of 20 *l.* how much will *A.* have got of *B?*

*Answer,* 6 *l.* 3 *s.* 9⅘ *d.*　That is to say,

*A.* lets *B.* have Currants to the Value of 20 *l.* which stood him in but ⅔ of the Money, or 13 *l.* 6 *s.* 8 *d.* In Return, *B.* gives him in Money 10 *l.* and to the Value of 10 *l.* in Goods, which Goods cost him 9 *l.* 10 *s.* 5 3/7 *d.*　The Difference in Account is as above to the Advantage of *A.*

(184) Three Persons entered joint Trade, to which *A.* contributed 210 *l.* *B.* 312 *l.* they clear 140 *l.* whereof 37 *l.* 10 *s.* belongs of right to *C.* That Person's Stock, and the several Gains of the other two, are required?

*Answer,, C.* Stock, 190 *l.* 19 *s.* 6 *d.*　*A.* Gained 41 *l.* 4 *s.* 8½ *d.*

(185) Four Figures of *Nine* may be so placed and disposed of, as to denote and read for 100, neither more or less: Pray how is that to be done?

*Answer,* 99 9/9.

(186) *A.* lets *B.* have a Hogshead of Sugar, of 18 Hundred Weight, worth 31 *s.* for 42 *s.* the Hundred, ⅓ of which he is to pay in Cash. *B.* hath Paper worth 14 *s.* the Ream, which it is agreed shall bear no more than 15 *s.* 6 *d.* and at that Rate truck for the rest: How stood the Account?

*Answer,* 7 *l.* 9 *s.* 2⅘ *d.* in *A*'s Favour.

(187) In the Partition of Lands in an American Settlement, *A.* had 757 Acres allotted to him, *B.* had 2104 Acres, *C.* 16410, *D.* 12881, *E.* 11008, *F.* 9813, *H.* 13800, and *J.* 8818 Acres: Now, how many Acres did the Settlement contain, since the Allotments made above want 416 Acres of ⅓ of the Whole?

*Answer,* 380035 Acres.

　　　　GENE-

## GENERAL DIRECTIONS for Penning LETTERS of BUSINESS.

A Tradefman's Letters fhould be plain, concife, and to the Purpofe; free from quaint or ftudied Expreffions; always pertinent, and conceived in fo clear Terms, as may neither give his Reader Hefitation or Doubt. And, as there ought to be nothing obfcure or fuperfluous in them, fo ought they to have no affected Abbreviations; for thefe will often make them ambiguous, or too generally ex-preffed.

All Orders, Commiffions, and material Circumftances of Trade, are to be plainly and explicitly delivered; nothing fhould be prefumed, underftood, or implied. Your Cor-refpondent is to be exprefsly told, what you would have done on his Part, and what he may depend on on yours. There fhould be no Poffibility of a Difappointment left, through his not being fully informed of your Intentions: For, when Orders are darkly given, they are doubtfully obferved; and a Miftake in Commerce muft always be of Confequence.

Nor ought the Correfpondent, on the Receipt of Letters, to be lefs punctual in anfwering every Article therein refer-ed to him; to each Particular whereof he is to reply dif-tinctly and directly. Nothing muft be omitted by him, or left in Sufpence, left the Correfpondence fhould fuffer for want of proper Intelligence.

The Stile fit for Letters fhould be fhort, familiar, neat, and fignificant; like that of Converfation. The Trader fhould converfe with his Correfpondent, by Letter, juft as he would do, was he to meet him Perfonally upon the Ex-change; and whatever he would fay Face to Face, that is proper to be written on any Point of Bufinefs.

## A Country Chapman's ORDER for Goods.

Mr Nicholas Candy,                    Chefter, May 25, 1764.

Having completed my feven Years Service with Mr Lawrence Dealwell, your old Chapman, I have now ventured into the World, and taken a Shop in the fame Town.

Town. I would defire you to fend me by the next Return, half a Butt of Currans; 5 Barrels of Raifins of the Sun; 8 Frails of Malaga; Sugars at 3 $d$. 4 $d$. and 5 $d$. ℔ Pound, each 4 $Cwt$. Cloves, Mace, Nutmegs, Cinnamon, each 3 $lb$. ½ $Cwt$. of Pepper; an $Cwt$. of Pymento; 16 Sugar Loaves of various Sorts; 4 $Cwt$. of Treacle; 5 $Cwt$. of Prunes; 2 Barrels of Figs; ¼ $Cwt$. of Ginger. Draw your Bill upon me for half the Value, it fhall be paid at Sight, the reft at three or four Months: So that I expect a Price according. For being a young Man, if I cannot buy and fell my Goods as low as others, I muft expect no Trade. As you deal with me in this, you fhall hear more frequently from

Your loving Friend,

Thomas Hopeful.

## The Apprentice's ANSWER, his Mafter being Sick, or out of the Way.

Mr Thomas Hopeful,

MY Mafter's Indifpofition confining him to his Bed, renders him unfit to write an Anfwer to yours of the 25th of May laft; however, he has ordered me to let you know, that the Confidence you have repofed in him he takes very kindly; and affures you, that he will ufe you fo well, and go fo low, that you fhall be very well fatisfied. I have taken Care to put up as choice Goods as any are in Town, and fent them by Lawrence Stager the Carrier. The particular Quantity and Prices, I have in a Bill of Parcels hereunto annexed; and, at your Defire, have drawn on you for ½ the Value, payable to Mr Charles Dean, or Order. For the Remainder, my Mafter would not have you ftraighten yourfelf for Time; and hopes he fhall have your farther Orders, as you find he deals with you in this; which is all that offers at prefent from

Your humble Servant,

London, June 11, 1764.      Ready Writer;

Servant to Mr Nich. Candy.

The

*The Apprentice's* LETTER, *advising the said* REMITTANCE *to another of his Master's Correspondents.*

Mr Charles Dean,
    Sir,          London, June 11, 1764.

MY Master has kept his Bed this Fortnight with the Gout, but is at present better. He orders me to acquaint you, that having an Opportunity of paying some Part of your Balance, he has inclosed remitted you a Bill for Sixty-five Pounds fourteen Shillings and one Peny, on Mr Thomas Hopeful, your Townsman, to be paid at Sight. He is beginning the World, and my Master being partly a Stranger to him, desires, when you write, to advise something of his Character and Circumstances. Please to give a Line upon Receipt of the Bill, and as Opportunity presents you may depend upon the rest. This at present, with the Family's Service, is all from,
          Sir,

            Your humble Servant,

*P. S.* My Master desires to be informed, what the Assignees have done in Mr Chapman's Affair; and whether Mr Indolent's Certificate will be allowed.

            *Ready Writer.*

## The BILL inclosed.

Sir,    London, June 11, 1764. for 65*l.* 14*s.* 1*d.*

At Sight, pay to Mr Charles Dean, or Bearer, the Sum of Sixty-five Pounds, fourteen Shillings and a Peny, the Value here delivered in Goods to Lawrence Stager, for your Use, and place it to Accompt of my Master Nicholas Candy, as ⅌ Advice from

To Mr Thomas Hopeful,    Your humble Servant,
  Grocer, Chester.       *Ready Writer.*

[*The Bill of Parcels upon the preceding Letter follows.*]

            Sold

Sold to Mr Thomas Hopeful of Chester, June 11, 1764.

| | | Cwt. qr. lb. | | lb. | | Cwt. qr. lb. | | d. | |
|---|---|---|---|---|---|---|---|---|---|
| ½ Butt of Currans | wt. Gr. | 9 . 0 . 7 | Tr. | 140 | Nt. | 7 . 3 . 7 | at | 4 | per *lb.* |
| 5 Barrels of Raisins of the Sun | | 15 . 0 . 0 | | 180 | | 13 . 1 . 16 | | 3½ | |
| 8 Frails of Malaga Raisins | | 4 . 0 . 0 | | 36 | | 3 . 2 . 20 | | 2½ | |
| 2 Barrels of Sugar | | 4 . 1 . 0 | | 28 | | 4 . 0 . 0 | | 3 | |
| Ditto | | 4 . 1 . 0 | | 28 | | 4 . 0 . 0 | | 4 | |
| Ditto | | 4 . 1 . 0 | | 28 | | 4 . 0 . 0 | | 5 | |
| Ditto | | 3 . 1 . 5 | | 33 | | 4 . 0 . 0 | | 9 | |
| Ditto | | 4 . 1 . 11 | | 39 | | 4 . 0 . 0 | | 8 | |

| | | | s. d. | |
|---|---|---|---|---|
| 3 Pound of Cloves | | at | 7 . 4 | per *lb.* |
| 3 *lb.* of Mace | | | 13 . 0 | |
| Ditto Cinnamon | | | 6 . 0 | |
| Ditto Nutmegs | | | 7 . 0 | |
| ½ *Cwt.* of Pepper | | | 3 . 3½ | |
| 1 *Cwt.* of Pimento | *lb.* | | 1 . 5 | |
| 4 Sugar-Loaves | wt. 32¼ | | 0 . 8 | |
| Ditto | 36 | | 0 . 9 | |
| Ditto | 27½ | | 0 . 9½ | |
| Ditto | 22 | | 0 . 10½ | |
| 4 *Cwt.* of Treacle | | | 13 . 0 | per *Cwt.* |
| 5 *Cwt.* of Prunes | | | 13 . 0 | |
| 2 Barrels of Figs, wt. Gr. 1 ¾ *Cwt.* Tr. 32 *lb.* Nt. 1 ¼ *Cwt.* 24 *lb.* | | | 29 . 2 | |
| ¾ *Cwt.* of Ginger | | | 0 . 7½ | per *lb.* |

*l.* 131 . 8 . 3

## Another Chapman's ORDER for Goods.

Exon, June 16, 1764.

Mr Nicholas Allom and Comp.

THIS is to defire you to fend ⅌ the next Veffel bound for Exeter, the Goods following, *viz.* Galls, 3 Bags; Indigo, 5 Barrels; Allom, 17 *Cwt.* Logwood, ½ a Ton; Madder, 14 *Cwt.* Copperas, 3½ Tons; Bahia Brazil, 4 *Cwt.* Bourdeaux Cream of Tartar, 6½ *Cwt.* Weft-India Fuftic, 5½ Ton; Red Sanders, 6½ *Cwt.* Valona Caps ground, 9½ *Cwt.* For the Balance of my laft Accompt, being 295 *l.* 14 *s.* 9 *d.* I have here inclofed fent you a Bill of Exchange, at 12 Days Sight, on Mr Lawrence Gemroy, Merchant in London, to whom I have given Advice this Day. Set the Prices as low as you can, and when you expect your Money for this Parcel, draw your Bills upon me, they fhall receive due Honour from

Your loving Friend,

*Zach. Careful.*

## The BILL inclofed.

Sir,   Ex°. 295 *l.* 14 *s.* 9 *d.*   Exon, June 16, 1764.

At twelve Days Sight, pay Mr Nicholas Allom, or Order, the Sum of Two hundred ninety-five Pounds fourteen Shillings and nine Pence, and place it to Accompt, as ⅌ Advice from

To Mr Lawrence Gemroy,      Yours,
  Merchant in London.

*Zach. Careful.*

A LETTER

## A LETTER of ADVICE upon the before-mentioned Draught to Mr Lawrence Gemroy.

Sir,

YOURS of the 20th paſt came to Hand the Day the Veſſel ſailed with your Goods on board; I ſhall however, take the firſt Opportunity to ſend the Stuffs mentioned in your laſt Order: Mean time, have this Poſt drawn on you for 295 *l.* 14 *s.* 9 *d.* at 12 Days Sight, to Mr Nicholas Allom, or Order, which pleaſe to honour as uſual, to oblige,

Sir,

Your affectionate Kinſman,

and humble Servant,

Exon, June 16, 1764.　　　　　　　　*Zach. Careful.*

## An Apprentice's ANSWER to the foregoing LETTER from Mr Zach. Careful.

Sir,　　　　　　　　　　　London, June 24, 1764.

MY Maſter received yours of the 16th Inſtant, with the Bill of Exchange incloſed, which is now accepted. The Parcel of Goods, wrote laſt for, I have this Day ſhiped on board the Coaſter of Exon, John Miller Maſter, being marked and numbered as ℔ Margin *. The Bill of Lading, and the Bill of Parcels, are both annexed. My Maſter and Partner are now out of Town; for that Reaſon, I have taken all poſſible Care to pleaſe you in both Goods and Prices. What you have further Occaſion for in our Way, be pleaſed to ſignify your Order, and it ſhall faithfully and diligently be performed by, Sir,

Your humble Servant,

*Ferdinando Failnone,*

Servant to Mr Nich. Allom and Comp.

* [*Theſe Numeros and Marks are to be ſet here as* ℔ *Margin of the ſubſequent Bill of Lading.*]

O　　　　　　　　　　　　The

The BILL of PARCELS on the preceding LETTER.

Sold to Mr Zachary Careful, June 24, 1764.

| | Cwt. gr. lb. | lb. | Cwt. gr. lb. | | £ s. d. | ⅌ Cwt. £ |
|---|---|---|---|---|---|---|
| 3 Bags of Galls—wt. Gr. 9 . 2 . 27 | Tr. 36 | | N 9 . 1 . 19 | at 3 . . 5 . 0 | | ⅌ Cwt. £ |
| 5 Barrels of Indigo | 15 . 2 . 19 | 72 | 15 . 2 . 0 | 3 | 9 . 7 . 0 | |
| 17 Cwt. of Allom | | | | | 0 . 12 . 0 | |
| ½ Ton of Logwood | | | | | 4 . 7 . 6 | ⅌ Ton. |
| 14 Cwt. of Madder | | | | | 2 . 18 . 6 | ⅌ Cwt. |
| 3¼ Ton of Copperas | | | | | 8 . 0 . 0 | ⅌ Ton. |
| 4 Cwt. of Bahia Brazil | | | | | 2 . 0 . 0 | ⅌ Cwt. |
| 6¼ Cwt. of Bourdeaux Cream of Tartar | | | | | 2 . 14 . 0 | |
| 5¼ Ton of West-India Fuffic | | | | | 0 . 14 . 3 | |
| 6¼ Cwt. of Red Sanders | | | | | 2 . 0 . 0 | |
| 9½ Cwt. of Valona Caps, ground | | | | | 0 . 11 . 6 | |

£ 374 . 16 . 6

## The BILL of LADING.

SHIPED, by the Grace of God, in good Order, and well Conditioned, by [Mr Nich. Allom and Company,] in and upon the good Ship, called the [Coaster of Exeter] whereof is Master, under God, for this present Voyage, [John Miller,] and riding at Anchor in [the River of Thames] and by God's Grace bound for [Exeter.] To fay, [eleven Parcels of several Sorts of Goods,] being marked and numbered as in the Margin, and are to be delivered in

like

like good Order, and well Conditioned, at the aforesaid Port of [Exeter] (the Danger of the Seas only excepted) unto [Zach. Careful] or to his Assigns, he or they paying for Freight of the said Goods, [sixteen Shillings four Pence] ꝑ Ton, with Primage and Average accustomed : In Witness whereof, the Master or Purser of the said Ship has affirmed to * three Bills of Lading, all of this Tenor and Date, one of which being accomplished, the other two stand void. And so God send the good Ship to her desired Port in Safety. Amen.

The Contents and Quality unknown,

John Miller.

Nᵇ 1 to 11.

Dated in [London, June the 24th, 1764.]

## The BILL of ENTRY at the Custom-House, June 24, 1764.

In the Coaster of Exon, John Miller; for Exon, Nich. Allom and Company.

NINE Hundred, one Quarter, and nineteen Pounds of Galls.
Fifteen Hundred and three Pounds of Indigo.
Seventeen Hundred of Allom, &c. [The Items as ꝑ foregoing Bill of Parcels here to be transcribed verbatim.]

## A Third ORDER from the Country for Goods.

Worcester, July 24, 1764.

Mr Nehemiah Holland,

I Am sorry you should meet with a Disappointment in the Return of Money, which I ordered Nich. Careless to pay you, when he was in London last Week: The first Opportunity that offers, I shall take Care to remit you a Bill, or if you have any Opportunity draw your Bill on me, it shall be paid at Sight. Be pleased to

* The three Bills of Lading mentioned, are disposed of in this Manner; one remains with the Person who shipped the Goods; one is kept by the Master of the Ship; and the third is sent to the Person who is to receive them.

O 2

to fend me by the Carrier, the next Return, 3 Ps. of Dow-
las; Hollands, at 2 s. 2 d. 2 s. 8 d. 3 s. 2 d 3 s. 9 d.
each 2 Ps. and 3 Ps. of Bag Holland, at 4 s. 8 d. five Ps.
of Cambrick, from 3 l. 10 s. to 5 l. 3 Ps. of Checks, 10 Ps.
of blue Hertfords, 6 Ps. of Ghentings, 4 Ps. of Muflins,
from 4 l. to 8 l. Send the loweft Price, and the Time of
Payment: I fhall be punctual, being

Your loving Friend,

Samuel Longell.

## A Servant's ANSWER.

Mr Samuel Longell,        London, Aug. 10, 1764.

YOURS of the 24th of July laft was received. I have,
⅌ John Surly, Worcefter Carrier, fent you the Goods
wrote for in your laft; the Bill of Parcels have hereunto
annexed. My Mafter's Affairs calling him to Briftol, I have
done my utmoft to content you, both in Goods and Prices;
being of Opinion you never had better Goods, or a better
Pennyworth. For what remains on the old Accompt, an
Opportunity will offer to draw a Bill on you next Week.
What you have Occafion for farther, fignify your Order, it
fhall be carefully followed; and as to Time of Payment, my
Mafter will be as reafonable as any Man. I add no more at
prefent, but that I am,

Your humble Servant,

*Thomas Meafurewell*, Servant to

Nehemiah Holland.

## The BILL mentioned to be drawn at Opportunity.

-----

58 l. 12 s. 6 d. London, Aug. 19, 1764.

Sir,

-----

Pay Mrs Charity Somerfield, or Order, the Sum of Fifty-
eight Pounds, twelve Shillings, fix Pence, eight Days after
Date, Value of Capt. Edward Somerfield, and place it to Accompt of my Mafter Nehemiah Holland, as ⅌ Advice from

To Mr Samuel Longell,     Your very humble Servant,
   Draper in Worcefter.         *The. Meafurewell.*

The

## The BILL of PARCELS.

Sold to Mr Samuel Longell, Aug. 11, 1764.

| | Ells. | | s. | d. | l. | s. | d. |
|---|---|---|---|---|---|---|---|
| 3 Ps. of Dowlas | Qt. 84½ | at 1 . 1½ ⅌ Ell | | | | | |
| 2 Ps. of Holland | 38 | | 2 | 2 | | | |
| Ditto | 38 | | 2 | 8 | | | |
| Ditto | 39½ | | 3 | 2 | | | |
| Ditto | 37½ | | 3 | 9 | | | |
| 3 Ps. of Bag Holland | 77½ | | 4 | 8 | 3 | 9 | 0 |
| | | | | | | | |
| 1 Ps. of Cambrick | Qt. 8 | ⅌ Yard | 11 | 6 | | | |
| Ditto | 8 | | 12 | 0 | | | |
| Ditto | 8 | | 13 | 6 | | | |
| Ditto | 8 | | 16 | 6 | | | |
| | | | s. | d. | | | |
| 10 Ps. of Hertfords | 247 | | 0 | 6¼ ⅌ Ps. | | | |
| 3 Ps. of Checks | 45 | | 35 | 0 | | | |

6 Ps. of Ghenting, viz.

| | Yds. | | s. | d. | | | |
|---|---|---|---|---|---|---|---|
| No 1. | Qt. 8 | at 1 . 10½ ⅌ Yard | 1 | 11 | | | |
| 2. | 8½ | | 2 | 0 | | | |
| 3. | 8¼ | | 2 | 3 | | | |
| 4. | 9 | | 2 | 5 | | | |
| 5. | 8½ | | 2 | 6 | | | |
| 6. | 8 | | | | | | |
| 1 Ps. of Muslin | 20 | | 4 | 0 | | | |
| Ditto | 20½ | | 5 | 6 | | | |
| Ditto | 21¼ | | 6 | 10 | | | |
| Ditto | 20 | | 8 | 0 | | | |

l. 119 . 5 . 2

# RECREATION XIV.

(188) *A.* and *B.* in Partnership equally divide the Gain; *A*'s Money, which was 84 *l.* 12 *s.* 6 *d.* lay for nineteen Months, and *B*'s for no more than 7: The Adventure of the latter is fought?

*Answer,* 229 *l.* 13 *s.* 11 ¾ *d.*

(189) In 117 times 406 Pieces of Coin, worth 3 *s.* 8 ⅔ *d.* a Piece, how many Reas at 20 for 3 *d.* English?

*Answer,* 14145040.

(190) *A.* has Kerſeys at 4 *l.* 5 *s.* a Piece, ready Money; in Barter they are charged by him at 5 *l.* 6 *s.* each, and ⅓ of that required down. *B.* has Flax at 3 *d.* a Pound; how ought he to rate it in Truck, not to be hurt by the Extortion of *A?*

*Answer,* 5 ⅝ *d* ¹¹⁴⁄₂₁₃

In all Solutions of Questions in Truck, the intrinsick Value of the Thing received, ought to tally with the like Value of the Thing delivered, where they deal upon the Par: If there be any Difference, some one of the Parties has the Advantage of the other by the Value of that Difference.

(192) Lent 109 Guineas, at 4 ᵱ *Cent.* which by the 18th of Aug. 1740, was raised, by the Intereſt, to as many Moidores, bating 2 *s.* 6 *d.* Pray on what Day did the Bond bear Date?

*Answer,* July 7, 1733.

(193) Put out 384 *l.* to Intereſt, and in 8 ¼ Years there were 542 *l.* 8 *s.* found to be due; what Rate of Intereſt could then be implied? *Answer,* 5 ᵱ *Cent.* ᵱ Annum.

(194) *A.* for nine Months Adventure received 20 *l.* *B.* for one of ſeven Months received 25 Guineas; and *C.* for lying out of his Contribution 5 Months, had a Title to 32 *l.* The Total of their Adventures, multiplied into their reſpective Times, was 640 *l.* What then were the Particulars?

*Answer,* *A.* 18 *l.* 3 *s.* 6 *d.* *B.* 30 *l.* 13 *s.* 5 *d.* *C.* 52 *l.* 6 *s.* 10 ¼ *d.*

(195) *A.* clears 13 *l.* in 6 Months; *B.* 18 *l.* in 5 Months; and *C.* 23 *l.* in 9 Months, with a Stock of 72 *l.* 10 *s.* What then did the general Stock amount to?

*Answer,* 131 *l.* 6 *s.* 10 *d.* neatly.

I have

(196) I have imported 80 Jars of Lucca Oil, each containing 1180 solid Inches: What came the Freight to at 4 s. 6 d. ⅌ Cwt. Tare, 1 in 10; counting 7½ Pounds of Oil to the Wine Gallon of 231 Cubic Inches?

*Answer, 5 l. 10 s. 9¼ d.*

(197) A. had 15 Pipes of Malaga Wine which he parted with to B. at 4⅓ ⅌ Cent. Profit, who fold them to C. for 38 l. 11 s. 6 d. Advantage; C. made them over to D. for 500 l. 16 s. 8 d. and cleared thereby, 6¼ ⅌ Cent. What did this Wine cost A. ⅌ Gallon?

*Answer, 4 s. 4¼ d.*

(198) If 19 Yards of Yard-wide Stuff, exactly line 14 Yards of Silk of another Breadth, how many Yards of the latter will line 184 Pieces of the former, each Piece holding 28¼ Yards?

*Answer, 3864 Yards.*

(199) A. has 50 Broad-Cloths, at 11 l. 10 s. a Piece, but in Change requires 13 l. taking Wool, at 2 s. 6 d. ⅌ Stone of B. in Return, that was really worth but 4 s. 4 d. a Tod: The Question is, how many Sacks of Wool will pay for the Cloth, and which of the Dealers has the better in the Bargain?

*Answer, 200 Sacks. B. got 33 l. 6 s. 8 d. by the Affair.*

(200) V. of Amsterdam, draws on X. of Hamburg, at 67 d. Flem. ⅌ Dollar of 32 Sols Lubeck; and on Y. of Nuremberg, at 70 d. Flem. ⅌ Florin of 65 Crutzers Current: If V. has Orders to draw on X. in order to remit to Y. at said Prices, how would run the Exchange between Hamburg and Nuremberg?

*Answer, 33 47/71 Sols Lub. ⅌ Florin.*

(201) M. of Amsterdam orders N. of London to remit O. of Paris, at 54 d. Sterl. ⅌ Crown, and to draw on P. of Antwerp, for the Value, at 33½ s. Flem. ⅌ Pound Sterling; but as soon as N. received the Commission, the Exchange was on Paris at 54½ d. ⅌ Crown: Pray at what Rate of Exchange ought N. to draw on P. to execute his Orders, and be no Loser? *Answer, 33 s. 2 44/109 d.*

(202) A. with Intention to clear 30 Guineas, on a Bargain with B. rates Hops at 16 d. ⅌ Pound, that stood him in 10 d. B. appriz'd of that, sets down Malt, which cost 20 s. a Quarter, at an adequate Price; How much Malt did they contract for? *Answer, 420 Bushels.*

A. and

(203) *A.* and *B.* venturing equal Sums of Money, clear by joint Trade 154 *l.* by Agreement *A.* was to have 8 ℔ *Cent.* because he spent Time in Execution of the Project, and *B.* was to have only 5: The Question is, what was allotted *A.* for his Trouble? *Answer,* 35 *l.* 10 *s.* 9 ¼ *d.*

(204) *A.* in order to put off to *B.* 720 Ells of damaged Holland, worth 5 *s.* an Ell, at 6 *s.* 8 *d.* proposes, in case he has half the Value in Money, to give *B.* thereon a Discompt of 10 ℔ *Cent.* The rest *A.* is to take out in Saffron, which *B.* apprized of the whole Management, rates in Justice at 30 *s.* the Pound: Pray what was it really worth in ready Money; and what Quantity of Saffron was he to deliver on the Change?

*Answer,* 20 *s.* a Pound, and 72 of them.

(205) *A.* lent his good Friend *B.* fourscore and eleven Guineas, from the 11th of December to the 10th of May following; *B.* on another Occasion, let *A.* have 100 Marks, from September 3 to Christmas following: Query, how long ought the Person obliged to let his Friend use 40 *l.* fully to retaliate the Favour? *Answer,* 170 Days, nearly.

(206) Laid out in a Lot of Muslin, 480 *l.* 12 *s.* upon Examination of which, two Parts in seven proved damaged: so that I could make but 5 *s.* 6 *d.* a Yard of the same; and by so doing find I lost 48 *l.* 18 *s.* by it. At what Rate ℔ Ell am I to part with the undamaged Muslin, to make up my said Loss? *Answer,* 12 *s.* 4 *d.* nearly.

(207) June the 23d. 1745, bought 900 *l.* of New South Sea Annuities, at 111 ⅛ ℔ *Cent.* viz. the Day before the closing of the Books, the Brokerage whereof is always 2 *s.* 6 *d.* ℔ *Cent.* on the Capital, whether you buy or sell. The Midsummer Dividend, 2 ℔ *Cent.* became due, and payable on the 10th of August following, by which Time the Rebellion growing considerable in the North, the said Annuities were down at 92 ¼ ℔ *Cent.* In the general Alarm sold 400 *l.* Capital at that Price; but continued the Remainder till a second, third, fourth, and fifth Dividend, as before, became due: And on opening the Books 10 August, 1747, sold out at 102 ¼ ℔ *Cent.* Now, reckoning I might have made 5 ℔ *Cent.* on my Money, had I kept it out of the Stocks, how stood this Article in Point of Profit or Loss?

*Answer,* to my Damage, 168 *l.* 13 *s.* 2 ¼ *d.*

A LET-

# A LETTER from a Merchant to his Factor.

Mr Iſaac Sharp,

Sir,

YOURS of the 11th current I received, and am glad to underſtand you will recover good Part of your Loſs of the Inſurers of the Swan. My Account of Sales incloſed I have examined, and am ſatisfied with the Net Proceed, and your Management therein. With Convenience, pleaſe to buy 10 Hhds. of white Biſcuit, and 49 Barrels of Beef, and ſend ℔ firſt Veſſel to Jamaica, conſigned to Mr Thomas Gunſton, for my Accompt: Pray engage your Victualler to get the Beef carefully ſalted and barreled, conſidering the Climate to which it is ſent. I am,

London, July 19, 1764.　　　　Sir,

　　　　　　　　Your Friend and Servant,

　　　　　　　　　　*Richard Allom.*

# ANSWER from the Factor to his Imployer.

Mr Richard Allom,

Sir,

INcloſed are the Invoyce and Bill of Lading of 49 Barrels of Beef, and 10 Hhds. of white Biſcuit, bought and conſigned, by your Order, to Mr Thomas Gunſton at Port-Royal; which being well caſked, I hope will prove well, and arrive to a good Market. An Opportunity preſents of drawing upon you for the Value, payable at one and twenty Days Sight, to the Commiſſioners of Cuſtoms at London, which I muſt entreat you to honour, and hope in a very ſhort Time to anſwer your Expectations, as to my Balance depending: In the mean Time, as Occaſion offers, let me have the Honour of your Commands, who am,

　　　　　　　　Sir,

　　　　　　　Your obliged humble Servant,

Dublin, Sept. 7, 1764.　　　　　　*Iſaac Sharp.*

*For Practice, the Learner may be put to draw Bills of Lading, Entry, and Exchange, conſequent to this Advice, by former Precedents.*

　　　　　　　P　　　　　　　Invoyce

Laus Deo, in Dublin, Sept. 5, 1764.

Invoyce of 49 Barrels of Beef, and 10 Hhds. of white Bifcuit, fhiped by me Ifaac Sharp on board the Dublin Merchant, Nich. Tory Mafter; and goes configned to Mr
Thomas Gunfton, Merchant, at Port-Royal in Jamaica;
for the proper Account and Rifque of Mr Richard Allom
of London; being marked and numbered as ℔ Margin.
Content, Coft, and Charges, *viz.*

*Imprimis,* To 49 Barrels of Beef, bought of ⎱ *l.*
    Jonas Long, at 15 s. 6 d. ℔ Barrel —— ⎰

To 10 Hhds. of white Bifcuit, bought of Will. ⎱
    Man, 29 *Cwt.* 26 *lb.* at 10 s. ℔ *Cwt.* —— ⎰

Nº 1. to 59.      **CHARGES.**

To Cuftom of the Beef, *L.* 2 . 9 . 0
Ditto of the Bifcuit, —— 0 . 10 . 0
Entry and Fees of Cocket, 0 . 5 . 6
Searcher, and Wharfin- ⎱
  ger's Fees of all, —— ⎰ 0 . 7 . 6
Carts to the Cuftom- ⎱
  houfe, 1½ d. ℔ Barrel, ⎰ 0 . 6 . 1
Carts for Hhds. to the ⎱
  Baker's, and to the ⎰ 0 . 3 . 4
  Cuftom-Houfe, ——
For 10 Hhds. 25 s. and ⎱
  Cooperage, Hoops, ⎰ 2 . 1 . 0
  and Heading, 16 s.
Porters and Shiping, —— 0 . 3 . 4
               —————— *l.* 6 . 5 . 9

To my Commiffion at 2½ ℔ *Cent. l.* 1 . 9 . 5
                    ————————

Suppofing the Exo Current to be 10
*per Cent.* in Favour of England; pray             *l.*
what Sum may Mr Sharp, at Dublin,
draw for on London, on Account of   Errors excepted, ————
the Factory above?

                                  ℔ *Ifaac Sharp.*
    *Anfwer, l.* 54 . 17 . 3

[Invoyce or Factory] *is the Account of Coft, Cuftom, Pro-
vifion, Charges,* &c. *of Goods fent from a Merchant or Factor, to his Correfpondent or Imployer, beyond Sea.*

    [Commiffion or Provifion] *is an Allowance to the Factor,
for his Pains in doing Bufinefs for his Imployer.*

Invoyce

Invoyce of 5 Barrels of Indigo, 5 Hhds. of Pymento, and 5 Hhds. of Sugar, shiped on board the Lyon, William Jones Mafter; for Accompt and Rifque of Nath. Owen, Merchant in London, being marked and numbered as under.

Port-Royal in Jamaica, Nov. 15, 1764.

Contents, Cofts, and Charges, *viz.*

**Indigo, 5 Barrels.**

| N° | |
|---|---|
| 1 | 142 |
| | 143 |
| | 146 |
| to | 152 |
| 5 | 173 |

756 lb. Nt. at 2 s. 1 d. $\bar{p}$ lb. — — — — — — lb.

**Pymento, 5 Hogfheads.**

| N° | Gr. 432 | Tr. 84 |
|---|---|---|
| 1 | 396 | 72 |
| | 410 | 81 |
| to | 376 | 70 |
| 5 | 412 | 82 |
| | 2026 | 389 |

lb.
Gr. 2026
Tr.  389

Nt. 1637 at 11½ d. $\bar{p}$ lb. — — — — l.

**Sugar, 5 Hogfheads**

| | Cwt. qr. lb. |
|---|---|
| Gr. | 52 . 1 . 20 |
| Tr. | 8 . 2 . 0 |
| Nt. | 43 . 3 . 20 at 24 s. $\bar{p}$ 100 lb. — — — — |

Charges, *viz.*
To Coft of 5 Barrels and 10 Hogfheads. — — — — 4 : 7 : 9
To Storage, 2½ per Cent. — — — — 5 : 4 : 11
To Commiffion, at 5 per Cent. — — — — 10 . 19 . 7

l. 230 . 10 . 10

Errors excepted, $\bar{p}$ Edwin and Bancroft.

Note, In the American Plantations 100 lb. is their Cwt.

## RECREATION XV.

(208) A Bond was made on the 7th of August, 1713, at 6 *per Cent. per Annum* for the Sum of 1114 *l.* 10 *s.* On the 11 of May, 1718, 140 *l.* was paid off, and a fresh Bond entered into for the Remainder at 5¼ *per Cent. per Annum.* At the Time the Interest of this last was 21 *l.* 16 *s.* 8 *d.* there was paid off 87 *l.* 11 *s.* 9 *d.* The old Bond being then taken up, a new one was given for the Residue; which being paid off on the 11th of September, 1724, the Bond-owner took no more than 1409 *l.* 16 *s.* 8 *d.* in full Payment. At what Rate then did he take Interest *per Cent. per* Annum upon the last Renewal of the Bond?

*Answer,* 2 *l.* 9 *s.* 6½ *d.*

(209) *A. B.* and *C.* will trench a Field in 12 Days; *B. C.* and *D.* in 14; *C. D.* and *A.* will do it in 15; and *D. A.* and *B.* in 18: In what Time will it be done by all of them together, and by each of them singly?

*Answer,* Together in 10,83 Days: By *A.* 47,848. *B.* in 38,931. *C.* in 27,194. *D.* in 111,176 Days.

(210) *A.* at Paris draws on *B.* of London 1200 Crowns, at 55 *d.* Sterling *per* Crown; for the Value whereof *B.* draws again on *A.* at 56 *d.* Sterling *per* Crown, besides reckoning Commission ¼ *per Cent.* Did *A.* get or lose by this Transaction, and what? *Answer,* he got 15 Crowns $\frac{11}{14}$.

(211) Amsterdam changes on London, 34 *s.* 4 *d. per* Pound Sterling, and on Lisbon at 52 *d. Flem.* for 400 Rees: How then ought the Exchange to go between London and Lisbon?

*Answer,* 75 $\frac{25}{103}$ *d.* Sterling for 1000 Rees.

(212) A Druggist has by him 4 Sorts of Green Tea, *viz.* of 5 *s.* 6 *s.* 8 *s.* and 9 *s. per* Pound: Out of these he is inclined to mix up a Tub, containing Nt. a Hundred and a half, so as to make the Commodity worth 7 *s.* the Pound: In what Proportion must those Teas be taken?

*Answer,* Either 42 *lb.* of each, or else 28 *lb.* of those of 8 *s.* and 6 *s.* with double that Quantity of the other two Sorts: And in Truth, as many Answers may be found to this Proposition, as there are different Ways of alligating properly the Prices of the Goods proposed. The Judgment of the Trader will, however,

rather

rather appear in confulting the Quality of his Goods, in order to the making an agreeable Mixture of them, than in taking any Direction from their Price or Value.

(213) *A.* has 100 Reams of Paper at 8 *s.* ready Money, which in Barter he fets down at 10 *s.* *B.* fenfible of this, has Pamphlets at 6 *d.* a piece, ready Money, which he adequately charges, and infifts, befides, on ¼ of the Price of thofe he parts with in Specie: What Number of the Books is he to deliver in lieu of *A*'s Paper? what Cafh will make good the Difference? and how much is *B.* the Gainer by this Affair?

*Anfwer.* They deal on the Par at 10 *s.* the Paper, and 7 ½ *d.* a piece for the 1600 Pamphlets, was no Money to pafs between them: But *B.* requiring ¼ of the 50 *l.* his Part of the Goods comes to in Money, reduces his own Outgoings, which intrinfically are 40 *l.* to 27 *l.* 10 *s.* and the juft Value of *A*'s Paper being full 40 *l.* gives *B.* in this Tranfaction, the Advantage of 12 *l.* 10 *s.*

(214) *A. B.* and *C.* company; *A.* put in his Share of the Stock for 5 Months, and laid claim to ¼ of the Profits; *B.* put in his for 8 Months, *C.* advanced 400 *l.* for 7 Months, and required on the Balance ²⁄₇ of the Gain: The Stock of the other two Adventurers is fought?

*Anfwer,* *A.* 168 *l.* *B.* 70 *l.*

(215) A young Hare ftarts 5 Rods before a Greyhound, and is not perceived by him, till fhe has been up 34 Seconds; fhe fcuds away at the Rate of 12 Miles an Hour, and the Dog, on view, makes after her, at the Rate of 20: How long will the Courfe hold, and what Ground will he run, beginning with the Outfetting of the Dog?

*Anfwer,* $58\frac{3}{32}$ Seconds, $1702\frac{1}{4}$ Feet run.

(216) *A.* and *B.* barter; *A.* has 140 *lb.* 11 *oz.* of Plate, at 6 *s.* 4 *d.* the Ounce, which in Truck he rates at 7 *s.* 2 *d.* an Ounce, and allows a Difcount on his Part, to have ¼ of that in ready Specie. *B.* has Tea worth 9 *s.* 6 *d.* the Pound, which he rates at 11 *s.* 2 *d.* When they come to ftrike the Balance, *A.* received but 7 *Cwt.* 2 *qr.* 18 *lb.* of Tea: Pray what Difcount did *A.* allow *B.* which of them had the

the Advantage, and how much, in an Article of Trade thus circumstanced?

*Answer*, Discount allowed 40 *l*. 6 *s*. 6 $\frac{6}{7}$ *d*. or 7 *l*. 15 *s*. 3 $\frac{1}{4}$ *d*. ⅌ *Cent*. B. the Advantage by 41 *l*. 7 *s*. 4 $\frac{6}{7}$ *d*.

(217) London changes with Amsterdam on Par, at 33 $\frac{1}{7}$ *s*. Flem. ⅌ Pound; Amsterdam changes on Middleburg at 2 ⅌ *Cent*. advance: How stands the Exchange between London and Middleburgh?

*Answer*, 34 *s*. Flem. ⅌ Pound Sterling.

(218) Q. of Rotterdam, remits to R. of Paris 2000 Crowns, at 91 *d*. Flem. ⅌ Crown, at double Usance, or 2 Months, and pays $\frac{1}{20}$ ⅌ *Cent*. Brokerage, with Orders to remit him again the Value, at 93 *d*. ⅌ Crown, allowing at the same Time $\frac{1}{3}$ ⅌ *Cent*. for Provision: What is gained ⅌ *Cent*. ⅌ Annum, by a Remittance thus managed?

*Answer*, 10 $\frac{42470}{182873}$.

(219) If I leave Exeter at 10 o'Clock on Tuesday Morning for London, and ride at the Rate of two Miles an Hour without Intermission; you set out of London for Exeter at 6 the same Evening, and ride 3 Miles an Hour constantly: The Question is, whereabout on the Road you and I shall meet, if the Distance of the two Cities be 130 Miles?

*Answer*, 61 $\frac{3}{7}$ Miles from Exeter.

(220) A Reservoir for Water has two Cocks to supply it; by the first it may be filled alone in 44 Minutes; by the second, in just an Hour; and it hath a discharging Cock, by which it may, when full, be emptied in half an Hour: Now, suppose these three Cocks, by Accident, should all of them be left open, and the Water should chance to come in: What Time, supposing the Influx and Efflux of the Water to be always alike, would this Cistern be in filling?

*Answer*, 2 $\frac{1}{4}$ Hours.

(221) A. sets out of London for Lincoln, at the very same Time that B. at Lincoln sets forward for London, distant 100 Miles. At 8 Hours End they meet on the Road, and it then appeared that A. had rode 2 $\frac{1}{2}$ Miles an Hour more than B. At what Rate an Hour did each of them travel?

*Answer*, A. 7 $\frac{1}{2}$ Miles. B. 5.

(222) Double my Money for me, said A. to B. and I will give thee 6 *d*. out of the Stock. With the Remainder he applied

plied in the like Manner to *C.* with equal Succefs, and gave him alſo alſo 6 *d.* He repeated this Propoſal to *D.* and then 6 *d.* was all he had to give. Pray what had he to begin with?

*Anſwer,* 5¼ *d.*

(223) My Water-tub holds 147 Gallons, the Pipe uſually brings in 14 Gallons in 9 Minutes. The Tap diſcharges at a Medium, 40 Gallons in 31 Minutes. Suppoſing theſe both careleſsly to be left open, and the Water to be turned on at 2 in the Morning. The Servant at 5, finding the Water runnung, ſhuts the Tap, and is ſolicitous in what Time the Tub will be filled after this Accident, in caſe the Water continues flowing from the Main?

*Anſwer,* at 3 Min. 48 Sec. after 6.

(224) If during the Tide of Ebb, a Wherry ſhould ſet out from London Weſtward, and at the ſame Inſtant another ſhould put off at Chertſey for London, taking the Diſtance by Water at 34 Miles: The Stream forwards this, and retards the other, ſay 2¼ Miles an Hour: The Boats are equally laden, the Rowers equally good, and in the ordinary way of Working, in ſtill Water, would proceed at the Rate of 5 Miles an Hour: The Queſtion is, where in the River the two Boats would meet?

*Anſwer,* 8¼ Miles from London.

(225) There are two Pieces of Clock-work, which, running with a Fly, will each of them lower a Weight uniformly, to the Depth of 35 Feet: The firſt Weight, or *A.* deſcends $\frac{11}{12}$ of an Inch in an Hour; and when it is let down, 12 Feet: The Second, or *B.* is put off, and the Train of Wheels belonging to this Machine, is ſo ordered, that the Weights will be in the ſame Level 100 Inches before they come to the Bottom: The Velocity of *B*'s Deſcent is required?

*Anſwer,* 1 $\frac{2}{11}$ Inch ℔ Hour.

(226) *A.* and *B.* truck, *A.* has 14 *Cwt.* 84 *lb.* of Farnham Hops, at 2 *l.* 19 *s.* ℔ *Cwt.* but in Barter, inſiſts on three Guineas. *B.* has Wine worth 6 *s.* ℔ Gallon, which he raiſes in Proportion to *A*'s Demand. On the Balance *A.* received but a Hogſhead and a half of Wine: Pray what had he in ready Money?

*Anſwer,* 16 *l.* 2 *s.* 1¼ *d.*

Amſter-

Amfterdam, Jan. 10, 1764.

Invoyce, or Factory of 10 Ps. of Holland, 10 Ps. of Cambrick, 9 Ps. of Ghentifh Cloth, laden by me Jonas Diligent, on board the Jofiah, Thomas Cock, Mafter; for the proper Account and Rifque of Henry Porter, Merchant in London, under the Mark ⅌ Margin: Contents, Cofts, and Charges, viz.

Gil. Sti. Pen.

10 Ps. of Holland.

| N° | Qt. | | | 5 Ps. | Qt. .. | | Gil. Sti. |
|----|-----|--|--|-------|--------|--|-----------|
| 1, | 31¼ | 33¾ | | | Ditto .. | | |
|    | 33¼ | 32 | | | | | |
| to | 32 | 34 | | | | In all 321¼ Ells at 1 . 11 ⅌ Ell. | |
|    | 31 | 31½ | | | | | |
| 5. | 30½ | 32¼ | | | | | |
|    | 10. | —— | | | | | |

9 Ps. of Cambrick, Qt. 124¾ Ells Flem. at 1 Gil. 3 Stiv. ⅌ Ell.
9 Ps. of Ghenting, Qt. 105½ Ells Flem. at 19 Stiv. ⅌ Ell.

CHARGES.

| | Gil. Sti. |
|---|---|
| To Cuftom and Brokerage of the Hollands, 3 Gil. ⅌ Ps. | 30 . 0 |
| To Charges in buying | 2 . 5 |
| To Cuftom of Cambrick and Ghentings | 19 . 11 |
| To Sledage and Boatage | 3 . 16 |
| To Warehoufe Room | 4 . 3 |
| To Average and Portage | 1 . 11 |
| | —— |

To my Commiffion, at 2½ ⅌ Cent.

Errors excepted,

From your humble Servant,

Jonas Diligent.

61 . 6 . 0
20 . 1 . 5
——
Flor.

Making at 34 s. 6 d. for
20 s. Sterl. 79 l. 9 s. 9 d.

## Port-Royal in Jamaica, Anno 1764.

An Account of Sales of 2765 Ells of Brown Ozenbrigs; 1112 Yards of Blue Hertfords; 2 Ps. of Black Cloth, Qt. 39 Yards; 40 Pair of Stockings; and 175 Ells of Bag-Holland, received from on board the Lion, Capt. Banister Master, from London, on Account of Mr Edward Luckey, is—Dr

|  | l. | s. | d. |
| --- | --- | --- | --- |
| To Portage of ditto | | | |
| To Commission on Sales, 5 ⅌ Cent. | 0 | 17 | 6 |
| To Storage, 2⅛ ⅌ Cent. | 12 | 16 | 9 |
| | 5 | 9 | 1 |
| To Mr E. Luckey his Accompt current, for the Nt. Proceed, bad Debts excepted, | 19 | 3 | 4 |
| | 237 | 14 | 11 |

## Port-Royal in Jamaica, Anno 1764.

Cr.  l. s. d.

*Contra*

By Benjamin Eaton, fold him 2765 Ells of Ozenbrigs, Yards, at 8¼d. ⅌ Yard
By 1112 Yards of Blue Linens, fold ditto, at 7¼ d. ⅌ Yard
By James Smart, for 39 Yards of Cloth fold him, at 15s. ⅌ Yard
By Lawrence Nunke, fold him 40 Pair of Hofe, at 7s. 10d. ⅌ Pair
By Ditto, for 175 Ells of Bag-Holland, at 6s. 3d. ⅌ Ell

Errors excepted, Apr. 16. 1764.
⅌ Your humble Servant,
*James Bradshaw.*

P

# INVOYCE from PORTUGAL.

Invoyce of Wine, laden ⅌ Nich. Strong and Owen Janyn, on board the Savanna, John Snap Mafter, for Account of P. Lilly and Comp. and confisgned to Paul Ludolph and Comp. in Dantzick.

Oporto, March 11. 1764.

| | Mill. Reas. |
|---|---|
| **P** To Coft of 10 Pipes of Wine, bought of Anth. de Minas, at 16 M. ⅌ Pipe | 160 . 000 |
| No. 1. To Cuftom, at 1055 Reas ⅌ Pipe | 10 . 550 |
| to 10. To Triming, &c. at 400 Reas | 4 . 000 |
| To Primage, at 60 Reas ⅌ Pipe | 0 . 600 |
| To Brokerage, at ½ ⅌ Cent. | 0 . 875 |
| To Commiffion, at 3 ⅌ Cent. | 5 . 280 |
| To Port-Charges of the faid Ship | 6 . 380 |
| | 187 . 680 |

Exo 40 Reas for 3 l.

Errors excepted,

⅌ Nich. Strong and Owen Janyn.

Anfw. l. 58 . 13 Sterling.

[Primage and Average] are fmall Allowances made to the Mafter and Mariners of a Ship, at Lading. [Average] alfo the Contribution of Infurers, in Cafe of Lofs; and fometimes the Affeffment made upon the reft of the Lading, to make good that Part which the Sailors caft overboard in Strefs of Weather, for the Security of the Whole.

# INVOYCE *from* SPAIN.

Laus Deo, in Cadiz, the 5th of Oct. 1764.

Invoyce of one Barrel cont. one Seron of Cascarilla, shiped on board the Sevilla-Merchant, Capt. Jonathan Braddel Commander, for Accompt and Risque, as ⅌ Advice; and go consigned to Mr Abra. Randal, Merchant in London; the Mark as ⅌ Margin. To Cost, &c. — — — Dr.

| Mark | Particulars | | Ry. | Pl. |
|---|---|---|---|---|
| AR | One Seron, Qt. Netto, 209¼ *lb.* of Cascarilla, at 9 Ps. ⅜ ⅌ *lb.* ——— | | | |
| | To Dispatch 4 Ps. ⅜ is ——— ——— ——— | 32 | | |
| | To Portage to the House, and Boats ——— ——— | 4 | | |
| | To Boat-hire, aboard ——— ——— ——— | 8 | | |
| | To Brokerage, at ½ ⅌ *Cent.* ——— ——— ——— | 39¼ | | |
| | | | | 83¼ |
| | To my Commission, at 2½ ⅌ *Cent.* ——— — | | | 378½ |
| | | | Ry. | |

At 8 Ryals of Plate, ⅌ Ps. of ⅜, what does the whole amount to, Exº. at 52*d.* Sterl. ⅌ Ps. of ⅜?

*Answ.* *l.* 420 . 10 . 10⅜

Errors excepted,

*James Langlow.*

[Brokerage] *is an Allowance to the Broker, to bring Persons to buy or sell Goods, &c.*

[To Balance an Accompt] *is to make the Total of the* Dr *and* Cr *Sides, when cast up, alike.*

# INVOYCE *from* FRANCE.

Bourdeaux, the 20th of Oct. 1764.

Invoyce of ½ Ton of Wine, and 20 Ps. of Prunes, shiped on the Canary-Merchant, John King Master, for Accompt of Valentine Austin, Merchant in London, marked as in the Margin.

|  |  |  | Liv. Sol. Den. |
|---|---|---|---|
| To 2 Hhds of Graves Claret, at 50 Cr. ℔ Ton | | — | 75 . 0 . 0 |
| To 20 Ps. of Prunes, bought of Mr Tart and Comp. cont. *viz.* | | | |

Tr. 97½ ℔. ℔ Cask.

| N°. | | | N°. | | |
|---|---|---|---|---|---|
| 1. | 1000 *lb.* | | 11. | 955 *lb.* | |
| 2. | 1000 | | 12. | 960 | |
| 3. | 1000 | | 13. | 960 | |
| 4. | 1005 | | 14. | 955 | |
| 5. | 990 | | 15. | 900 | |
| 6. | 995 | | 16. | 925 | |
| 7. | 955 | | 17. | 950 | |
| 8. | 1045 | | 18. | 981 | Gr. — 10 Qt. |
| 9. | 1000 | | 19. | 930 | Do. |
| 10. | 1000 | | 20. | 1040 | Tr. — 20 Qt. |

℔. 17596 Nt. at 2 . 17 . 7 ℔ ℔ Quintal.

Liv. Sol. Den.

( Continued as under )

## C H A R G E S.

| | | Liv. | | |
|---|---|---|---|---|
| To Custom and Brokerage of Wine, 20 *liv.* ꝑ Ton. —— | Liv. | 10 | 0 | 0 |
| To Charges in buying, 15 *sol.* ꝑ Ton —— | | 0 | 7 | 6 |
| To Sledage and Boatage of the said Wine —— | | 0 | 15 | 0 |
| To Custom of Prunes, *liv.* 4. 15 ꝑ Ps. —— | | 95 | 0 | 0 |
| To Sledage and Boatage, 9 *sol.* ꝑ Ps. —— | | 9 | 0 | 0 |
| To the Ship-Broker, for the Prunes, 10 *sol.* ꝑ Ton — | | 4 | 17 | 9 |
| To Average and Poor's Box, 27 *sol.* ꝑ Ton, Gr. —— | | 13 | 3 | 10 |
| | | 133 | 4 | 1 |

To my Commission, at 2 ¼ ꝑ Cent.    Liv.    17 . 17 . 6

Errors excepted,    Liv.

Leon. Moulson.

What Sterling is Mr Austin to charge himself with, on Account of this Factory, at 57¾ *d.* ꝑ Cr. And what ought the Prunes to weigh at London, the Kintal or 100 *lb.* Bourdeaux, being 110 at London?

*Answ.* l. 58 . 10 . 3    Cwt. 172 . 3 . 7

# RECREATION XVI.

(227) A Ciftern holds 103 Gallons, and being brim full, has 2 Cocks to run off the Water; by the firft of which, a three Gall. Pail will be filled in 60 Seconds; by the other in 75 : In what Time will this Ciftern be emptied, through both thefe Apertures together, fuppofing the Efflux of the Water all along the fame?

*Anfwer,* 19 Minutes, 4 ⅗ Seconds.

(228) *A.* of Amfterdam owes *B.* of Paris 2000 Florins of current Specie, which he is to remit him, by Order, the Exchange 90½ *d. Flem. de Banco,* ℔ Crown of 60 Sols Tournois, the Agio of the Bank being 4 ℔ *Cent.* better than Specie; but when this was to be negotiated, the Exchange was down at 89½ *d.* ℔ Crown, and the Agio, let us fuppofe, raifed to 5 ℔ *Cent.* What did *B.* get by this Turn of Affairs?

*Anfwer,* 1 *cr.* 18 *fol.* 9 *den.*

(229) Sound, not interrupted, is by Experiments found uniformly to move about 1150 Feet in a Second of Time: How long then, after firing the Warning-gun in Hyde-Park, may the fame be heard at Highgate, taking the Diftance at 5⅔ Miles?

*Anfwer,* 26 Seconds, 1 9/11 Third?

(230) *Y. Z.* made the following Bett for 1000 Guineas, to be decided the Monday, Tuefday, and Wednefday in Whitfun Week, on Barham Downs, between the Hours of 8 in the Morning and 8 at Night. The Propofer has 10 choice Cricketers in full Exercife, who, on this Occafion, are to be diftinguifhed by the firft 10 Letters of the Alphabet. Thefe are to run and gather up, and carry fingly, 1000 Eggs, laid in a right Line, juft two Yards afunder, putting them gently into a Bafket placed juft a Fathom behind the firft. They are to work one at a Time, in the following Order: *A.* is to fetch up the firft 10 Eggs, *B.* the fecond, *C.* the third ten, and fo forward to *K.* whofe Turn it will be to fetch up the 100th Egg. After which *A.* fets out again for the next 10, *B.* takes the next, and fo forward alternately, till *K.* fhall have carried up the 1000th Egg, at 100 Eggs ℔ Man. The Fellows are to have 300 *l.* for their 3 Days Work, if they do it, and it is to be diftributed in Proportion to the Ground each Man fhall in his Courfe have gone over. It is required,

required, firſt, How many Miles each Perſon will have run? Secondly, What Part of the 300 *l.* will come to his Share? Thirdly, Whether, if the Men had been poſted at proper Places, they had not better have run from London to York twice, and back in the Time, taking the Meaſure at 180 Miles?

*Anſwer,* *A.* 27 *l.* 6 *s.* *C.* 28 *l.* 10 *s.* *E.* 29 *l.* 14 *s.* *G.* 30 *l.* 17 *s.* 11 *d.* *J.* 32 *l.* 1 *s.* 11 *d.* The Fractions come to 5 *d.* and the Journey mentioned would have fallen ſhort of their preſent Undertaking, 417 ¼ Miles.

(231) If I ſee the Flaſh of a Piece of Ordnance, fired by a Veſſel in Diſtreſs at Sea, which happens, we will ſuppoſe, nearly at the Inſtant of its going off, and hear the Report a Minute and 3 Seconds afterwards; How far is ſhe off, reckoning for the Paſſage of Sound as before?

*Anſw.* 13 Miles, 5 Furl. and 31 Poles, nearly.

(232) The Quantity of Matter contained in all Spheres, is directly in Proportion to the Cubes of their Diameters; if then a Bullet of caſt Iron, 4 Inches diameter, weighs experimentally 9 *lb.* what is the Difference of the Weight of one that is 13½ Inches, and another that is no more than 7½ Inches?

*Anſwer,* About 287 *lb.*

(233) If the Diameter of the Earth is 7970 Miles, of the Moon 2170 Miles, ſuppoſing them both to be exact Spheres, as they are not: What Compariſon is there between them in Point of Magnitude?

*Anſwer,* The Earth is 49,5446 times bigger than the Moon.

(234) *A.* and *B.* are on oppoſite Sides of a Wood, 134 Toiſes about. They begin to go round it both the ſame Way at the ſame Inſtant of Time, *A.* goes 11 Toiſes in 2 Minutes, and *B.* 17 in 3: The Queſtion is, How many Times will they ſurround this Wood, before the Nimbler overtakes the Slower?

*Anſwer,* 17 times.

(235) There are three Orders of Leavers, or three Varieties, wherein Weights, Props, and Moving-Powers may be differently applied to the Vectis, or inflexible Bar, in order to effect mechanical Operations in a convenient Manner. The firſt hath the Power placed at one of its Ends, the Weight to be raiſed is put at the other, and the Prop is
ſome-

fomewhere between. A Leaver of the fecond Order, has the Power alfo at one End, the Prop is fixed directly at the other, and the Weight fomewhere between them. Where the Prop is planted at one End of the Bar, the Weight at the other, and the Moving-Force is applied fomewhere between, it is then a Leaver of the third Order.

If a Leaver, 40 effective Inches long, will by a certain Power thrown fucceffively thereon, in 13 Hours raife a Weight 104 Feet: In what Time will two other Leavers, each 18 effective Inches long, raife an equal Weight 73 Feet; the Force of ftraight Leavers being in a direct Proportion of their Lengths ? *Anfw.* 10 Hours, $8\frac{1}{7}$ Minutes.

(236) A Leaver of the firft Order equally divided, and juftly poifed, is the Balance-Beam: To this, if a Power be applied at one End, it will always move an equal Weight at the other. In like Manner, a Leaver equally poifed, and unequally divided, having a Power applied at one End, will move a Weight at the other which will be reciprocally proportionable to the Diftances of thofe Ends from the Fulcrum, or Point fupported: Of this kind is the Steelyard. What Weight then hung on, at 70 Inches Diftance from the Prop of this Machine, will equipoife a Hogfhead of Tobacco of $9\frac{1}{4}$ *Cwt.* freely fufpended at two Inches Diftance on the contrary Side? *Anfwer,* $30\frac{7}{16}$ *lb.*

(237) Again: What Weight will a Fellow be able to raife, who preffes with the Force of a Hundred and a half, on the End of an equipoifed Handfpike 100 Inches long, which is to meet with a convenient Prop exactly $7\frac{1}{2}$ Inches above the nether End of that Machine? *Anfwer,* 2072 *lb.*

(238) In giving Directions for making an Italian Chair, the Shafts whereof were fettled at 11 Feet between the Axle-Tree, whereon the principal Bearing is, and the Backband, by means of which the Weight is partly thrown upon the Horfe; a Difpute arofe whereabout on the Shafts the Center of the Body of this Machine fhould be fixed. The Coach-Maker advifed this to be done at 30 Inches from the Axle: Others were of Opinion, that at 24 it would be a fufficient Incumbrance to the Horfe. Now, admitting the two Paffengers, with their Baggage, ordinarily to weigh 2 *Cwt.* apiece, and the Body of the Vehicle to be about 70 *lb.* more:

Pray

Pray what will the Beast, in both those Cases, be made to bear more than his Harness; observing only, that these Shafts are no other than Leavers of the second Order, and that the Weight to be supported will be always reciprocally as the Distance of the Center of the Machine's Gravity shall be from the Prop and moving Power?

*Answer*, $117\frac{8}{11}lb$. in the former, and $94\frac{2}{11}lb$. in the second Case.

(239) A Person with a Hand-spike 100 Inches long, is said, in the last Proposition save one, by bearing on the upper End of it with the Force of 168 *lb.* to sustain 2072 *lb.* at the other, a convenient Prop being pitched $7\frac{1}{2}$ Inches above it. If now we change the Nature of the Leaver, and, bearing on the Pavement with the nether End, we suppose the Weight to be moved presses at $7\frac{1}{2}$ Inches, or where the Prop in the other Case was fixed, and the Hand lifting at the upper End with the Force of 168 *lb.* as before; the Question is, what Difference there will be in Point of Power between these different Applications of the same Leaver?

*Answer*, The Power gained in either Case will be as 37 to 3, exactly the same. A Person is capable, indeed, generally, of lifting more than his own Weight: The latter Application seems to be the more advantageous on that Account; but when equal Forces are applied to Leavers of the first two Orders, *cæteris paribus*, equal Effects will be produced.

(240) A Water-wheel turns a Crank, working 3 Pump-Rods, fixed just 6 Feet from the Joint or Pin, by which their several Leavers, each 9 Feet in length, are fastened, for sake of the intended Motion, at one End; the Suckers of the Pumps being worked by the other, shews them to be Leavers of the third Order. Now, I would know what the Length of the Stroke in each of the Barrels will be, if the Crank be made to play just 9 Inches round its Center?

*Answer*, 27 Inches.

(241) Once more: With what Force ought that Water-wheel to be driven, which, circumstanced as above, raises 3 Cubic Feet of Water at every Revolution of the Wheel, each experimentally weighing $62\frac{1}{2}lb$. Avoirdupoiz; the Friction of the Machine rejected?

*Answer*, Without forcing it any higher, the Lift must be $281\frac{1}{4}lb$.

R

Factory

## INVOYCE *from* ITALY.

Factory of the Cost and Charges of One hundred Barrels of Anchovies, shiped on board the Tortois, Capt. James Snat, for Accompt of Mr Samuel Tanqueray of London, Merchant; and consigned to himself, under Mark ⅌ Margin.

| | Liv. | Sol. | Den. |
|---|---|---|---|
| To prime Cost of said 100 Barrels of Anchovies, at Ps. ⅝ ⅌ Bar. 2¼ | 1650 | — | — |
| To Portage and Warehouse — Liv. 6 . 0 . 0 | | | |
| To Jessing, with Cooper's Pains — 15 . 0 . 0 | | | |
| To Warehouse-Room and Leviation — 25 . 0 . 0 | | | |
| To Portage and Boatage aboard — 20 . 0 . 0 | | | |
| To Brokerage, ½ ⅌ Cent. — 8 . 5 . 0 | | | |
| To Brimage — 5 . 0 . 0 | | | |
| To my Provision, 3 ⅌ Cent. | 79 | 5 | — |
| | 51 | 17 | 6 |

Livorn, Nov. 26, 1764.

Liv.

Errors excepted,

⅌ *Emanuel Luxena.*

At 115 Sols ⅌ Ps. of ⅝ for how much Sterling may Mr Tanqueray credit his Factor, Exo at 4s. 6d. Sterling ⅌ Ps. of ⅝?

*Ansv. l.* 69 . 13 . 11

[ *Italy changes upon the Dollar, containing at Leghorn 6 Livres; at Genoa but 5.* ]

# INVOYCE *from* LONDON.

Invoyce, or Factory of 6 Hhds of Tobacco, and 3 Bales of Woollen Cloth, shiped on board the Streights-Merchant, Theophilus Thoroughpaid Master, for the proper Accompt and Risque of Nicol. Neapolitano, Merchant in Leghorn, and configned to himself, marked and numbered as under. Contents, Cofts, and Charges, *viz.*

Best bright Tobacco, 6 Hhds. *viz.*

| | Cwt. qr. lb. | Tr. qr. lb. |
|---|---|---|
| N° 1. Qt. | 2 . 3 . 7 | 2 . 14 |
| 2. — | 3 . 1 . 10 | 2 . 20 |
| 3. — | 3 . 3 . 0 | 2 . 0 |
| | 9 . 3 . 17 | 1 . 3 . 6 |
| | 12 . 3 . 1 | |

| | Cwt. qr. lb. | Tr. qr. lb. |
|---|---|---|
| N° 4. Qt. | 4 . 1 . 27 | 3 . 4 |
| 5. — | 2 . 2 . 20 | 2 . 10 |
| 6. — | 5 . 2 . 10 | 3 . 12 |
| | 12 . 3 . 1 | 2 . 0 . 26 |
| | | 1 . 3 . 6 |

Total, Gr. 22 . 2 . 18
4 . 0 . 4

Tot. Tr. Cwt. 4 . 0 . 4

Cwt. 18 . 2 . 14

| | lb. |
|---|---|
| Suttle, | 2086 |
| Tret, | 80 |

lb. 2006 Nt. at 7¼d. ℔ Pound. ———— l.

Cloth, 3 Bales, *viz.*
N° 27, 28, 29. Qt. each 10 Short Cloths, at 12 l. ℔ Cloth, ———— l.

## CHARGES.

Brought forward from Folio ult°.

| | l. |
|---|---|
| To Custom of all | 53 . 18 . 6 |
| To Cost of 3 Wrappers | 0 . 10 . 6 |
| Brokerage at ¼ ꝑ Cent. | 2 . 2 . 3 |
| Storage | 1 . 0 . 0 |
| Cartage and Porterage | 0 . 10 . 6 |

To my Commission, at 2½ ꝑ Cent.    12 . 0 . 4

Errors excepted,    1492 . 16 . 4

ꝑ Ship's Husband.

Laus Deo, Lond. Aug. 4. 1764.

## A LETTER of ADVICE. To Messieurs Edw. Martin and Tho. Harvey.

Hamburgh, April 10. 1764.

Sirs,

THIS is to advise you, that I have shiped on board the Marigold, John Getall Master, 10 Rolls of Oznabrigs; amounting to, as ꝑ inclosed Invoyce, 5833 Marks Lubeck, at 16s. Lubeck each Mark. Ex° at 152s. Lubeck, for 20s. Sterling, for your proper Accompt and Risque; 25 Barrels of Mum; and 16 Cwt. of Latten Wire, from,

This Consignment makes in Sterl. l. 614

Your humble Servant,

*James Jermyn.*

[To Consign Goods] Is when a Merchant, or Factor, sends Goods directed to his Correspondent or Imployer.

Bourdeaux, Anno 1764.   Dr

Mr Valentine Auftin,

| | | Liv. | Sol. | Den. |
|---|---|---|---|---|
| Oct. 20. | To Coft and Charges of 20 Ps. of Prunes, with ¼ a Ton of Wine, shiped ⅌ the Canary-Merchant, John King Mafter, as ⅌ Invoyce fent | 732 | 13 | 10 |
| | To my Bill of 70 Cr. 5 Sol. remitted him on Mr John Strong, at 1½ Ufance, at 55¼ d. ⅌ Cr. is | 210 | 5 | 0 |
| Dec. 7. | To Coft and Charges of 10 Ps. of Brandy, fhiped ⅌ Edward Shaw, as ⅌ Invoyce | 1291 | 1 | 6 |
| Jan. 10. | To Coft and Charges of one Tierce of White-Wine, ½ Hhd. of Vinegar, fhiped on the Truelove of Yarmouth, Nich. Rope Mafter | 44 | 15 | 0 |
| | To Poftage of Letters to this Day | 1 | 16 | 2 |
| Feb. 16. | To Balance transferred to your Credit in new Accompt | 18 | 4 | 8 |
| | Liv. | 2298 | 16 | 0 |

Errors excepted

Bourdeaux, Anno 1764.   Cr

Contra

| | | Liv. | Sol. | Den. |
|---|---|---|---|---|
| Oct. 30. | By my Bill on him in Favour of Mr Francis Amot, of 312 Cr. 11 Sol. at 2 Ufance, at 55¼ d. ⅌ Cr. | 936 | 11 | 0 |
| Dec. 14. | By his Remittance at 10 Days Sight, of 270 Cr. on Meffieurs Power and Jean Laroon | 810 | 0 | 0 |
| 15. | By his Remittance, at 8 Days Sight, 185 Cr. on Mr Richard Lee, of Rochel, negotiated at ½ ⅌ Cent. Lofs with Mr Strange | 552 | 5 | 0 |
| | Liv. | 2298 | 16 | 0 |

The 19th of Feb. 1764.

By your humble Servant,

Lenard Morfon.

Dr

Mr Anthony Fountain

| 1764. | Cwt. qr. lb. | Nt. at l. | |
|---|---|---|---|
| Mar. 26. To Raisins, 19 Barrels | wt. 72.2.3 | Nt. at l. 1.16.0 | |
| Apr. 5. To Figs, 12 Barrels | 9.3.14 | 1.4.6 | |
| 17. To Sugar, 3 Hhds. | 31.2.12 | 1.12.6 | |
| June 16. To Currans, 3 Butts. | 64.1.0 | 1.16.8 | |
| July 11. To Tobacco, 5 Hhds. | 17.1.15 | 5.10.7 | |
| Aug. 5. To Wormseed, 1 Bale | 15.2.22 | 3.14.6 | |

Cr    l. 45.16.10

Contra

| 1764. | | |
|---|---|---|
| Apr. 19. By Cash, received of Capt. John Marlow | | |
| May 16. By Ditto, for a Bill of 419 Gilders, Exchange at 34s. 6d. Flem. | | |
| 19. By a Bill of 957 Liv. 10 Sol. Exchange at 57⅜d. ⅌ Crown | | l. 104.15 : 7 |
| June 14. By Cash received of Mr Richard Perry | | 76.10 : 0 |
| 24. By a Bank of England Note | | 107.2.4 |
| By Balance due to me | | |

l.

[An Accompt of Sales] *Specifies the Sale of Goods received from your Imployer, with the Charges on Receipt, and their Net Proceed.*

[An Accompt Current] *is that wherein your Correspondent is made Dr for whatever he ought to make good, or allow, and Cr for what he ought to be allowed or made good to him; and is an Accompt that sums up the Heads of your Dealing with him, and decides how Affairs stand betwixt you, to the Time of its being made out.*

# RECREATION XVII.

(242) A Weight of $1\frac{1}{2}$ *lb.* laid on the Shoulder of a Man, is no greater a Burden to him, than its abfolute Weight, or 24 Ounces: What Difference will he feel, between the faid Weight applied near his Elbow, at 12 Inches from the Shoulder, and in the Palm of his Hand, 28 Inches therefrom; and how much more muft his Mufcles then draw to fupport it at Right Angles; that is, having his Arm extended right out?

*Anfwer,* 24 *lb.* Avoirdupoiz.

(243) It is conceived, that the Effects or Degrees of Light, Heat, and Attraction, are reciprocally proportional to the Squares of their Diftances from the Center, whence they are propagated: Suppofing then, the Earth to be 81000000 Miles diftant from the Sun, I would know at what Diftance from him another Body muft be placed, fo as to receive Light and Heat, double to that of the Earth?

*Anfwer,* 57275650 Miles nearly.

(244) Suppofe with Dr Keil, the Diftance of the Sun to be from us 115 of his Diameters: How much hotter is it then at the Surface of the Sun, than under our Equator?

*Anfwer,* By 13225 Degrees.

(245) The Diftance between the Earth and Sun is accounted 81000000 of Miles; the Diftance between Jupiter and the Sun 424000000 of Miles: The Degree of Light and Heat received by Jupiter, compared with that of the Earth, is required?

*Anfwer,* $\frac{6561}{179776}$, or about $\frac{1}{27}$ of the Earth's Light and Heat.

(246) Mercury, the nearest of the Planets to the Source of Heat, Light and Life, in our Syftem appointed, the Sun, is about 32 Millions of Miles from him; Saturn, the remoteft of the Planets, is ufually diftant about 777 Millions of Miles: What Comparifon or Proportion is there between the Solar Influences on thefe two Bodies?

*Anfwer,* As 1024 to 603729.

(247) A

(247) A certain Body on the Surface of the Earth, weighs 112 *lb.* the Queſtion is, whither this Body muſt be carried that it may weigh but 10 *lb.*

>    *Anſwer,* To 3,3466 Semi-diameters from the Earth's Center.

(248) If a Body weighs 16 Ounces upon the Surface of the Earth, what will its Weight be 50 Miles above it, taking the Earth's Diameter at 7970 Engliſh Miles ?

>    *Anſwer,* 15 Ounces, 9 Dr. $\frac{11312575}{16261345}$.

(249) The leſs porous a Body is, the greater its Denſity; now the Moon's Denſity or Compactneſs is to that of the Earth as 123$\frac{2}{4}$ to 100 : What Proportion then is there between the Quantity of Matter in the Earth, and that in the Moon, ſince the Earth's Diameter is 7970 Miles, and that of the Moon 2170 ?

>    *Anſwer,* There is 40$\frac{117}{1000}$ times more Matter in the Earth than in the Moon.

(250) There is a vaſt Country in Ethiopia Superior, to whoſe Inhabitants the Moon doth always appear to be moſt enlightened when ſhe is leaſt enlightened; and to be leaſt when moſt, according to the 21ſt Paradox of Gordon's Geographical Grammar; admitting the mean Diſtance of the Earth and Moon's Centers 240,000 Miles : In what Proportion is this Illumination ?

>    *Anſwer,* The Side turned from the Earth, at the New, is more enlightened than that obverted to the Earth at Full, in the Proportion of 4152 to 4076 nearly.

(251) The Cubic Inch of Marble is 1,5688 *oz.* Avoirdupoiz; what Difference is there, in Point of Weight, between a Figure, containing a ſolid Foot and half of Stone, and another of equal Dimenſions in Braſs, 4,63 Ounces whereof make a Cubic Inch ?

>    *Anſwer, Cwt.* 4 . 1 . 19.

(252) The Sum Total of any Rank of Numbers equally increaſing, is found by multiplying the Sum of the firſt and laſt, by half the Number of Terms.

How many Strokes do the Clocks of Venice (which go on to 24 o'Clock) ſtrike in the Compaſs of a natural Day?

>    *Anſwer,* 300.

(253) The Length of my Garden is 94 Feet; now if Eggs be laid along the Pavement a Foot aſunder, and be fetched up

ſingly

ingly to a Basket, removed one Foot from the last : How much Ground must he traverse that does it ?

*Answer*, 1 Mile, 5 Furl. 21 Pol. 3½ Feet.

(254) By multiplying 16 Feet, the Descent of an heavy Body, near the Earth's Surface, in one Second of Time, by as many of the odd Numbers, beginning from Unity, as there are Seconds in any given Time, *viz.* by 1 for the first; 3 for the second; 5 for the third; 7 for the fourth, and so on; the Sum total will give the Space it has passed, any where on this Side the Center of the Earth, in that Time : Suppose a Stone let go into an Abyss, should be stopped at the End of the 11th Second, after its Delivery, what Space would it have gone through ?  *Answer*, 1936 Feet.

It may also be proved, that the Velocities acquired by Bodies in falling, are in Proportion to the Squares of the Times in which they fall.  For Instance, let go three Bullets together; stop the first at one Second, it will have passed 16 Feet as before: Stop the next at the End of the Second; it will have fallen four times 16 Feet, or 64; and stop the last at the third Second, and the Distance will be 144, or 9 times 16; and so forward.

(255) What then is the Difference between the Depth of 2 Wells, into each of which, should a Stone be droped at the same Instant, one will meet with the Bottom at 6 Seconds, the other at 10 ?  *Answer*, Difference 1024 Feet.

(256) If a Stone be 19½ Seconds in descending from the Top of a Precipice to the Bottom ; what is the Height of the same, according to the foregoing Canon ?

*Answer*, 1014 Fathoms.

On the contrary; to determine in what Time a heavy Body will, by Virtue of its natural Tendency towards the Center of the Earth, reach any Place assigned, on this Side of the same; say, as 16 Feet are to the Square of one Second, or 1, so is any given Distance, to the Square of the Seconds required.

(257) In what Time will a Musquet-Ball, droped from the Top of Salisbury-Steeple, said to be 400 Feet high, be at the Bottom ?  *Answer*, 5 Seconds.

(258) If a Hole could be bored through to the Center of the Earth, and the half Diameter of this Planet was proved to be 3923 times 5000 Feet; in what Time, after the Delivery of a heavy Body on its Surface, would it arrive at its Center ?

*Answer*, 18 Min. 27 Sec. $\frac{488}{1207}$.

S  (259) The

(259) The Length of Pendulums are to one another reciprocally as the Squares of the Number of their Vibrations, made in the same Space of Time. If then a Pendulum, 39,2 Inches long, in our Latitude, swings Seconds, or 60 times in a Minute; what Difference is there between the Length of one, that vibrates half Seconds, or 120 times in a Minute; and another that swings double Seconds, or 30 times in a Minute?
*Answer*, 12 Feet, 3 Inches.

(260) Again, What Difference will there be in the Number of Vibrations made by a Pendulum of 6 Inches long, and another of 12 Inches long, in an Hour's Time?
*Answer*, 2695,14.

(261) What Difference is there in the Length of two Pendulums, the one swings 30 Times, the other 100 Times in an Hour?  *Answer*, 6036$\frac{4}{5}$ Feet.

(262) Give the Length of a Pendulum that will swing once in a Third; Ditto in a Second; Ditto in a Minute; Ditto in an Hour; Ditto in a Day.
*Answer*, In a Third ,653 Inch; Second 39,2 Ditto; Minute 196 Feet; Hour 2$\frac{1}{14}$ Miles; Day 53$\frac{5}{11}$ Ditto.

(263) Observed, that while a Stone was descending to measure the Depth of a Well, a String and Plummet (that from the Point of Suspension, or the Place where it was held, to the Center of Oscillation, or that Part of the Bob, which being divided by a circular Line struck from the Center abovesaid would divide it into two Parts of equal Weight) measured just 18 Inches; had made 8 Vibrations: Pray what was the Depth, allowing (1150 Feet per Second) for the Return of Sound to the Ear?  *Answer*, About 400 Feet.

The Sum Total of any Rank of Numbers, not equally progressive, but multiplied from first to last, by one common Factor, may be universally found by multiplying the last of the Terms by the common Multiplier, and from the Product deducting the first Term, divide the Remainder by the said Multiplier less 1; the Quotient will be the Total sought.

(264) On New-Year's Day, a Gentleman married, and received of his Father-in-law a Guinea, on Condition that he was to have a Present on the first Day of every Month, for the first Year, which should be double still to what he had the Month before: What was the Lady's Portion?
*Answer*, 4299*l.* 15*s.*

(265) What

(265) What is an Annuity to expire in a Dozen Years worth, diſcounting 10 ℔ *Cent.* ℔ Annum, by compound Intereſt? *Anſwer,* 6 Years, 297 Days Purchaſe.

---

## The Form of an Engliſh BOND, to which may be put any CONDITION.

KNOW all Men by theſe Preſents, That I [*Benjamin Bidfair* of Stepney, in the County of Middleſex, Ropemaker] am held and firmly bound to [*William Wellmeant,* of Sutton-Colefield, in the County of Warwick Eſq;] in One hundred Pounds, lawful Money of Great Britain ; to be paid to the ſaid [*William Wellmeant*] his certain Attorney, Executors, or Adminiſtrators : For the Payment whereof, I bind myſelf, my Heirs, Executors and Adminiſtrators, firmly by theſe Preſents : Sealed with my Seal    Dated this [firſt Day of September] in the [Fourth] Year of the Reign of our Sovereign Lord [GEORGE THE THIRD] by the Grace of God, of Great Britain, France, and Ireland [KING] Defender of the Faith, and ſo forth. And in the Year of our LORD [One thouſand Seven hundred and Sixty-four.]

---

## A CONDITION for Money lent.

THE Condition of this Obligation is ſuch, That if the above bounden [*Benjamin Bidfair*] his Heirs, Executors, or Adminiſtrators, do well and truly pay, or cauſe to be paid, unto the above-mentioned [*William Wellmeant*] his Executors, Adminiſtrators, or Aſſigns, the full Sum of [Fifty Pounds] of good and lawful Money of Great Britain, on the [Firſt Day of December] next enſuing the Date hereof, with lawful Intereſt for the ſame; then this Obligation to be void, or elſe to remain in full Force.

Sealed and delivered, (being
    firſt legally ſtamped) in  ·  *Benjamin Bidfair,* (L. S.)
    Preſence of *A. B. C D.*

*When a Bond is given in Conſideration of the Value received, the Obligation is always to be made for double the Value in the Condition.*

*The*

*The Dates of legal Instruments, Sums of Money, and the Number of all other Things specified in them, must be written in Words at length, never in Figures, for fear of Alterations. The Instruments themselves, as well as all Proceedings at Law, must be written wholly in English, according to a late Act of Parliament.*

---

# A CONDITION to stand to the AWARD of Arbitrators.

Jan. 1. 1764.

THE Condition of this Obligation is such, That if the above bounden [*Benjamin Bidfair* of London, Merchant] his Heirs, Executors, and Administrators, and every of them, do and shall in all Things well and truly stand to, obey, abide by, perform, fulfil, and keep the Award, Order, Arbitrement, final End and Determination of [*Anthony Aimwell*, and *Michael Makepeace* of London, Merchants] Arbitrators indifferently named, elected, and chosen, as well on the Part and Behalf of the above bounden, [*Benjamin Bidfair*] as of the above named [*William Wellmeant*] to arbitrate, award, order, judge, and determine of, and concerning all Manner of Action and Actions, Cause and Causes of Actions, Suits, Bills, Bonds, Specialties, Judgments, Executions, Extents, Accompts, Debts, Dues, Sum and Sums of Money, Controversies, Trespasses, Damages, and Demands whatsoever; at any Time or Times heretofore had, made, moved, brought, commenced, sued, prosecuted, done, suffered, committed, or depending by or between the said Parties, so as the Award may be made and given up in Writing, under their Hands and Seals, ready to be delivered to the said Parties, on or before the [first of February next ensuing the Date hereof.] But if the said Arbitrators do not make such their Award of and concerning the Premises, by the Time aforesaid, that then, if the said [*Benjamin Bidfair*] his Heirs, Executors, and Administrators, for his and their Parts and Behalf, do in all Things, well and truly stand to, obey, abide by, perform, fulfil, and keep the Award, Order, Arbitrement, Umpirage, final End, and Determination of [*Ferdinando Finishall* of London Esq;] Umpire indifferently chosen between the said Parties, to end the said Matter and Differences, so as the

said

said Umpire do make his Award or Umpirage of and concerning the Premises, and deliver the same in Writing, under his Hand and Seal, to the said Parties, on or before the [sixth Day of February] next ensuing the Date abovesaid : Then this Obligation to be void, or else to remain in full Force.

Sealed and Delivered, (being
   legally stamped) in the    *Benjamin Bidfair,* (L. S.)
   Presence of, *A. B. C. D*

*Both Parties are, in this Case, to be mutually bound to each other, and if there be no Umpire admitted, the latter Part of the Condition, beginning* [But if the said Arbitrators] *is to be omitted.*

*A Clause ought to be added to this Instrument, and signed by each Party, directing such Award to be entered and given as a Plea, in either of the King's Courts in Westminster, in order to corroborate and render it final to them.*

---

## The FORM of an UMPIRAGE of Award.

TO all People to whom this present Writing shall come : [I *Ferdinando Finishall,* of London Esq;] Umpire indifferently chosen between [*Benjamin Bidfair,* and *William Wellmeant* of London, Merchants] send Greeting. Now know ye, That I the said *Ferdinando Finishall,* having deliberately heard, considered, and understood the Griefs, Allegations, and Proofs of both the said Parties; and being willing, as much as in me lieth, to set the said Parties at Unity and good Accord, do by these Presents, Arbitrate, Award, Order, Deem, Decree, and Judge; that the said [*Benjamin Bidfair*] his Executors, Administrators, or Assigns, do and shall well and truly pay, or cause to be paid, unto the said [*William Wellmeant*] his Executors, Administrators, or Assigns, the full Sum of [One hundred Pounds] of lawful Money of Great Britain, on the [Seventeeth Day of March] next, ensuing the Date of these Presents ; and that upon Payment thereof; the said [*Benjamin Bidfair,* and *William Wellmeant*] shall, at their own proper Costs and Charges, seal, subscribe, and, as their several Acts and Deeds, deliver each to the other
a general

a general Releafe in Writing, of all Matters, Actions, Suits, Caufes of Actions, Bonds, Bills, Covenants, Controverfies, and Demands whatfoever; from the Beginning of the World, to the [Firft Day of May laft paft] and in the [Fourth] Year of our Sovereign [Lord GEORGE, King of Great Britain, &c.] In Witnefs whereof, I have hereunto fet my Hand and Seal, the [Fourth Day of February, in the Year of our LORD, One thoufand Seven hundred Sixty-four.]

Sealed and delivered (being
    firft duly ftamped) in      *Ferdinando Finifhall*, (L.S.)
    Prefence of      *E. F.*
                 *G. H.*

---

## LETTER of LICENCE to a Debtor.

TO all People to whom this prefent Writing fhall come: We whofe Names are hereunder fubfcribed, and Seals affixed, Creditors of [*A. B.* of London, Merchant] fend Greeting. Whereas, the faid [*A. B.*] on the Day of the Date of thefe Prefents, is indebted unto us feverally, in divers confiderable Sums of Money; which at prefent he is not able to fatisfy unto us, without Refpite and Time to be given him for the Payment thereof: Know ye therefore, That we the faid Creditors, for divers good Caufes and Confiderations us thereunto moving, have given and granted, and by thefe Prefents do give and grant unto the faid [*A. B.*] our fure and fafe Conduct and free Licence, that he the faid [*A. B.*] fhall, and may fafely come and go, and refort unto us, and every one of us, his faid Creditors, to compound and take Order with us, and every one of us, for all and every of our faid Debts, and may go about any other Bufinefs, to any other Perfon or Perfons whatfoever, without any Trouble, Suit, Arreft, Attachment, or other Moleftation to be offered and done unto him, the faid [*A. B.*] his Wares, Goods, Monies, or other Merchandizes whatfoever, by us or any of us, or by the Heirs, Executors, Adminiftrators, Partners, or Affigns of us, or any of us, or by our, or any of our Means and Procurement, to be fought or procured to be done, from the Day of the Date hereof, unto the full End and Term of
[One

[One whole Year] next enfuing. And we the faid Creditors, whofe Names are here under-written, do hereby Covenant and Grant, and every one of us for his own Part, his Executors and Adminiftrators, covenanteth and granteth, to and with the faid [*A. B.*] that if any Trouble, Wrong, Damage, or Injury, fhall be done unto him the faid [*A. B.*] either in his Body, Goods, or Chattels, or any of them, within the faid Term of [One Year] next coming after the Date hereof, by us, or any of us, his faid Creditors, or by any other Perfon or Perfons, by or through the Procurement, Confent, or Knowledge of us, or any of us, contrary to the true Intent and Meaning of this our prefent Writing of fafe Conduct ; that then the faid [*A. B.*] by Virtue of thefe Prefents, fhall be difcharged and acquitted for ever, towards and againft him and them, of us, his and their Heirs, Executors, Adminiftrators, Partners, or Affigns, and every one of them, by whom, and by whofe Means, he fhall be arrefted, troubled and attached, or damnified, of all Manner of Actions, Suits, Quarrels, Debts and Demands, either in Law or Equity, from the Beginning of the World, to the Day of the Date hereof : In Witnefs whereof, we have hereunto fet our Hands and Seals, the [Fourth Day of May, in the Year of our LORD, One thoufand Seven hundred and Sixty-four.]

Sealed and delivered, (being firft
    duly Stamped) in Prefence of,
       *R. S.*
       *W. X.*

| | | |
|---|---|---|
| *A. B.* (L.S.) | *R. D.* (L.S.) |
| *C. D.* (L.S.) | *P. Q.* (L.S.) |
| *E. F.* (L.S.) | *E. L.* (L.S.) |
| *G. H.* (L.S.) | *M. T.* (L.S.) |
| *J. K.* (L.S.) | *Y. Z.* (L.S.) |
| *S. P.* (L.S.) | *W. N.* (L.S.) |
| *L. W.* (L.S.) | |

# RECREATION XVIII.

(269) ONE at a Country Fair, had a Mind to a String of 20 fine Horfes; but not caring to take them at 20 Guineas *per* Head, the Jockey confented, that he fhould, if he thought good, pay but a fingle Farthing for
the

the firſt, doubling it only to the 19th, and he would give the 20th into the Bargain: This being preſently accepted, how were they ſold? *Anſwer*, at 27*l.* 6*s.* 1$\frac{47}{60}$*d.* each.

(270) What ought a Man to give down, in ready Money, for the Reverſion of 1000*l.* a Year, to continue 20 Years on a Leaſe, which cannot commence till five Years are at an End, allowing the Purchaſer compound Intereſt at 6 *&c* Cent.? *Anſwer*, 8571*l.* 7$\frac{1}{4}$*d.*

(271) A Minor of 14, had an Annuity left him of 70*l.* a Year, the Proceed of which, by Will, was to be put out, both Principal and Intereſt yearly, as it fell due, at 5 *&c* Cent. till he ſhould attain to 21 Years of Age. The utmoſt Improvement being thus made of this Part of his Fortune: What had he then to receive? *Anſwer*, 569*l.* 18*s.* 10*d.*

(272) Value the Leaſe of a Houſe in tolerable Repair, the Rent 54*l.* 17*s.* a Year; the Ground Rent 7 Guineas; 3 Years of it only to come; the Rent payable every Six Months: Diſcompt *&c* compound Intereſt on this kind of Purchaſe, at 10*l.* *&c* Cent. *Anſwer*, 120*l.* 10*s.* 11$\frac{1}{2}$*d.*

(273) A Fine for the Leaſe of a Tenement is ſettled at 153*l.* under a reſerved Rent of 16*l.* a Year: Now the Tenant cannot conveniently pay more than 50*l.* but for the 6 Years to come of the Term, is willing rather to pay an adequate Rent, computing 10*l.* *&c* Cent. *&c* compound Intereſt: What ought that Rent to be? *Anſwer*, 39*l.* 13*s.* *&c* Year.

(274) Another Leaſe for 7 Years is agreed for at 250*l.* Fine, on the old Rent 44*l.* a Year; but conſidering the Contractor deſires to reduce the Rent to 20*l.* a Year, and pay a proper Fine, computing, as before, after the Rate of 10*l.* a Year: To what muſt the Fine be advanced? *Anſwer*, 366*l.* 16*s.* 9$\frac{1}{2}$*d.*

(275) Suppoſe I would add 5 Years to a running Leaſe of 15 Years yet to come, the improved Rent being 186*l.* 7*s.* 6*d.* *&c* Annum: What ought I to pay down for this Favour, diſcounting 4 *&c* Cent. *&c* compound Intereſt? *Anſwer*, 460*l.* 13*s.* 10*d.*

(276) Held

(276) Held of a College 486 *l.* 10 *s.* a Year on a reserved Rent of 94 *l.* Money being at 5 ♅ *Cent.* Interest: What Fine ought severally to be paid on a 7, a 14, and a 21 Year's Lease?

*Answer,* For 7 Years, 2271 *l.* 3 *s.*

14 Years, 3885 *l.* 4 *s.* 4 *d.*

21 Years, 5032 *l.* 6 *s.*

(277) A Son, previous to his Marriage, is minded to have 50 *l.* a Year, Freehold, settled on his Family; and, to have immediate Possession of it, offers his Father in lieu an Annuity for his Life, valued at 12 Years Purchase, discompting 4 ♅ *Cent.* thereon; whereas he is content the Estate should be valued at a Discompt of 3 ♅ *Cent.* and consequently will be worth 33½ Years Purchase: Pray what had the Father for his Life?

*Answer,* 177 *l.* a Year.

(278) A Gentleman took a College Lease of 237 *l.* a Year, for 21 Years, and paid the full Fine: The Rent reserved was 10 *l.* a Year; but when 4 Years were lapsed, against his Marriage he renewed the Lease, and filled up the 21 Years. In 14 Years after that his Wife dying, he again renewed it in Favour of his Daughter, then 7 Years of Age; and by the Time she was 19, it was a Third Time renewed, in order to her Settlement: The Question is, what Money the Society must have received from this Family from first to last, allowing 5 *l.* a Year Discompt on the Fines?

*Answer,* 4823 *l.* 18 *s.* 10¼ *d.*

1. If the Quantities of Matter in any two or more Bodies, put in Motion, be equal, the Forces wherewith they are moved, will be in Proportion to their Velocities.

2. If the Velocities of these Bodies be equal, their Forces will be directly as the Quantities of Matter contained in them.

3. If both the Quantities of Matter and the Velocities be unequal, the Forces with which Bodies are moved, will be in a Proportion compounded of the Quantities of Matter they contain, and of the Velocities wherewith they move.

(279) The Battering-Ram of Vespasian, weighed, suppose 100000 Pounds, and was moved, let us admit, with such a Velocity, by Strength of Hands, as to pass through 20 Feet

T

in

in one Second of Time, and this was found sufficient to demolish the Walls of Jerusalem; with what Velocity must a Bullet, that weighs but 30 *lb.* be moved, in order to do the same Execution? · *Answer,* 66666⅔ Feet in a Second.

(280) There are two Bodies, the one contains 25 times the Matter of the other, (or is 25 times heavier) but the lesser moves with 1000 times the Swiftness of the greater; in what Proportion are the Forces by which they are moved?

*Answer,* The less is moved with a Force 40 times greater than the other.

In comparing the Motions of Bodies, the Ratio, or Proportion between their Velocities, will be compounded of the direct Ratio of the Forces wherewith they are moved, and the reciprocal of the Quantities of Matter they contain.

(281) A Body weighing 20 *lb.* is impelled by such a Force as to send it 100 Feet in a Second; with what Velocity would a Body of 8 *lb.* Weight move, if it were impelled by the same Force?

*Answer,* 250 Feet in a Second.

(282) There are two Bodies, one of which weighs 100 *lb.* the other 60, but the lesser Body is impelled by a Force 8 times greater than the other; the Proportion of the Velocities wherewith these Bodies move is required?

*Answer,* The Velocity of the greater to that of the less, as 3 to 40.

(283) There are two Bodies, the greater contains 8 times the Quantity of the Matter in the less, and is moved with a Force 48 times greater; the Ratio of the Velocities of these two Bodies is required?

*Answer,* The greater to the less, as 6 to 1.

1. In comparing the Motions of Bodies, if their Velocities be equal, the Spaces described by them shall be in the direct Proportion of the Times in which they are described.

2. If the Times be equal, then the Spaces described will be as their Velocities.

3. If the Times and the Velocities be unequal, the Spaces will be in a Proportion compounded of the Times and Velocities.

There

(284) There are two Bodies, one of which moves 40 times swifter than the other; but the swifter Body has moved but one Minute, whereas the other has been in Motion two Hours: The Ratio of the Spaces described by these two Bodies is required?

*Answer*, The swifter to the slower, as 1 to 3.

(285) Again, supposing one Body to move 30 times swifter than another, as also the swifter to move 12 Minutes, the other only 1: What Difference will there be between the Spaces by them described, supposing the last has moved 60 Inches?

*Answer*, 1795 Feet.

(286) In comparing of Motions as above, the Ratio of the Times is compounded of the direct Ratio of the Spaces described, and the reciprocal of the Celerities. There are two Bodies, one whereof has described 50 Miles, the other only 5; the first had moved with 5 times the Velocity of the second: What is the Ratio then of the Times they have been describing those Spaces?

*Answer*, As 2 to 1.

(287) When an heavy Body is weighed in any Fluid, it loses therein so much of its Weight, as an equal Bulk of that Fluid is found to weigh. Upon this Principle, suppose then, a cubic Inch of standard Gold in the Air, weighs 10 Ounces Troy, and that by Experiments, a solid Inch of fresh Water is found to weigh 256 Grains Troy: What will a gold Chain weigh in Water, that raises a Fluid an Inch in a Vessel 3 Inches square, when put into it?

*Answer*, 85 Ounces, 4 dwts. In Air 90 Ounces.

(288) Again, as the cubic Inch of Silver is found to be about 4,444 Ounces Troy, lighter than one of Gold, supposing the Workman had adulterated the said Chain with 14 Ounces and a half of Silver: How much higher would the Water, upon its Immersion, have been raised in the said Vessel?

*Answer*, ,12885 of an Inch higher than so much Gold.

(289) An irregular Piece of Lead Ore, taken from the Yorkshire Pit, weighs in the Scale just 12 Ounces, but weighed in Water loses 5 Ounces of that Weight; so that a Quantity of Water of the Bigness of the Ore weighs just

T 2　　　　　5 Ounces,

5 Ounces, as had been faid. From the Derbyfhire Pit, a rough Fragment of Ore weighs, out of Water, 14½ Ounces, and in Water 9 Oz. the comparative, or the fpecific Weight of thefe two Ores is required?

*Anfwer*, 145 to 132, or 12 to 11 in Favour of the fecond.

(290) An irregular Fragment of Glafs in the Scale, weighs 171 Grains; another of Magnet 102 Grains. In Water the firft fetches up no more than 120 Grains, and the other 79. Then 51 and 23 are the feveral Weights of their comparative Bulks of Water: What then will their fpecific Gravities turn out to be?

*Anfwer*, Glafs is to Magnet, as 3933 to 5202, or nearly, as 10 to 13 reciprocally.

(291) Hiero, King of Sicily, ordered his Jeweller to make him a Crown, containing 63 Ounces of Gold. The Workman thought, fubftituting part Silver therein, a proper Perquifite; which taking Air, Archimedes was appointed to examine it, who, on putting it into a Veffel of Water, found it raifed the Fluid, or that itfelf contained 8,2245 cubic Inches of Metal; and having difcovered, that the cubic Inch of Gold more critically weighed 10,36 Ounces, and that of Silver but 5,85 Ounces, he, by Calculation, found what Part of his Majefty's Gold had been changed: And you are defired to repeat the Procefs.

*Anfwer*, ℔ Alligation 28,8 Ounces.

(292) In the Walls of Balbeck in Turkey, there are three Stones laid end to end, now in Sight, that meafure in Length 61 Yards; one of which in particular is 63 Feet long, 12 Feet thick, and 4 Yards over: Now, if this Block was Marble, every cubic Inch of which is at leaft an Ounce and half in weight; what Power would balance it, fo as to prepare it for moving?

*Anfwer*, 656$\frac{1}{16}$ Tons, the Burden of a good Eaft-India Ship.

(293) The cubic Inch of common Glafs weighs about 1,36 Oz. Troy; ditto of Salt Water ,5427; and of Brandy ,48926 ditto. Suppofe a Seaman hath a Gallon of this Liquor in a Glafs Bottle, that weighs 3½ *lb.* Troy out of Water; and, to conceal it from the King's Officers, throws

i

it overboard: The Question is, if it will sink, how much Force would just buoy it up?

*Answer*, It is 12,8968 Ounces heavier than the same Bulk of Salt Water.

(294) Another of the Mariners has half an Anchor of Brandy, of the specific Gravity above; the Cask, suppose, measures ½ of a cubic Foot, and the solid Inch of Oak is known to be 192¼ Grains Troy: What Quantity of Lead, 5,984 Ounces Troy to the cubic Inch, is just requisite to keep the Cask and Liquor under Water?·

*Answer*, 84 Ounces Troy will just do it.

(295) The absolute Weight of a Body floating in a Fluid, is precisely equal to the Weight of such Part of the Fluid as shall be thrust away thereby and displaced, or, in other Words, to the immersed Part of the Body: Suppose then it be by Measurement found, that a Man of War, with all its Ordnance, Rigging and Appointments, draws so much Water as to displace 1300 Tuns of Sea Water, weighing ,5949 of an Ounce Avoirdupois to the cubic Inch, and that the Measure be taken according to that of London Beer; the Weight of this Vessel is required?

*Answer*, Cwt. 26287 . 2 . 19 . 9

---

## A GENERAL RELEASE.

KNOW all Men by these Presents, That I [*Henry Haveall*, of London, Founder] have remised, released, and for ever quitted Claim, and by these Presents, do for me, my Heirs, Executors, and Administrators, remise, release, and for ever quit Claim, unto [*Lewis Lightpocket* Citizen and Lorimer of London] his Heirs, Executors, and Administrators, all and all manner of Actions, Cause and Causes of Actions, Suits, Bills, Bonds, Writings obligatory, Debts, Dues, Duties, Accompts, Sum and Sums of Money, Judgments, Executions, Extents, Quarrels, Controversies, Trespasses, Damages, and Demands whatsoever, both in Law and Equity, or otherwise howsoever; which against the said [*Lewis Lightpocket*] I ever had, now have, and which I, my Heirs, Executors, and Administrators, shall, or may

have,

have, claim, challenge, or demand, for or by Reason or Means of any Matter, Cause, or Thing, from the Beginning of the World, to the Day of the Date of these Presents. In Witness whereof, I have hereunto set my Hand and Seal, [this Tenth Day of June, in the Year of our Lord One thousand Seven hundred and Sixty-four.]

Signed, Sealed, Delivered,
  (being first legally stamped)    *Henry Havrall*, (L. S.)
in Presence of

         *L. M.*
         *N. O.*

---

# A Letter of Attorney.

KNOW all Men by these Presents, That I [the Lady *Elizabeth Goring*, of the Parish of Hampton, in the County of Middlesex, Widow] have made, ordained, constituted, and appointed, and by these Presents do make, ordain, constitute, and appoint [*Edmund Wingate* of Gray's-Inn Esq; to be my true and lawful Attorney, for me, and in my Name, and for my Use, to ask, demand, and receive of, and from *Henry Long* of St Mary-le-bonne Esq; *Peter Randal* of Pancras Gent. *Philip Ryley* of Wandsworth, Dyer; and *Jeremiah Holcomb* of Islington, Innholder] their Executors, Administrators, or Assigns, as well all such Sum and Sums of Money as now are, or which shall, or may, at any Time hereafter become due and owing to me, for or on Account of Rent, for the respective Tenures, by them, or some of them now occupied and possessed; and upon Non-payment thereof, the said Person or Persons, his or their Executors and Administrators, for me, and in my Name, to sue, arrest, imprison, implead, and prosecute for the same, and upon such Suit to proceed to Judgment and Execution; and thereupon, the said Person or Persons, their or either of their Executors and Administrators, in Prison to hold and keep, until Payment thereof be made, with all Costs and Damages sustained, and to be sustained, by reason of the detaining of the same: And upon Payment thereof, the said

Person

Person and Persons, their and either of their Executors and Administrators, forth of Prison to discharge, and Acquittances for me in my Name to make, seal, and deliver; and also to perform, pursue, and execute all and every such other lawful and reasonable Acts, Means, and Things whatever, both for recovering and discharging the same, as shall be needful to be done. Giving, and by these Presents, granting to my said Attorney, not only my full and absolute Power in the Premises himself, but also Power to substitute and appoint one or more Attorney or Attornies in his Stead, to act, execute, do, and perform all lawful Acts, Deeds, or Things, with relation to the Premises, and ratifying and holding firm all and whatsoever my said Attorney, or his Substitutes beforesaid, shall lawfully do, or cause to be done, in or about the Premises, by Virtue of these Presents. In Witness whereof, I have hereunto set my Hand and Seal [the Fourth Day of July, in the Year of our LORD One thousand Seven hundred and sixty-four.]

Sealed and Delivered, (being first legally stamped) in Presence of        *Eliz. Goring*, (L. S.)

             *Y. Z.*
             *P. D.*

---

## The FORM of a WILL.

### *In the Name of GOD.* Amen.

I [the Lady *Arabella Earnly*] of [Bromley, in the County of Kent, Widow] being of perfect Mind and Memory, make this my last Will and Testament: First, I desire to be privately buried [in the Parish Church of St Ann, in the Liberty of Westminster, and that the Charges of my Funeral may not exceed Forty Pounds.] My temporal Estate I bequeath and dispose of in the following Manner: Imprimis, [To my Daughter *Alice*, I bequeath the Sum of Two thousand Five hundred Pounds, my Indian Trunk, a Table Clock, and

and my Picture done by *Dabl*.] Item, [To my Niece and God-daughter, *Mary Peters*, I bequeath my Diamond Ring, my Pearl Pendants set with Brilliants, and an Hundred Pounds to buy her Mourning.] Item, To Mr *William Vernon*, my Cousin, I bequeath the Sum of One Guinea to buy him a Ring.] Item, [To the Poor of the Parish of Bromley aforesaid, I bequeath the Sum of Ten Pounds to be paid to the Minister and Churchwardens, within Ten Days after my Funeral, to be by them distributed as they see good, among their said Poor.] The Residue, and Remainder of my Estate, Lands, Tenements, Hereditaments, with my Goods, Chattels, Plate and Jewels, India Bonds, Arrears of Rent, with all other Properties of what kind soever, to me appertaining, I give, devise, and bequeath [to my Son *Thomas*] whom I constitute and appoint [the whole and sole] Executor of this my last Will and Testament; and I do hereby utterly revoke, disallow, and disannul all former Bequests, Wills and Legacies by me heretofore in any wise left or made, declaring, ratifying, and confirming this, and no other, to be my last Will and Testament: In Witness whereof, I have hereunto set my Hand and Seal, this [First Day of May, in the Year of our LORD One thousand Seven hundred and Sixty-four.]

Signed, Sealed, Published, and Declared, by the within named Testatrix [the Lady *Arabella Earnly*] to be her last Will and     (*Arabella Earnly*, L. S.) Testament, in Presence of us, who subscribed our Names in Presence of the said Testatrix and of each other,

C. D.
E. F.
I. H

*Three Witnesses are requisite to a Will, if it concern a real Estate; which Witnesses are to see each other sign it, as well as the Testator. If the Estate be personal only, two may do. The Law exempts Wills from being made on stamped Paper.*

A BILL.

## A BILL of SALE.

KNOW all Perfons whom it may concern: That I [*Lazarus Lackcafh* of Norwich, in the County of Norfolk, Goldfmith] for and in Confideration of the Sum of [Fifty Pounds] of lawful Money of Great Britain, to me in Hand paid by [*Dives Doubledun* of London, Efq;] the Receipt whereof I do hereby acknowledge, have bargained, fold, and delivered; and by thefe Prefents, according to the due Form of Law, do bargain, fell, and deliver unto the faid [*Dives Doubledun,* Four Caraɛts of Oriental Pearl; Nine Grains of Brait Diamonds; One Silver Teapot, weight Twenty Ounces; One Silver Salver, weight Ten Ounces; Two Sets of Silver Cafters, weight Thirty Ounces; and Ten Cornelian Rings, fealed up, by Confent, with my Seal.] To have and to hold the faid bargained Premifes, unto the faid [*Dives Doubledan*] his Executors, Adminiftrators, and Affigns, for ever. And I the faid [*Lazarus Lackcafh*] for myfelf, my Executors, and Adminiftrators, the faid bargained Premifes unto the faid [*Dives Doubledun*] his Executors, Adminiftrators, and Affigns, againft all Perfons, fhall and will warrant, and for ever defend by thefe Prefents: Provided neverthelefs *, that if I the faid [*Lazarus Lackcafh*] my Executors, Adminiftrators, and Affigns, or any of us, do and fhall well and truly pay, or caufe to be paid unto the faid [*Dives Doubledun*] his Executors, Adminiftrators, or Affigns, the Sum of [Fifty-one Pounds Five Shillings, as Principal and Intereft] lawful Money of Great Britain, on the [Firft of November next enfuing the Date hereof] for Redemption of the bargained Premifes; then this prefent Bill of Sale fhall be void and of none Effeɛt: But if Default be made in the Payment of the faid [Fifty-one Pounds Five Shillings] in Part, or in the Whole, contrary to the Manner and Form beforefaid; that then it fhall remain and be in full Force and Virtue. In Witnefs whereof, I have hereunto fet my Hand and Seal, the [Firft Day of May, in the Year of our Lord, One thoufand Seven hundred and Sixty-four]

Sealed and Delivered, (being
    firft legally ftamped) in
    Prefence of    *P. D.*        *Lazarus Lackcafh,* (L. S.)
                  *R. M.*

* *If the bargained Premifes be redeemable by a limited Time, a Provifo of this Nature is added.*

U            A WAR-

## A WARRANT of ATTORNEY to confefs Judgment.

*To* [ John Carpenter, John Davis, *and* John Hodges, *Gent.*] *Attorneys of His Majefty's Court of Common-Pleas, at Weftminfter*] *jointly and feverally, or to any other Attorney of the fame Court.*

THESE are to defire, and authorife you, the Attornies above-named, any of you, or any other Attorney of the Court of [Common-Pleas] aforefaid, to appear for me [*John Morris* of Yatton, in the County of Somerfet, Yeoman, in the faid Court of Common-Pleas, the next Trinity-Term, or any fubfequent Term] and then and there to receive a Declaration for me, in an Action of [Debt for Two hundred Pounds, befides Cofts of Suit] at the Suit of [*Robert Creyghton* of the Liberty of St Andrew in Wells, in the County aforefaid, Doctor of Divinity.] And thereupon to confefs the fame Action, or elfe to fuffer a Judgment, by *He faith nothing*, or *I am not informed*, or otherwife, to pafs againft me, in the fame Action, and to be thereupon forthwith entered up againft me of Record [in the fame Court of Common-Pleas.] And, for your fo doing, this fhall be to you, or any of you, or to any other Attorney as aforefaid, your, his, their, or any of their fufficient Warrant: In Witnefs whereof, I have fet my Hand and Seal, this [Twenty-fifth Day of February, One thoufand Seven hundred Sixty-four.

Sealed and Delivered, (being
    firft legally ftamped) in
    Prefence of               *John Morris,* (L. S.)
          G. S.
          R. M.

Note, *This Inftrument is of great Force and Validity, and wards off that Opprobrium of our Conftitution, the Expences and Delays of Law-Proceedings; efpecially if a Claufe be inferted, promifing no Writ of Error fhall be brought or profecuted upon it in Bar.*

A POLICY

## A POLICY of ASSURANCE of a Ship and Cargo OUT and HOME.

KNOW all Men by thefe Prefents, That *Clement Cautious* of London, Merchant, as well in his own Name, as for and in the Name and Names of all and every other Perfon and Perfons, whom the fame may or fhall concern, doth make Affurance, and hereby caufe himfelf and them, and each of them, to be affured, loft or not loft, at and from the Port of London, to the Port of Alicant, in the Kingdom of Spain, and at and from thence back to London, upon all Kinds of Goods and Merchandizes, and alfo upon the Body, Tackle, Apparel, Ordnance, Munition, Artillery, Boat, and other Furniture, of and in the good Veffel, called The Bonny Tack, Burden Two hundred and Eighty Tons, or thereabout, whereof *Leonard Lookout,* for the prefent Voyage, is Mafter, beginning the Adventure upon the faid Ship and Cargo, from and immediately following the Date hereof, and fo to continue and endure, until the faid Ship, with her faid Wares and Merchandizes on board, her Tackle, Apparel, Ordnance, Munition, Artillery, Boat, and other Furniture, fhall arrive at the Port of Alicant as aforefaid, and during her abode and ftay there; and farther until the faid Ship, with her Goods and Merchandizes on board, with all her Appointments and Furniture beforefaid, fhall arrive back at the Port of London, and hath there moored at Anchor Four and twenty Hours in Safety, and upon the Goods and Merchandizes till they be there difcharged and landed. And it fhall be lawful for the faid Ship in this Voyage, to proceed and fail to, and touch and ftay at any Ports and Places whatfoever; efpecially at Lifbon and Gibraltar, without Prejudice to this Affurance. The faid Ship and Cargo, for fo much as concerns the Affureds, is and fhall be rated and valued at Six thoufand Five hundred Pounds Sterling, without farther Account to be given by the Affureds for the fame. And touching the Adventures and Perils, which we the Affurers are content to bear, and do take upon us in this Voyage, they are of the Seas, Men of War, Fire, Enemies, Pirates, Rovers, Thieyes, Jetzons,

Letters

Letters of Mart and Countermart, Surprisals and Takings at Sea, Arrests, Restraints, and Detainments of all Kings, Princes, and People, of what Nation, Condition, or Quality soever, Baratry of the Master and Mariners, and of other Perils, Losses, and Misfortunes, that have or shall come to the Hurt, Detriment, or Damage of the said Ship, Wares and Merchandizes on board her, or any Part thereof. And in case of any Misfortune, it shall be lawful for the Assureds, their Factors, Servants, and Assigns, to sue, labour, and travel for, in and about the Defence, Safeguard, and Recovery of the said Ship, Wares and Merchandizes, or any Part thereof, without Prejudice to this Assurance; to the Charges whereof, we the Assurers will contribute each of us according to the Rate and Quantity of his Sum herein insured. And so we the Assurers are contented, and do hereby promise and bind ourselves, each for his own Part, our Heirs, Executors, Goods, and Chattels, to the Assureds, their Executors, Administrators, and Assigns, for the true Performance of the Premises, confessing ourselves paid the Consideration due to us for this Assurance, by the said *Clement Cautious,* at and after the Rate of Two ⅌ *Cent.* and in case of Loss, to abate Ten ⅌ *Cent.* and to pay without farther Proof of any Interest whatsoever, more than this present Policy, any Use or Custom to the contrary notwithstanding. In Witness whereof, we the Assurers have subscribed our Names and Sums by us severally assured in London, as follows, viz.

I *A. B.* am contented with this Assurance, for One thousand Five hundred Pounds: Witness my Hand,　　　　　London,
　　　　Day of　　　　Anno 1764.
　　　　　　　　　　　　　　*A. B.*
} 1500 *l.*

I *C. D.* am contented with this Assurance, for Eight hundred Pounds, &c.
　　　　　　　　*C. D.*
} 800 *l.*

*The Assureds choose to have this Business transacted by several Hands, when a private Assurance is taken, to have the more certain Security.*

A 5

AS Skill in MEASURING is almoſt neceſſary to make young People competent Judges of general Buſineſs; and the caſting up the Contents of ſuch Things, as are the Subject of GEOMETRY, is to be effected by Numbers, as well as any Calculation whatever, ſome few Examples, expreſſed in a familiar Way, for the Sake of the Beginner, are here ſubjoined; with Intention to give him a ſmall Inſight into this Affair, and to excite his Curioſity to look into Authors that have treated this uſeful and delightful Subject more at large : Mean time, the judicious Maſter will take the Trouble to delineate and explain the Figures intended by the Propoſitions, in order to aſſiſt his Pupil in the Conception of what he is about : And ſuch Eye-draught will, in great Meaſure, point out, or ſuggeſt, the Method of Inveſtigation.

---

## RECREATION XIX.

### SUPERFICIAL MEASUREMENT.

(296) WHAT is to be meaſured upon the Surface only, as Land, Glaſs, Painting, Flooring, Tyling, Paving, Plaiſtering, &c. if it be a four-ſided Figure, whoſe oppoſite Sides are equal, multiplying the Length into the perpendicular Height, finds the ſuperficial Content. And, conſequently, the ſuperficial Content, and any one of thoſe Dimenſions being given, the other of them will be found by ſimple Diviſion.

The biggeſt of the Egyptian Pyramids, near Grand Cairo, being Square, and meaſuring according to Mr Greaves's Account, 693 Feet Engliſh on a Side: How many Acres then of Ground doth it ſtand on ?

*Anſwer*, Acres 11. Poles 4.

(297) What Difference is there between a Floor 28 Feet long, by 20 broad, and two others, that meaſure 14 Feet apiece by 10; and what do all Three come to, at 45 s. ℔ Square, viz. 10 Feet by 10 ?

*Anſwer*, 280 Sq Feet Diff. Amount 18 l. 18 s.

(298) A rectangular four-ſided Room meaſures 120 Feet 6 Inches about, and is to be Wainſcoted, at 3 s. 6 d. ℔ Yard :

Yard square: After the due Allowances, for girt of Cornice and Members, it is 16 Feet 3 Inches high: The Door is 7 Feet by 3 Feet 9: The Window-Shutters, 2 Pair, are 7 Feet 3, by 4 Feet 6: The Cheek-boards round them, come 15 Inches below the Shutters, and are 14 Inches in breadth: The Lining-boards round the Door-way, are 16 Inches broad: The Door and Window-Shutters, being wrought on both Sides, are reckoned as Work and half, and paid for accordingly: The Chimney, 3 Feet 9, by 3 Feet, not being inclosed, is to be deducted from the superficial Content of the Room; and the Estimate of the Charge is required?

*Answer,* 43 *l.* 4 *s.* 6 *d.*

(299) When a Roof is of a true Pitch, the Rafters are ¾ of the Breadth of the Building; now supposing the Eaves-boards to project 10 Inches on a Side: What will the new ripping an Out-house cost, that measures 32 Feet 9 Inches long, by 22 Feet 9 Inches broad upon the Flat, at 15 *s.* ♏ Square?

*Answer,* 8 *l.* 15 *s.* 9¼ *d.*

(300) If my Court-Yard be 47 Feet 7 Inches square, and I have laid a Foot-way of Purbeck Stone, 4 Feet wide, along one Side of it: What will paving the rest, with Flints, come to, at 6 *d.* ♏ Yard square? *Answer,* 5 *l.* 15 *s.* 2½ *d.*

(301) A square Cieling contains 114 Yards 6 Feet of Plaistering, and the Room 28 Feet broad: What was the Length of it? *Answer,* 36 6/7 Feet.

(302) An Elm Plank is 14 Feet 3 Inches long, and I would have just a Yard square slit off: At what Distance from the Edge must the Line be struck? *Answer,* 7 29/71 Inches.

(303) Having a rectangular Marble Slab, 58 Inches by 27, I would have a Foot square cut off, parallel to the shorter Edge; I would then have the like Quantity divided from the Remainder, parallel to the longer Side; and this alternately repeated, till there should not be the Quantity of a Foot left: What will the Dimensions of the Remnant be?

*Answer,* 20,7 Inches by 6,086.

(304) Being about to plant 10584 Trees equally distant in Rows, the Length of the Grove must be 6 times the Breadth: How many of the shorter Rows will there be?

*Answer,* 252 Rows, viz. ⅙ of the Trees are to form an exact Square, the Side whereof shews how many of them come into a short Row.

(305) A

(305) A common Joift is 7 Inches deep, and $2\frac{1}{2}$ thick but I want a Scantling juft as big again, that fhall be three Inches thick: What will the other Dimenfion be?

*Anfwer*, $11\frac{2}{3}$ Inches.

(306) I have a fquare Girder 19 Inches by 11; but one of a quarter of the Timber in it, provided it be 9 Inches deep, will ferve: How broad will it be?

*Anfwer*, $5\frac{20}{38}$ Inches.

(307) I have a Wooden Trough, that at 6 *d.* ⅌ Yard, coft me 3 *s.* 2 *d.* Painting within; the Length of it was 102 Inches, the Depth 21 Inches: What was its Breadth?

*Anfwer*, 2 Feet, $3\frac{1}{4}$ Inches.

(308) My Plummer has put 28 *lb.* ⅌ Foot fquare into a Ciftern 74 Inches and twice the thicknefs of the Lead long, 26 Inches broad, and 40 deep; he has put three Stays within acrofs it 16 Inches deep, of the fame Strength, and reckons 22 *s.* ⅌ *Cwt.* for Work and Materials: I being a Mafon, have paved him a Work-fhop, 22 Feet 10 Inches broad, with Purbeck Stone, at 7 *d.* ⅌ Foot, and upon the Balance, I find there is 3 *s.* 6 *d.* due to him: What was the Length of his Work-fhop?          *Anfwer*, 31 Feet, $9\frac{1}{4}$ Inches.

(309) The rectangular powdering Trough of a Man of War meafures 27 fquare Feet 112 Inches, the Depth is 20 Inches, the Breadth 16: The Length is fought?

*Anfwer*, 5 Feet.

(310) In 110 Acres of Statute-Meafure, in which the Pole is $16\frac{1}{2}$ Feet long, how many Chefhire Acres, where the cuftomary Pole is 6 Yards long? and how many Yorkfhire, where the Pole in ufe is 7 Yards in Length?

*Anfwer*, Chefhire Acres, 92 . 1 . 28.
Yorkfhire Acres, 67 . 3 . 25.

(311) I would fet 3584 Plants in Rows, each 4 Feet afunder, and the Plants 7 Feet apart, in a rectangular Plot of Ground: What Land will this take up?

*Anfwer*, 2 Acres, $48\frac{1}{2}$ Poles.

(312) A triangular, or three-fided Figure, (being the half of a four-fided one of the fame Height and Length) if you multiply the Bafe, or longeft Side, by the fhorteft Height, you have double the Content.

A triangular Field, 738 Links long, and 583 in the Perpendicular, brings in 12 *l.* a Year: What is it fet at an Acre?

*Anfwer*, 5 *l.* 11 *s.* $6\frac{3}{4}$ *d.* nearly.

(313) The End-Wall of an Houſe is 24 Feet 6 Inches in breadth, and 40 Feet to the Roof; $\frac{1}{3}$ of which is 2 Bricks thick; $\frac{1}{3}$ more, $1\frac{1}{2}$ Brick thick; and the reſt 1 Brick thick: Now the Gable riſes 38 Courſe of Bricks (4 of which uſually make a Foot in depth) and this is but 4 Inches, or half a Brick thick: What will this Piece of Work come to, at 5 *l*. 10 *s*. ℔ Statute Rod, the Dimenſions of which are given Page 52 of this Treatiſe?

*Anſwer,* 20 *l*. 11 *s*. 7 $\frac{1}{2}$ *d*. nearly.

(314) When the Perpendicular of a Triangle cannot readily be taken, the Content may be found by the Meaſure of the Sides, thus: Subtract each of the three Sides, from half the Sum of the three Sides ſeverally; then multiply the ſaid half Sum, with the three Differences found, continually; and the ſquare Root of the Reſult, ſhall be the Area or Content of the Triangle ſought.

Having a Fiſh-pond of a triangular Form, whoſe three Sides meaſure 400 Yards, 348, and 312: What Quantity of Ground does it cover?

*Anſwer,* 52284 $\frac{1}{2}$ ſquare Yards.

(315) The Quarry of Glaſs 3 $\frac{1}{4}$ Inches on every Side, and as much croſs the Middle, coſts 1 *d*. the Square is 5 $\frac{1}{4}$ Inches, by 3 $\frac{1}{2}$, and coſts 1 $\frac{1}{2}$ *d*. What will be ſaved, glazing 1000 Feet, the cheaper of the two Ways; ſuppoſing the Leading of the Lights to be nearly equal in either kind of Work?

*Anſwer,* 5 *s*. 10 *d*.

(316) Every other right-lined Figure, be it regular or not, may be divided into Triangles; the Sum of whoſe Areas is the Content; for Example,

A Piece of Garden-Box lies in Form of a regular Pentagon, or Figure of five equal Sides, each 48 Feet; and from the Center of the Figure, to the Middle of one of theſe, it meaſures 41;57 Feet nearly. The Area of the Figure will be the Content of theſe five Triangles: Pray what is that?

*Anſwer,* 4988,4 Feet.

(317) The Square of the Hypothenuſe, or the longeſt Side of a right-angled Triangle, is equal to the Sum of the Squares of

the

the other two Sides, and confequently the Differences of the Squares of the Hypothenufe, and either of the other Sides, is the Square of the remaining Side.

I want the Length of a Shoar, that being to ftrut 11 Feet from the Upright of a Building, will fupport a Jamb 23 Feet 10 Inches from the Ground ?

*Anfwer*, 26 Feet, 3 Inches nearly.

(318) A Line 27 Yards long, will exactly reach from the Top of a Fort, on the oppofite Bank of a River, known to be 23 Yards broad : The Height of the Wall is required ?

*Anfwer*, 42 Feet, 5 Inches.

(319) Two Ships fet Sail from the fame Port, one of them goes due Eaft, 50 Leagues; the other due North, 84 : How far are they then afunder ?

*Anfwer*, 97 ½ Leagues.

(320) The Height of an Elm, growing in the Middle of a circular Ifland, 30 Feet in Diameter, plumbs 53 Feet, and a Line ftretched from the Top of the Tree, ftraight to the hither Edge of the Water, 112 Feet : What then is the Breadth of the Moat, fuppofing the Land on either Side the Water to be level ?

*Anfwer*, 83⅓ Feet.

(321) Suppofe a Light-houfe built on the Top of a Rock ; the Diftance between the Place of Obfervation, and that Part of the Rock level with the Eye, and directly under the Building, is given 310 Fathoms ; the Diftance from the Top of the Rock, to the Place of Obfervation, is 423 Fathoms; and from the Top of the Building 425 : The Height of the Edifice is required ?

*Anfwer*, 17 Feet, 7 Inches, nearly.

(322) A Ladder 40 Feet long, may be fo planted, that it fhall reach a Window 33 Feet from the Ground, on one Side the Street ; and without moving it at the Foot, will do the fame by a Window 21 Feet high, on the other Side : The Breadth of the Street is required ? *Anfwer*, 56 6/10 Feet.

(323) An ancient Bath was found, of a triangular Form, the Sum of whofe Three equal Sides was 125 Feet : The Area of the Bottom is required ? *Anfwer*, 752 fquare Feet.

(324) The paving of a triangular Court, at 18 *d.* ⅌ Foot, came to 190 *l.* the longeft of the three Sides was 88 Feet : What then was the Sum of the other two equal Sides ?

*Anfwer*, 106,85 Feet.

X

(325) I would plant 10 Acres of Hop-Ground, which muſt be done, either in the ſquare Order as the Number 4 ſtands on the Dice, or in the quincunx Order, as the Number 5; the three neareſt Binds, in both Caſes, muſt be ſet lineally juſt 6 Feet aſunder: How many Plants more will be required, for the laſt Order than for the firſt; admitting the Form of the Plot to lay the moſt advantageous for the Plantation in either Caſe?

> *Anſwer*, 1872, nearly. Every Plant in the ſquare Order will require the Space of 36 ſquare Feet, and in the Quincunx 31,177. In Practice they leave a Verge of 6 Feet all round the Plot, which in this Calculation is not conſidered.

(326) A Summer-houſe is a Cube of 10 Feet in the clear, the Cornice of which projects juſt 15 Inches on a Side, and being of Timber and Stucco, the Sides are 6 Inches thick, ſo that the whole Front of the Roof, from out to out, is $13\frac{1}{2}$ Feet. This is hipped from each of the Corners to the Center, and being truly Pediment-pitch, it riſes $\frac{2}{5}$ of the Front, or 3 Feet. I would, by help of theſe Dimenſions, meaſure the Slating, without venturing to climb for more, and compute the coſt at $3\frac{1}{2}d$. $\cancel{p}$ ſquare Foot. This may be done by firſt diſcovering what the diagonal Line on the Flat is tranſverſely from the Corner. And, ſecondly, from thence and the perpendicular Riſe of the Roof, the Length of each of the 4 principal Rafters. And then, thirdly, from the Breadth of the Front given, a Perpendicular may be found, which will determine the Coſt of this Piece of Work to be 2*l*. 18*s*. 2*d*. nearly.

(327) There are two Columns in the Ruins of Perſepolis, left ſtanding upright; one is 64 Feet above the Plane, the other 50: Between theſe, in a right Line, ſtands an ancient Statue, the Head whereof is 97 Feet from the Summit of the higher, and 86 Feet from the Top of the lower Column; the Baſe whereof meaſures juſt 76 Feet to the Center of the Figure's Baſe: By theſe Notices, the Diſtance of the Top of the Columns may be, by Numbers, eaſily found?

> *Anſwer*, 157 Feet nearly.

(328) A triangular Bath, 6 Feet deep, is exactly incloſed by 3 ſquare Pavilions, and rectangular, the Sum of whoſe Plans, together, make juſt 50 Poles: The Area of *A* the leſs, is to that of *B*. the middle one, as $4\frac{1}{2}$ to 8; and the Sum of the Areas of *A*. and *C*. the biggeſt, is to that of *B*. as $8\frac{1}{4}$ to 4: How many Wine Hogſheads of Water will this Bath receive?

> *Anſwer*, 1163 Hogſheads, $47\frac{1}{2}$ Gallons.

(329) A four-sided Figure, whose Sides are unequal, is called a Trapeze: I have an Orchard of that Form, containing 3¼ Acres, which being divided by a Diagonal, or a Line, from Corner to Corner, the Perpendicular of one of the Triangles is 430 Links, and the other 360: The Length of the said Diagonal, or common Base of those Triangles, is required?

*Answer*, 949 ⁷⁸⁄₇₈ Links.

The Areas of Circles are found either by multiplying half the Circumference by half the Diameter, or by multiplying the Square of the Diameter by ,7854, that being the Area of the Circle, whose Diameter is 1.

(330) Give the Area of a circular Bowling-Green, that is 16 Poles a-cross the Middle; the Circumference being 3,1416 times the Diameter of a Circle?

*Answer*, 1 Acre, 41 Poles, &c.

(331) The surveying Wheel is so contrived, as to turn just twice in the Length of a Pole, or 16½ Feet: What then is its Diameter? *Answer*, 2,626 Feet.

(332) I would turf a round Plot, measuring 130 Feet about, and would know the Charge at 4 d. ℔ Yard square?

*Answer*, 2 l. 9 s. . 10 d. nearly.

(333) I want the Length of a Line, by which my Gardener may strike a round Aurangerie, that shall contain just half an Acre of Land? *Answer*, 27¾ Yards, nearly.

(334) Agreed for an oaken Curb to a round Well, at 8 d. ℔ Foot square; it is exactly 42 Inches in Diameter, within the Brick-work, and the Breadth of the Curb is to be 14¼ Inches: What will it come to? *Answer*, 11 s. 11 d. nearly.

(335) It is observed, that the extreme End of the Minute-hand of a public Dial, moves just 5 Inches in the Space of 3¼ Minutes: The Question is, what is the Length of that Index? *Answer*, 14,69 Inches.

(336) A. B. C. join for a Grindstone 36 Inches over, value 20 s. toward which A. paid 7 s. B. 8 s. and C 5 s. The Waste-hole, through which the Spindle passed, was 5 Inches square: To what Diameter ought the Stone to be worn, when B. and C. begin severally to work with it? Begin your Calculation from the Center.

*Answer*, For B. to 29,324 Inches; for C. to 19,013 Inches.

X 2 (337) As

(337) As the Diameter of a Circle, is the only neceſſary Dimenſion to find the greateſt Square that may either be inſcribed, or the ſmalleſt that may be circumſcribed: I demand what Difference there is in the Area of the Section of a round Tree, 20 Inches over, conſidered both thoſe ways; and how far the Reſult, from each of thoſe Dimenſions, differs from the Truth in the circular Meaſure?

*Anſwer*, Within 114,16 Inches too little.
Without 85,84 Inches too much.

(338) Having paved a Semi-circular Alcove with black and white Marble, at 2s. 4d. ℔ Foot, the Maſon's Bill was juſt 10l. what then was this Arch in Front, conſidering, that as ,7854, the Area of the Circle, the Square of whoſe Diameter is 1, ſo is the Area of any other Circle to the Square of its Diameter? *Anſwer*, 14 Feet, 9 Inches.

(339) What Proportion is there between the Arpent of France, which contains 100 ſquare Poles, of 18 Feet each, and the Engliſh Acre, containing 160 ſquare Poles, of 16½ Feet each, conſidering that the Length of the French Foot is to that of the Engliſh, as 16 to 15. *Anſwer*, As 13 to 11 nearly.

(340) In turning a one Horſe Chaiſe within a Ring of a certain Diameter, it was obſerved, that the Outer Wheel made two Turns while the Inner made but one: The Wheels were equally high, and ſuppoſing them fixed at the ſtatutable Diſtance, or 5 Feet aſunder on the Axletree: Pray what was the Circumference of the Track deſcribed by the Outer Wheel? *Anſwer*, 63 Feet, nearly.

Multiplying half the Arch by half the Diameter, alſo finds the Area of a Sector; that is, any Part of a Circle cut through from the Center to the Circumference.

(341) The Area of a Sector (ſuppoſe one of the Diviſions of a Wilderneſs) which being ſtruck from a Center, with a Line 30 Yards long, makes the Sweep, or circular Part, 63 Feet, is required? *Anſwer*, 315 Yards.

(342) The Curvature of one of theſe Sectors being parted off by a ſtraight Line, drawn through its Limits, leaves a Segment of a Circle, to be meaſured, by deducting the Content of the Triangle, cut off from the Area of the whole Sector, to diſcover the Area of the Segment.

The

The Propofition above may ferve as an Example to this, allowing the Chord, or ftraight Line, drawn through the two Ends of the Curve (as it will be found) about 15 Inches fhorter than the arched Line abovefaid.

*Anfwer*, Content of the Segment 25 Yards, nearly.

An Ellipfe, or Oval, is meafured by multiplying the Product of the long and fhort Diameters by .7854, as in the Circle, and this will give the fuperficial Content.

(343) The Ellipfe in Grofvenor-Square meafures 840 Links the longeft Way, and 612 acrofs, within the Rails; the Walls are 14 Inches thick; what Ground do they inclofe, and what do they ftand upon?

*Anfwer*, Inclofe 4 Acres, 6 Poles.

Wall ftands on 1758¼ fquare Feet, nearly.

The Dimenfions of all fimilar Figures are in Proportion to their Areas, as the Squares of their refpective Sides, *et contra*.

(344) If a round Pillar, 7 Inches over, has 4 Feet of Stone in it, of what Diameter is the Column, of equal Length, that meafures ten times as much?

*Anfwer*, 22,136 Inches over.

(345) A Pipe of fix Inches Bore will be 3 Hours in running off a certain Quantity of Water: In what time will 4 Pipes, each 3 Inches Bore, be in difcharging double the Quantity?                                    *Anfwer*, 6 Hours.

(346) A Yard of Rope 9 Inches round weighs, fuppofe, 22 *lb.* what will a Fathom of that weigh, which meafures a Foot about?                                    *Anfwer*, 78⅜ *lb.*

(347) If 20 Feet of Iron Railing fhall weigh half a Ton, when the Bars are an Inch and Quarter fquare, what will 50 Feet of ditto come to, at 3½ *℔* Pound, the Bars being but ¾ of an Inch fquare?                          *Anfwer*, 20 *l.*

(348) A Looking-glafs is 16 Inches by 9, and contains a Foot of Glafs: What will the Content of the Plate be that has twice the Length, and three times the Breadth?

*Anfwer*, 6 Square Feet.

(349) A Sack that holds Three Bufhels of Corn is 22⅔ Inches broad when empty: What would the Sack contain that, being of the fame Length, had twice its Circumference, or twice its Breadth?    *Anfwer*, A Quarter and a Half.

(350) My

(350) My Plumber has set me up a Cistern, and his Shop-book being burnt, he has no Means of bringing in the Charge, and I do not chuse to take it down to have it weighed; but by Measure he finds it contains 64 square Feet $\frac{3}{16}$, and that it is $\frac{1}{8}$ of an Inch precisely in Thickness. Lead was then wrought at 21 *l.* ℔ Fodder. Let the Accomptant, from these Items, make out the poor Man's Bill, considering farther, that $4\frac{4}{11}$ *oz.* is the Weight of a cubic Inch of Lead?

*Answer,* 9 *l.* 2 *s.* 1 *d.*

---

# RECREATION XX.

## MEASUREMENT of SOLIDS.

MULTIPLY the Area by the Depth, to find the Solidity of uniform Bodies, or such as are equal from Top to Bottom.

(351) What is the Difference of a solid half Foot, and half a Foot solid?

*Answer,* One is but $\frac{1}{4}$ of the other.

(352) What is the Proportion, in Point of Space, between a Room 25 $\frac{1}{2}$ Feet long, 20 Feet 2 Inches broad, 14 Feet high, and Two others of just $\frac{1}{2}$ the Dimensions?

*Answer,* As 4 to 1.

(353) Another Room is 17 Feet 7 Inches long within, 13 Feet 10 Inches broad, and 9 Feet 6 Inches high; it has a Chimney carried up straight in the Angle, the Plan whereof is just the half of 5 Feet 6 Inches, by 4 Feet 2: The Question is, how many cubic Feet of Air the same will contain, allowing the Content of the Fire-place and Windows at 4 solid Yards?

*Answer,* 2309 Feet, 10 $\frac{4}{5}$ Inches.

(354) A Ship's Hold is 112 Feet 6 Inches long, 32 broad, and 5 Feet 6 deep: How many Bales of Goods, 3 Feet 4 Inches long, 2 Feet 4 Inches broad, and 3 Feet deep, may be stowed therein, leaving a Gang-way the whole Length of 4 Feet and $\frac{1}{2}$ broad?

*Answer,* The Quantity of 729 $\frac{1}{2}$, nearly.

(355) I want a rectangular Cistern, that at 16 *lb.* to the Foot square shall weigh just a Fodder of Lead, it must be 8 Feet long, and 4¼ over: How many Hogsheads, Wine-measure will this contain, taking it at ¼ of an Inch from the Top?
*Answer*, 16 Hogsheads, 40 Gallons.

(356) A Log of Timber is 18 Feet 6 Inches long, 18 Inches broad, and 14 thick, Die-square all through: Now, if 2 solid Feet and ⅛ be sawed off the End, how long will the Piece then be?       *Answer*, 17 Feet $\frac{711}{1008}$.

(357) The solid Content of a square Stone is found to be 126¼ Feet, its Length is 8 Feet 6 Inches: What is the Area of one End, and what the Depth, if the Breadth assigned be 38½ Inches?       *Answer*, 55,55 Inches deep.

(358) The Dimensions of the circular Winchester Bushel are 18½ Inches over, and 8 Inches deep: How many Quarter of Grain then will the square Bin hold, that measures 7 Feet 10 long, 3 Feet 10 broad, and 4 Feet 2 deep within?
*Answer*, 12, &c.

(359) Taking the Dimensions of the Bushel, as above, what must the Diameter of the circular Measure be, which at 12 Inches deep will hold 9 Bushels of Sea-coal struck?
*Answer*, 45 Inches $\frac{1}{15}$.

(360) A Prism of two equal Bases, and six equal Sides, that measures 28 Inches cross the Center, from Corner to Corner: The superficial and the solid Content is required, taking the Length at 134 Inches?
*Answer*, Superf. 9 Yards, 4 Feet, 3 Inches.
Solid 39 Feet, 843 Inches.

(361) I have a rolling Stone 44 Inches in Circumference, and am to cut off three cubic Feet from one End: Whereabouts must the Section be made?
*Answer*, At 33,66 Inches.

(362) I would have a Syringe an Inch and ¼ in the Bore, to hold a Pint Wine-measure of any Fluid: What must the Length of the Piston, sufficient to make an Injection with it, be?       *Answer*, 23,5294 Inches.

(363) I would have a cubic Bin made capable of receiving just 13½ Quarters of Wheat, Winchester Measure: What will be the Length of one of its Sides?
*Answer*, 61,4678 Inches.

(364) A

(364) A Bath Stone, 20 Inches long, 15 over, and 8 deep, weighs 220 *lb.* how many cubic Feet thereof will freight a Ship of 290 Tons?　　　　　*Anſwer,* 4101 Feet.

(365) The common Way of meaſuring Timber, being to girt a round ſtraight Tree in the Middle, and to take ¼ of the Girt for the Side of a Square, equal to the Area of the Section there; if this be not conſidered in the Price appointed, pray on which Side lies the Advantage?

　　　　*Anſwer,* For the Buyer, near 13 Feet in a Load.

(366) The Cylinder, Globe, and Cone, are in Proportion to one another, as 3, 2, and 1. The Cube therefore of the Diameter, of any Cylinder of equal Height and Breadth, multiplied ,7854, the Area of the Circle whoſe Diameter is 1, will always give the Solidity of that Cylinder. The Cube of the Diameter of a Globe again multiplied by ⅔ thereof, or ,5236, gives the ſolid Content. And the ſaid Cube, multiplied by ⅓ of that, or ,2618, produces in general the Solidity of any Cone whoſe Breadth and Height are equal. By this Rule the ſolid Content of a Globe, 20 Inches in Diameter, a Cylinder of the ſame Diameter, 20 Inches long; and a Cone 20 Inches Diameter at Baſe, and 20 Inches high, are ſeverally required?

　　　　*Anſwer,* Cone, 2094,4.　Globe, 4188,8.
　　　　　　Cylinder, 6283,2.

The ſuperficial Content of theſe is found by conſidering the Cylinder, as a ſquare Surface 20 Inches by the Circumference, adding a double Area for the two Baſes. The Globe, as a Rectangle of the Diameter and Circumference; and the Cone, as a Triangle, whoſe Baſe is the Circuit, and Perpendicular the ſlope Height, adding once the Area of the Baſe. At 8 *d.* ⅌ Yard, the Painting of them is found to amount to 2 *s.* 1⅔ *d.*

(367) Our Satellite the Moon is a Globe in Diameter 2170 Miles; I require how many Quarters of Wheat ſhe would contain, if hollow, 2150 4/10 ſolid Inches being the Buſhel; and how much Yard-wide Stuff would make her a Waiſtcoat was ſhe to be clothed?

　　*Anſwer,* Content 791070349484701 44000 Quarters.
　　　　Surface 45824284391424 Yards ſquare.

(368) Suppoſing the Atmoſphere, or Body of the Air and Vapours, ſurrounds the Globe of the Earth and Sea, to 60 Miles above the Surface; the Earth is 7970 Miles in Diameter;
　　　　　　　　　　　　　　　　　how

how many cubic Yards of Air then hang about, and revolve along with this Planet; and what is the Weight of the whole Mafs of fluid Matter in the Atmofphere contained, if at a Medium 12*lb.* Avoirdupois be found experimentally, as in Fact it is, to prefs upon every circular Inch, on the Surface of the Earth ?

    *Anfwer*, Meafure 6626425427414876 1600 folid Yards, Weight 12240191636776672000 Pds. Avoirdupois.

(369) A Cork may be cut into fuch a Form, that it may, without Alteration, feverally fill the Cavity of a Circle an Inch in Diameter, of an equilateral Triangle, whofe Sides are each an Inch, and a geometrical Square, alfo an Inch on a Side: What muft be the Shape ?

    *Anfwer*, It will be a Wedge, whofe Bafe, being circular, will fill the Round: The Ridge-Front will replenifh the Square, and the End-Section make out the Triangle.

When Figures run uniformly taper (but not to a Point) they are to be confidered as Fruftrums or Portions of the Cone or Pyramid; by fupplying therefore what is wanting to make the Figure entire, and then deducting the Part cut off, we find the Solidity of the Part propofed.

(370) A round Mafh-Vat meafures at the Top 72 Inches over within, at the Bottom 54, the perpendicular Depth being 42 Inches; the Content in Ale Gallons is required ?

    In order to complete the Cone; ufe this Analogy: As half the Difference of the Top and Bottom 9 Inches, are to the Depth 42 Inches, fo is half the greater Diameter 36 Inches, to the Altitude of the whole Cone.

    *Anfwer*, It holds Gall. 467, and almoft an half.

    Or elfe; to the Areas of the Top and Bottom, add the fquare Root of the Products of thofe Areas, and this multiply by $\frac{1}{3}$ of the Height of the Fruftrum, for the Solidity.

    The Shaft of a round Pillar, 16 Inches in Diameter at the Top, is about 8 of the Bottom Diameters in Height, $\frac{1}{7}$ whereof is truly cylindrical, and the other $\frac{2}{3}$ fwelling, but we will fuppofe it tapers ftraight; it is $\frac{1}{8}$ lefs at Top than at Bottom; the Price of the Stone and Workmanfhip is fought at 3*s.* 6*d.* ⅌ cubic Foot; and farther, the fuperficial Content, including both Ends ?

    *Anfwer*, 3*l.* 10*s.* 4½*d.* &c. Superf. 61$\frac{1}{10}$ Feet.

(372) A triangular Pyramid, whofe Sides, at Bafe, meafure 30 Inches apiece, and is 21 Feet high, ⅌ the Slope, is
to be fold at 7 s. ⅌ folid Foot; and if the polifhing the Surface of the Sides will be 8 d. ⅌ Foot more, I would know
the Coft of this Stone when finifhed !

*Anfwer*, 9 l. 4 s. 11 d.

(373) A Stick of fquare Timber tapers ftraight; the Side
at the greater End is 19¼ Inches, at the lefs, 13½ Inches,
the Length 16 Feet 6 Inches, the Value, at 2 s. 6 d. ⅌ Foot
folid, is demanded ?

*Anfwer*, 3 l. 18 s. 10 d.

To meafure a common Cafk : Find the Areas at Head
and Bung, add ⅓ of the lefs, and ⅔ of the greater, for a
mean Area; this multiplied by the Length of the Cafk is its
Solidity in Inches, which reduce.  Or, II.  To double the
Square of the Bung Diameter add that of the Head; then
multiply by the Length of the Cafk, and divide by 1077,24
for Beer, or by 882,42 for Wine Gallons.

(374) What Quantity of Brandy will the Diftiller's Tun
contain, that meafures 40 Inches within at Head, 52 at Bung,
and is 100 Inches long; and how many Barrels of London
Ale would fill it ?

*Anfwer*, Brandy 794, &c.
Ale 20 Barrels, 10¼ Gallons.

(375) The famous Tun of Heidelburgh, that being heretofore annually replenifhed with Rhenifh, had in it fome
Wine that was many Ages old; before the French demo-
lifhed it in the late War, it was 31 Feet in Length, and
21 Feet in Diameter, and pretty nearly cylindrical : Pray
how many Tuns of Wine would the fame contain ?

*Anfwer*, 318 Tuns, 183 Gallons, &c.

SOLUTIONS

# SOLUTIONS

## TO THE

Most Difficult of the aforegoing

# QUESTIONS;

### WITH THE

Manner of Performing the several OPERATIONS.

By BENJ. WEBB, Writing-Master and Accountant,
and Master of the Haberdashers-School in Bunhill-Row.

APOLOGY.

# A P O L O G Y.

BEING engaged to revise and examine this Edition of Mr CLARE's excellent *Introduction to Trade and Business*, and it being judged that the Methods of Solution to the most difficult Questions in the Recreative Part of it would make an agreeable Appendix, I undertook to perform the Task: In what Light it will be received by the Public I hope I need not be solicitous, since the Intent was the Encouragement of the Pupil, and the Ease of the Instructor.

*B. W.*

---

Explanation of the Symbols made use of in the Appendix.

| | |
|---|---|
| + | Signifies more or added to. |
| — | less or taken from. |
| × | multiplied by. |
| ÷ | divided by. |
| = | equal to. |
| : :: : | direct Proportion. |
| ◻ | squared. |
| √ | square Root. |

APPENDIX.

# APPENDIX.

### QUESTION XIII.

| | |
|---|---|
| The Bell at Pekin | 120.000 *lb.* |
| Excefs — — | 94.600 |
| The German Bell | 25.400 |
| The Bell at Nankin | 50.000 |
| Difference is — | 24.600 nearly half above the |
| | German Bell. |

### QUESTION XIV.

| | |
|---|---|
| Grandfather's Age is . 119 |
| Subtract — — 83 |
| Grandfon's Age is — 36 |
| The Father's Age is 63 |
| The Difference is — 27 between Father and Son. |

### QUESTION XXII.

| | |
|---|---|
| Charlotte's Fortune — — | 13200 |
| Mifs Kitty's — — — | 13200 |
| Charlotte's raifed to — — | 15000 |
| To Ditto left by Grandmother | 1800 |
| Mifs Kitty's raifed to — — | 20000 |
| To Ditto left by Grandmother | 6800 |
| Left between them — — | 8600 |

QUES.

QUESTION XXVII.

| | | | |
|---|---|---|---|
| When Seth was born, Adam was | — | 130 | Years old. |
| When Enos was born, Seth | — — | 105 | |
| When Ditto was Father to Cainan | — | 90 | |
| When Cainan had Mahaliel | — — | 70 | |
| Mahaliel had Jared | — — — | at | 65 |
| Jared had Enoch | — — — | at | 162 |
| Enoch had Mathufelah | — — | at | 65 |
| Mathufelah had Lamech | — — | at | 187 |
| Lamech had Noah | — — | at | 182 |
| Noah, when the Flood happened, was | | 600 | |

Years 1656 To the Flood.
Years 930 To Adam's Death.

726 Years after Adam's
Deceafe.

QUESTION XXX.

Mean Diftance between the Earth and Sun is Miles 81.000.000
Ditto Earth and Moon — — — 240.000

In an Eclipfe of the Moon — — — 81.240.000
Then from — — — — 81.000.000
Subtract — — — — 240.000

In an Eclipfe of the Sun — — 80.760.000

QUESTION XXXIII.

1600 Guineas are — £ 1722
Multiplied by 4

Mother's Part — 6888
Subtract — 1383

Daughter's Part is — 5505
Then ¼ — 2752 . 10

The eldeft Son's Part 8257 . 10
Collected as under.

£ 1722 . — . — 6888
6888 . — . —
5505 . — . — 2) 12393
8257 . 10 . —
6196 . 10 . — 6196 . 10 = Youngeft Son.
988 . 10 . — Funeral Expences.

29557 . 10 . —
30000 . — . —

442 . 10 . — Remainder.

## QUESTION XXXVII.

| | | £ | | | |
|---|---|---|---|---|---|
| Due to the Guardian | | £ | 74 | 18 | 4 |
| Paid off — — — — | | | 41 | 14 | 8 |
| | | | 33 | 3 | 6 Brother's Debt. |
| | ½ — | | 16 | 11 | 9 |
| Paid off by Sifter — — | | | 49 | 15 | 8 |
| | | | 13 | 12 | 10 |
| | Add | | 36 | 2 | 5 Sifter's Debt. |
| | | | 33 | 3 | 6 Brother's Debt. |
| Paid off by Uncle — — | | | 69 | 5 | 11 |
| | | | 24 | 7 | 3 |
| Then colle&t Brother's Debt | | | 44 | 18 | 8 Uncle's Debt. |
| Sifter's Ditto | | | 33 | 3 | 6 |
| | | | 36 | 2 | 5 |
| | | | 114 | 4 | 7 |
| | | | 35 | 15 | 5 Father's Gain. |
| | | £ | 150 | 0 | 0 Proof. |

## QUESTION XXXIX.

| | | £ | | | |
|---|---|---|---|---|---|
| 100 Guineas are — — | £ | 105 | — | — | |
| Deduct 10 Marks, viz. | | 6 | 13 | 4 | |
| S's Part is — — | | 98 | 6 | 8 | |
| Deduct — — | | — | 16 | 8 | |
| T's Part is — — | | 97 | 10 | 0 | |
| Deduct — — | | 6 | 6 | 0 | |
| R's Part is — — | | 91 | 4 | 0 | |
| Add — — | | 3 | 17 | 2 | |
| W's Part is — — | | 95 | 1 | 2 = W |
| Then colle&t — | | 91 | 4 | 0 = R |
| | | 97 | 10 | 0 = T |
| | | 98 | 6 | 8 = S |
| | £ | 382 | 1 | 10 = Anſwer. |

### Question XL.

| | | |
|---|---|---|
| Troy built before the Temple | 440 | Years. |
| London Ditto ———— | 260 | |
| Difference | 183 | |
| | 3000 | |
| In the Year | 2827 | London was built. |
| Carthage built before Rome | 113 | |
| Rome before Chrift ———— | 744 | |
| | 857 | |
| Chrift born A. M. ———— | 4000 | |
| In the Year | 3143 | Carthage built. |
| | 2827 | London. |
| London older than Carthage | 316 | Years. |

### Question XLV.

| | | |
|---|---|---|
| 20 Piers, each 60 Feet thick | 1200 | Feet. |
| 21 Arches, each 170 Feet | 3570 | Feet. |
| The Length of Trajan's Bridge | 4770 | |
| Deduct the Length of Weftminfter | 1200 | |
| | 3570 | the Anfwer. |

### Question LXIII.

The Snail goes up 8 Feet the firft Day, comes down 4; then goes up 8 the fecond Day, and defcends 4 at Night, &c. fo that on the fourth Day fhe is 20 Feet high, and need not come back again.

### Question LXVI.

| | | | s. | d. |
|---|---|---|---|---|
| The Value of the Purfe and Money is | | | 12 . | 8 |
| Value of Purfe ———— | $\frac{1}{8}$ | is | 1 . | 7 |
| Money in the Purfe ———— | | is | 11 . | 1 |

Ques-

## QUESTION LXXIII.

From 20 the Number of Terms, and 21 the laſt Term.
Take 1 = Com. Diff.

$\overline{19} \times 1\frac{1}{2} = 28\frac{1}{2}$ Then
24
$28\frac{1}{2}$
21
—
73 The Father's Age.

## QUESTION LXXIV.

This Queſtion may be eaſily traced by proceeding as under. On the laſt Night the Number of Sheep was reduced to 20, when 21 had been ſtolen the Number then being 41, for the $\frac{1}{2}$ of 41 is $20\frac{1}{2}$, and $\frac{1}{2}$ a Sheep make 21, ſo then 41—21=20 ; and in like manner for the reſt, the Double of $41\frac{1}{2}$ is 83, and the Double of $83\frac{1}{2}$ is 167, the Number of Sheep at firſt.

## QUESTION LXXXIV.

360 the Sum of 2 Numbers.
114 the Leſs.
———
246 then $246 \times 114 = 28044$ = Product.
114
———
132 = Difference. $\frac{246}{114} = 2\frac{3}{19}$ the larger Quote.

## QUESTION LXXXV.

$\frac{2072}{14} = 148$ and $148 \times 25 = 3700$ and

$\frac{3700}{6}$ Feet = 1 Fathom = $616\frac{2}{3}$ Fathoms.

## QUESTION XCI.

$360° \times 69'\frac{1}{2} = 25020$ Miles, then
H. M.    H.
As 23.56 : 25020 : : 1 : $1045\frac{145}{356}$ Miles.

## QUESTION XCII.

$2 \times 3 \times 4 \times 5 \times 6 = 720$
Add    1
———
721

Then $\frac{721}{7} = 103$ even.

$\frac{721}{2.3.4.5.6}$ reſpectively will leave an odd one.

Z

## QUESTION C.

As $5 : 8 :: 75 : 120$

Then $120 \square = 14400$

$\quad\quad 75 \square = 5625$

$\quad\quad\quad\quad\quad 8775 = $ Diff.

$\dfrac{120}{75} = \dfrac{8}{5} = $ Ratio or largest Quote.

$\dfrac{75}{120} = \dfrac{5}{8} = $ Lesser Quote.

Then $\frac{8}{5} \square = \frac{64}{25}$ } These reduced $= \dfrac{4096 + 625}{1600} = 2\dfrac{1521}{1600}$

And $\frac{5}{8} \square = \frac{25}{64}$

## QUESTION CII.

$L + M + N + O = £\,10000$     Then $6050 - 420 = 5630$

$L + M + N \quad\quad = \quad 8500$     And $\dfrac{5630}{2} = 2815 = M$

$\quad$ Then $O = £\,1500$     And $6050 - 2815 = 3235 = N$

$\quad M + N \quad = \quad 6050$

$\quad M + N + O = \quad 7550$     Proof.

Then from $L + M + N + O = 10000$    $L = 2450$

$\quad$ Take $\quad M + N + O = 7550$    $M = 2815$

$\quad$ Remains $\quad L \quad = \quad £2450$    $N = 3235$

Then $L + \quad\quad\quad\quad O = 1000$    $O = 1500$

Take $L + \quad\quad\quad\quad O = 3950$

Rem. $M + N \quad\quad\quad = 6050$     $£\,10000$ as before.

## QUESTION CIV.

$\quad\quad\quad\quad £ \quad\quad s \quad\quad d$

$A + B = 13 . 10 . 0$

$B + C = 12 . 12 . 0$

$A + C = 11 . 16 . 6$

$\quad\quad\quad\quad 37 . 18 . 6$

Then divide by the Number of Players at each Time will give the Sum Total won.

Thus $\quad 2)\; 37 . 18 . 6$

$\quad\quad + \quad 18 . 19 . 3 = A + B + C$

Then $\quad - \quad 13 . 10 . 0 = A + B$

$\quad\quad\quad\quad\quad 5 . 9 . 3 = \quad\quad$ C's Gain.

Then $\quad - \quad 12 . 12 . 0 = B + C$

$\quad\quad\quad\quad\quad 6 . 7 . 3 = \quad\quad$ A's Gain.

Then $\quad - \quad 11 . 16 . 6$

$\quad\quad\quad\quad\quad 7 . 2 . 9 = \quad\quad$ B's Gain.

QUES-

## QUESTION CV.

$$W + X + Y = £ \; 350 . 10$$
$$W + X + Z = \quad 344 . 10$$
$$X + Y + Z = \quad 400 . —$$
$$W + Y + Z = \quad 378 . 4$$

$$3) \; \overline{1473 . 4}$$

Gain.       491 . 1 . 4

Subtract 450 - - - -   472 . 10 . 0

Remains     £ 18 . 11 . 4

## QUESTION CVI.

                s. d.

120 at 2 a Penny = 5 . 0

120 at 3         3 . 4

             d.    8 . 4

And 240 at 5 for 2   -   8 . 0

Loss    0 . 4

## QUESTION CVII.

1st   2d   3d

5 : x :: 8 Then    To find the 4th. Say as $5 : 9.8 :: 8 : \frac{78.4}{5} =$

                 15.68 = the fourth. Then

$8x = 78.4$         15.68

and $x = 9.8 =$ 2d No    — 9.8

            5.88   The Answer required.

## QUESTION CVIII.

    s. d.    G.     £

If   4 . 6 —   1 — 33 facit   $146\frac{4}{3}$ Wine and Water.

                      126 = Wine 1 Pipe.

Gallons $20\frac{2}{3}$ = Water.

## QUESTION CIX.

Gall.   S. I.

$13\frac{1}{4} \times 282 = 3760$ Solid Inches, and this $\times 52835 = 1986.596$

and this $\div 7\frac{1}{2}$ lb. or 120 Ounces, gives $16\frac{4}{5}$ Gall. nearly.

## QUESTION CXI.

Put $a =$ the Expence, this doubled $= 2a$

Put $a =$ the Profit, this halved $= \frac{1}{2}a$    therefore $\frac{1}{2}a$ must

be $\times 4$ to make $2a$, consequently the Proportion is 4 to 1.

### Question CXII.

£ 39 . 19 . 8 = 39 . . 983 decimally, then divide 39 . 983 by 12 Years, and it will quote 3 . 3327.

Then $\dfrac{100}{3 . 3327}$ = 30 Years.

### Question CXIV.

| Miles | | Min. | | Mile | | Sec. Tb. |
|---|---|---|---|---|---|---|

Say If $37\frac{11}{10}$ —— 4 —— 1 facit 6 . 26 nearly.

### Question CXV.

| | Ap. | | P. | Multiply the Antecedents together |
|---|---|---|---|---|
| If | 12 | - - - | 12 | for a Divisor, and the Consequents |
| | 3 | - - - | —$\frac{1}{2}$ d. | together for a Dividend, as under. |

What will — — 84 Cost.

$$\begin{array}{cc} 12 & 21 \\ 3 & \frac{1}{2}d. \\ \hline \end{array}$$

Anteced. 36   10.5

84

$$\overline{\phantom{84}}\ d.$$

36) 882. (24 $\frac{1}{2}$

### Question CXVI.

Divide the Sum Total of the Notches by the Number of Players at a Time, and add their Deficiency to the Quotient, and you will have 356.

### Question CXVII.

| | S | Sacks | £ | Sacks |
|---|---|---|---|---|

Say If 36 —— 12 —— 41 facit 273 $\frac{1}{3}$ and this multiplied by $\frac{7}{6}$ will give 318 $\frac{8}{9}$ People.

### Question CXVIII.

Now $\frac{8}{10}$ = $\frac{4}{5}$ and $\frac{4}{4}$ = $\frac{4}{20}$ = $\frac{2}{10}$ = $\frac{1}{5}$ = Tax.

Then 1 Fifth - - £ 8 . 10 - - 5 Fifths facit £ 42 . 10

### Question CXIX.

If £ 3 . 10 —— £ 130 —— £ 4 . 5 facit £ 57 . 17 . 1 $\frac{1}{7}$

### Question CXX.

| | £ | S D | £ | S D |
|---|---|---|---|---|

If 105 —— 31 . 9 —— 110 facit 33 . 3 $\frac{1}{2}$

### Question CXXI.

If 45 Persons —— £ 20 what will 58 Pers. facit 25 . 15 . 6 $\frac{3}{4}$ and if £ 25 . 15 . 6 $\frac{3}{4}$ —— Gall. 17 —— 63 facit 43 . 12 . 6.

Ques-

### QUESTION CXXII.

Miles  Day  Mile         Miles  Day  Mile

If 22 —— 1 —— 1 facit $\frac{1}{22}$ and if 32 —— 1 —— 1 —— $\frac{1}{32}$

Day      Mile  Day

then $\frac{1}{22} - \frac{1}{32} = \frac{10}{704}$ Day. Then say, if $\frac{10}{704}$ —— 1 —— 4 facit

Mile  Mile

$\frac{2816}{10}$ = 281$\frac{6}{10}$ and 350 — 281$\frac{6}{10}$ = 68$\frac{4}{10}$.

### QUESTION CXXIV.

£    £      £  £  £  S

From 100 take 17 remains 83. Then if 83—100—52 . 10 facit

£  S  D    £  £  £  S  D    £  S  D

63 . 5 . 0$\frac{80}{83}$ and if 100—120— 63 . 5 . 0$\frac{80}{83}$ facit 75 . 18 — 7$\frac{2}{83}$

£  S  £  S  D

—52 . 10 = 23 . 8 — 7$\frac{2}{83}$.

### QUEST. CXXV. See QUEST. CXV.

### QUESTION CXXVI.

℔.  D  £  S  D    £  S  D    £  S  D

112 at 25$\frac{2}{3}$ = 11 . 19 . 6$\frac{2}{3}$ the $\frac{11 . 19 . 6\frac{2}{3}}{2}$ = 5 . 19 . 9$\frac{1}{3}$ subtracted from £ 8 gives the Answer.

### QUESTION CXXVII.

Work Men Work Men    Time Men Time        Men

If 1 — 30 — 4 = 120. And if 1 — 120 — $\frac{1}{5}$ facit $\frac{1}{5}$) $\frac{120 \times 1}{1}$ (600

### QUESTION CXXVIII.

Ft In.  Ft In.  Ft In.    Ft In.

If 50 . 11 — 98 . 6 — 300 . 8 facit 581 . 7$\frac{48}{211}$ then subtract

Ft In.  Ft In.      Ft In.

20 . 6 + 30 . 9 and remains 530 . 4$\frac{48}{211}$.

### QUESTION CXXIX.

S  D  D    S      D      S  D

4 . 3 = 51 Sold for 6 Loss ₱ Cent. is 8$\frac{1}{2}$ + . 56 then 6

Charges 2 a Pair                  — . 0 . 8$\frac{1}{2}$ . 56

      ——                                    ——

    53       D  S  D                5 . 3$\frac{1}{4}$ . 44

Then if 53 — 5 . 3$\frac{1}{4}$ + . 44 — £100 facit £19 . 10 . 11$\frac{17}{53}$

### QUESTION CXXX.

D  £  S  D    £      £        £  S

If 1$\frac{1}{2}$ — 1 — 6 . 7$\frac{1}{4}$ facit 53 then if 4 fifths — 53 — 5 fifths facit 66 , 5

Then £ 66 . 5 = whole Rent.

53 . 0 = $\frac{4}{5}$ of Rent.

    ——

13 . 5 = King's Tax = $\frac{1}{5}$ of the Rent.

QUESTION CXXXI.

300 Barrels each 14 $lb$. at $12\frac{1}{2}d$. amount to 140000 $l$.

$$\begin{array}{cccc} lb. & D & lb. & D \\ \text{Then if } 7490 \longrightarrow 140000 \longrightarrow 1 \text{ facit } 18\frac{5180}{7490}. \end{array}$$

$$\begin{array}{cccc} l & l & D & D \\ \text{And if } 117 \longrightarrow 100 \longrightarrow 18\frac{5180}{7490} \text{ facit } 15\frac{11091}{11731}. \end{array}$$

QUESTION CXXXII.

$$1700 + 400 + 400 + 400 = 2900 \text{ for } 1700 \overset{Days}{=} 11 - 400 = 3 \&c.$$
$$= 20 \text{ Days.}$$

QUESTION CXXXIII.

To $\pounds 3179 . 11 . 8$ add $\pounds 25 = 3204 . 11 . 8$. Then for $\frac{1}{7}$ of the Year the Increase at $\frac{1}{7}$ the Year is $\frac{1}{12}$ and the whole Estate $= \frac{13}{12}$ consequently $\frac{12+1}{12} = \frac{13}{12}$. Then $\pounds 3204 . 11 . 8 \div \frac{13}{12} =$ $\pounds 2958 . 1 . 6 \frac{4}{13}$. Again for 1 Year with the Increase of $\frac{1}{3} = \frac{4}{3}$, then $\pounds 100 + \pounds 2958 . 1 . 6\frac{1}{2} \div \frac{4}{3} = \pounds 2295 . 11 . 1\frac{1}{4}$. And this last Sum $+ 100 \div$ by $\frac{4}{3} = \pounds 1795 . 3 . 4\frac{1}{2}$, and this $+ \pounds 100 \div \frac{4}{3}$ $= \pounds 1421 . 7 . 6$ the Answer required.

QUESTION CXXXV.

$1 \times 2 \times 3 \times 4 \times 5 \times 6 \times 7 \times 8 \times 9 = 362880$ Days $= 999\frac{225}{365}$ Years Board for 200 Guineas $= $ about $50\frac{2}{7}d$. a Year.

QUESTION CXXXVI. Is an easy Sum in Position.

QUESTION CXXXIX.

$$\begin{array}{ccc} & \pounds & S & D \\ \text{If } \pounds 17 \longrightarrow \pounds 3 \longrightarrow \pounds 140 \text{ facit } 24 . 14 . 1. \end{array}$$ Then from $\pounds$ $\pounds$ $S$ $D$ $\pounds$ $S$ $D$
140 deduct 24 . 14 . 1 remains 115 . 5 . 11 then $\frac{1}{5}$ of $\pounds 140 = \pounds 28$ and $\pounds 28 \div 17 = \pounds 1 . 12 . 11$. Then to $\pounds 115 . 5 . 11 +$ 1 . 2 . 11 facit $\pounds 116 . 18 . 10$.

QUESTION CXL.

$$\begin{array}{ccc} Day & W & Day & W \\ \text{If } 10 \longrightarrow 1 \longrightarrow 1 \text{ facit } \frac{1}{10} \end{array} \text{ then } \frac{1}{10} + \frac{1}{13} = \frac{23}{130} \text{ in one Day}$$
$$13 \longrightarrow 1 \longrightarrow 1 \quad \frac{1}{13}$$
consequently $5\frac{15}{23}$ Days finishes the Whole.

QUESTION CXLI.

$$\begin{array}{lcl} A+B+C+D & = & 25000 \\ E+C+D+E & = & 33000 \\ A \phantom{+B}+C+D+E & = & 30000 \\ A+B+C \phantom{+D}+E & = & 28000 \\ A+B \phantom{+C}+D+E & = & 32000 \\ \hline & & 148000 \\ \hline \end{array}$$

Then

Then 148000 ÷ 4 the Number combined
= 37000 the Sum of their Fortunes.

Then $A+B+C+D+E = 37000$
And $A+B \quad +D+E = 32000$
_____

$5000 = C$ the third Daughter.

## QUESTION CXLII.

Day Work Day

$B+C = 18$ then if $18 - 1 - 1 - \frac{1}{18}$ then $A+B+C = \frac{7}{11}$

$A+B+C = 11$ then if $11 - 1 - 1 - \frac{1}{11}$ and $-B+C = \frac{9}{18}$

$\phantom{xxxxxxxxxxxxxxxxxxxxxxxxxxxxxxxxxx}198$

$\phantom{xxxxxxxxxxxxxxxxxxxxxxxxxxxxxxxxxx}\overline{\phantom{xx}7}$

$\phantom{xxxxxxxxxxxxxxxxxxxxx} = 28\frac{2}{7}$ Days.

## QUESTION CXLIII.

$A+B = \frac{2}{7} = .2857$
$A+C = \frac{3}{8} = .375$
$B+C = \frac{3}{10} = .3$

$\phantom{xxxxx}9607 ÷ 2$ the combined $N^{o} = .48035 = A+B+C$ &

$\phantom{xxxx} W \phantom{xx} S \phantom{xxxx} W \phantom{xxxxx} S \phantom{xx} D \phantom{x} .2857 = A+B$

Then if $.4804 - 30 - .19465$ facit $12 . 1 \phantom{x} \overline{.19465} = C$ and in
like manner proceed for the rest.

## QUESTION CXLIV. CXLV. CXLVI.

May be solved by Position, or by a Simple Algebraic Equation.

### Example of QUESTION CXLIV.

Put $x = C$'s Crowns. Then by the Question B's Crowns are
$= x - 178$ and A's Crowns $= x - 178 + 129$, then these added
together equal 1000 Crowns thus:

$C = x$
$B = x - 178$
$A = x - 178 + 129$
_____

$3x - 356 + 129 = 3x - 227 = 1000$ conseq. $= 3x = 1000 + 227$

$\phantom{xxxxxxxxxxxxxx} = 1227$ and $x = \frac{1227}{3} = 409 = C$'s Crowns.

Whence $B = 409 - 178 = 231$ and $A = 409 - 49 = 36$ A.

## QUESTION CXLVII.

$\phantom{x} S \phantom{xxxxxxxxxxxx} S \phantom{x} D \phantom{xxxxxxxx} S \phantom{x} D$

At 11 he cleared $\frac{3}{4} = 4 . 1\frac{1}{4}$ remains $6 . 10\frac{1}{4}$ prime Cost.

$\phantom{x} S \phantom{x} D \phantom{xxxxxxxxx} S \phantom{x} D \phantom{xxxxxxxx} S \phantom{x} D$

$13 . 6$ raised deduct $6 . 10\frac{1}{4}$ remains $6 . 7\frac{1}{4}$ Gain.

$\phantom{xxx} S \phantom{x} D \phantom{xxxxxx} S \phantom{x} D$

Then if $6 . 10\frac{1}{4} - 6 . 7\frac{1}{4} - 100£$ facit £96 . 7 . 3$\frac{2}{3}$

$\phantom{xxxxxxxxxxxxxxxxxxxxxxxxxxxxxxxxxxxxxxxx}$ QUES-

QUESTION CXLVIII.

Is performed by the Rule of Three Indirect.

QUESTION CLI.

$x + y + z = 12$ Then if $12 - 1 - 1$ facit $\frac{1}{12}$ Work.

$x = 24$      $24 - 1 - 1$      $\frac{1}{24}$

$x = 34$      $34 - 1 - 1$      $\frac{1}{34}$

Then $x + z = \frac{1}{14} + \frac{1}{24} = \frac{38}{816}$ then $\underline{x + y + z = \frac{1}{12}}$

$-x \quad + z = \frac{38}{816}$

Conseq. $y = \frac{120}{5792}$ in 1 Day.

If $\frac{\text{Work}}{\frac{120}{5792}} \longrightarrow \frac{\text{Day}}{1} \longrightarrow \frac{\text{Work}}{1}$ facit $\frac{\text{Days}}{81\frac{6}{10}}$.

QUESTION CLIV.

From 90° take 23°$\frac{1}{2}$ remains 66°$\frac{1}{2}$ then to 11°.48′ add 23°.30′ facit 35°.18′ to this add 66°.30′ facit 101°.48′ and this laft Sum ÷ by 2 gives 50°.54′.

QUESTION CLVI.

Sloop and Cargo $= £16131\frac{7}{10}$ then $\frac{7}{8}$ of $\frac{1}{2}$ of $\frac{1}{2} = a$. $\frac{1}{3}$ of $\frac{4}{5}$ of $a = b = B$. Then $a - b = A$ and $A + B$ reduced $= \frac{84}{320}$ and $\frac{320}{320} - \frac{84}{320} = \frac{236}{320}$ the Remainder of the Sloop and Cargo, then $\frac{9}{11}$ of $\frac{236}{320} = \frac{2124}{3520} = P$. Then fay by the Rule of Three,

                                         £

If 3520 $\longrightarrow$ £16131.7 $\longrightarrow$ 2124 facit $9734\frac{127}{3500}$.

QUESTION CLVII.

Is performed by Alligation, and is very eafy.

QUESTION CLIX.

If, allowing him to make £5 ꝑ Cent. of his Money,

The Intereft of £100 $= £5$      £40 a Year allowed.

           of   200 $= 10$        55

           of   300 $= 15$        70

                         ——       ——

                        30    3) 165

                                  ——

                              55 Mean Sum.

                    deduct  30

                              ——

                            25 $=$ his Allowance for

                            ——      Attendance.

QUEST.

# APPENDIX. 177

### QUESTION CLXIV.

Put $4000 = n$ then $\frac{1}{4}$ of $\frac{2}{3}$ of $n = \frac{5n}{12}$ now $\frac{12n-5n}{12} = \frac{7n}{12}$.

Then $\frac{1}{4}$ of $\frac{7n}{12} = \frac{7n}{48}$ and $\frac{28n-7n}{48} = \frac{21n}{48} = \frac{7n}{16}$.

Then $\frac{7}{10}$ of $\frac{17}{20} = \frac{119}{200}$ of $\frac{7n}{16} = \frac{833n}{3200}$ and $\frac{7n}{16} - \frac{833n}{3200} =$

$\frac{1400n-833n}{3200} = \frac{567n}{3200}$ and $\frac{3}{16}$ of $\frac{567n}{3200} = \frac{1701n}{51200}$ then $\frac{567n}{3200} - \frac{1701n}{51200} =$

$\frac{9072n}{51200} - \frac{1701n}{51200} = \frac{7371 \times 4000}{5120} = 575\frac{11}{64}$ Nuts.

### QUESTION CLXV.

May be performed by two Operations in double Position.
Operation the first brings out $376\frac{8}{17}$ Bushels of Malt.
$225\frac{15}{17}$      Meal.
$197\frac{11}{17}$      Oatmeal.

800 Bushels.

Operation the second brings out $1 s. 7\frac{240}{1111}d.$ whence the rest may be readily had.

Or by two simple Equations in Algebra.

By the question $x + \frac{3x}{5} + \frac{21x}{40} = 800$ whence $x = 376\frac{8}{17}$ Bush. of Malt.

and $\frac{3x}{5} = 225\frac{15}{17}$    Meal.

$\frac{21x}{40} = 197\frac{11}{17}$    Oatmeal.

Then these Fractions reduced we shall have for the next Equation
$3360x + 7680x + 19200x = £142 \times 17 = 2414$, which reduced into Shillings $= 48280 s.$

Then $x = \frac{48280}{30240} = \frac{2414}{1512} = 1 s. 7\frac{240}{1512}d.$ as before.

### QUESTION CLXVI.

$\frac{44}{17}$) $\frac{361}{17}$ ( $\frac{361}{17} = 9\frac{23}{17}$ and this $\square = 95\frac{266}{1369}$.

### QUESTION CLXVII.

$\frac{77}{48} \times \frac{44}{77} = \frac{1}{3}$ Cube of $\frac{44}{17} = \frac{110592}{410513} = \frac{995328}{4102797}$.

### QUESTION CLXX.

$£2000 \times \frac{1}{4} = 1500$ and $1500 + 2000 = £3500 = \frac{2}{3}$ of the Fortune.
and $\frac{1}{2}$ of $\frac{2}{3} = 1750 = \frac{1}{3}$ ditto.

$5250 =$ whole Fortune.

If she had had a Daughter, the Mother would have had— £3500
If a Son £1750, but as she had both, she had no more than 1500

Lost in Equity £2000

A a        QUES-

### Question CLXXIV.

This Question is performed by Alligation alternate.

$$24 \begin{cases} 30 \\ 20 \\ 18 \\ 15 \end{cases} \quad \begin{array}{c} 9+6+4 \\ 6 \\ 6 \\ 6 \end{array} \quad \begin{array}{c} 19 \\ 6 \\ 6 \\ 6 \end{array}$$

| | lb. | | lb. | | lb. | | lb. |
|---|---|---|---|---|---|---|---|
| Then say if 19 | — | 120 | — | 19 | facit | 120 |
| 19 | — | 120 | — | 6 | | $37\frac{17}{19}$ |
| 19 | — | 120 | — | 6 | | $37\frac{17}{19}$ |
| 19 | — | 120 | — | 6 | | $37\frac{17}{19}$ |

The true Answer is   lb. $233\frac{13}{19}$

### Question CLXXVII.

$\frac{3}{8}+\frac{1}{7}=\frac{45}{56}$ and $1-\frac{45}{56}=\frac{11}{56}$ then if $11 - £140 - 45$ facit $£572\frac{8}{11}$.

### Question CLXXVIII.

Say if £45 —— £100 —— £52 . 10 facit £116 . 13 . 4 the whole Stock.

Then A=10 and B 7=17, then if 17 —— £116 . 13 . 4 —— 10 facit A's Stock, and then proceed to find B's.

### Question CLXXIX.

£ 74 . — = A's Gain.
52 . 10 = B's.

——————

21 . 10 = Difference.
126 . 10 = Sum.

Then if £ 21 . 10 —— £ 19 . 19 . 8 —— £ 126 . 10 facit £117 . 6 = Sums advanced. Then £117 . 6 = Principal.
126 . 10 = Gain.

       s.      Ank.

If 55 —— 1 —— 243 . 16 facit 88 Ankers.

If Ank. 88 —— £126 . 10 —— 1 Anker facit 28s. 10$\frac{1}{4}$d.

### Question CLXXXVI.

| 18 Cwt. at 42s. = 756 |    s. 15 . 6 |
|---|---|
| —————— | 14 . — |
| $\frac{1}{3}$ 252 | ———— |
| | 1 . 6 |
| 504 | 2 |
| | 3 . — |

If 31 s. —— 3 s. —— 504 s. facit £ 2 . 8 . 9$\frac{1}{3}$

Then 42      18 Cwt. at 11s. = 19s. 8d. = £9 . 18 . —
—31                     2 . 8 . 9$\frac{5}{3}$
————

11 Gained.      In A's favour £7 . 9 . 8$\frac{2}{3}$,

Ques-

## QUESTION CXC.

$£ 5 . 6$

$\frac{1}{2} 2 . 13$

$\overline{7 . 19}$

Then if $£4 . 5$ —— $£7 . 19$ —— $3d$. facit

$5\frac{1}{2}d. + \frac{£14}{215}$ *Error*

## QUESTION CXCII.

The whole Interest is $65s. 6d.$ then say if $£4$ was gained by $£100$ in $365$ Days, in how long time will $2289s.$ gain $65s. 6d.$ facit 7 Years 41 Days, to be deducted from the 18th of August, gives the 7th of July, 1783.

## QUESTION CXCIII.

$£ 542 . 8 =$ Principal and Interest.

$384 . 0 =$ Principal.

$\overline{158 . 8}$

Then if $£384$ —— $£158 . 8$ —— $100$ facit $£82\frac{1}{2}$, this ÷ $8\frac{1}{4}$ gives $100s. = £5$.

## QUESTION CXCIV.

| $£$ | $s.$ | | | | $£$ | $s.$ | $d.$ | $£$ | $s.$ | $d.$ |
|---|---|---|---|---|---|---|---|---|---|---|
| 20 . 0 | If $£78 . 5$ —— 640 —— $£20$ facit | | | | 162 . 11 . 6 | | | = 18 . 3 . 6 |
| 26 . 5 | | | | | 9mo. | | | | | |
| 32 . 0 | Ditto ditto 26 . 5 | | | | 214 . 13 . 11 | | | = 30 . 13 . 5 | | |
| | | | | | 7mo. | | | | | |
| 78 . 5 | Ditto ditto 32 | | | | 461 . 14 . 6 | | | = 52 . 6 . 10¼ | | |
| | | | | | 5mo. | | | | | |

## QUESTION CXCIX.

50 Cloths at $£13 = £650$.

Then if $2 . 6$ —— $14$ —— $650$ facit $7.2800 ÷ 364 =$ in a Sack, facit 200 Sacks.

Now if $11 . 10$ —— $13$ —— $2 . 1$ facit $28.261$ fere, and from $30$, take $28.261$

$\overline{1.739}$

50 Cloths at $£11 . 10$ $\oplus$ Cloth facit $£575$.

Then if $30$ —— $1.739$ —— $575$ Answer $33 . 6 . 8$

## QUESTION CCII.

If $10$ —— $6$ —— $20$ facit $12$

If $12$ —— $8$ —— $31 . 10$ facit 420 Bushels.

## QUESTION CCIII.

$8 + 5 = 13$ and $8 - 5 = 3$ Then if $13$ —— $3$ —— $£154$ facit $£35 . 10 . 9\frac{1}{4}$

QUES-

## QUESTION CCIV.

$$72 \times 30 = 108 \times 20 = 1296 \text{ for } 720 \text{ at } 6.8 \text{ or } \frac{1}{3} \pounds = 240$$

deduct 10 per Cent.    24

           216

$\frac{1}{2}$ in Cash    108

720 Ells at 5s    180

Pounds of Saffron =    72

## QUESTION CCVI.

$\pounds 480 . 12 . —$

$137 . 6 . 3$ damaged.

$\pounds 343 . 5 . 9$

$\pounds 137 . 6 . 3$

$48 . 18 . —$ loft.

If $88 . 8 . 3$ —— $137 . 6 . 3$ —— $5 . 6$ facit $8 . 6\frac{1}{4}$

Then if $8s. 6\frac{1}{4}d.$ —— 1 Yard —— $\pounds 480 . 12$ facit 1128 Yards in all. Then $\frac{2}{7}$ of 1128 Yards $= 322\frac{1}{4}$ Yards damaged ——$895\frac{3}{4}$ Yards undamaged. Now $\pounds 343 . 5 . 9 =$ Value of the undamaged. And to this add $\pounds 48 . 18$ we shall have $\pounds 392 . 3 . 9$, then say If $805\frac{3}{4}$ Yards —— $\pounds 392 . 3 . 9$ —— 1 Ell facit $12s. 2d.$

## QUESTION CCVII.

Remark, if I am supposed to make Interest of the $\pounds 400$ Stock sold out, and of the Dividends received, it will be to my damage about $\pounds 132$.

## QUESTION CCVIII.

The Interest of $\pounds 1114 . 10$ for 1461 Days is $\pounds 318 . 8 . 2\frac{1}{4}$.

Paid off $\pounds 140$ remains    $1292 : 18 . 2\frac{1}{4}$

Then add the Interest of this last to September 5, 1718, found thus,

If $\pounds 100$ —— $\pounds 5\frac{1}{4}$ —— $\pounds 1292 . 18 . 2$ facit $\pounds 67 . 17 . 6\frac{1}{4}$ and       $21 . 16 . 8$

If $\pounds 67 . 17 . 6\frac{1}{4}$ — 365 Days —$\pounds 21 . 16 . 8$ facit 116 Days $=$ September 5, 1718,

Paid off    $\pounds 1314 . 14 . 10\frac{1}{4}$

            $87 . 11 . 9$

Then the Sum taken for the Bond on the 11th of September, 1724, is ——    $\pounds 1227 . 3 . 1\frac{1}{4}$

            $1409 . 16 . 8$

Interest taken $\pounds$    $182 . 13 . 6\frac{1}{4}$

Then

Then to find the Rate of Intereſt taken ſay,

If £1227 . 3 . 1½ — £1409 . 16 . 8 — £100 facit £114 . 17 . 6

Then this Intereſt divided by 6 Years = the Time from September 1718 to September 1724, gives the Anſwer thus

Intereſt £14 . 17 . 6 ÷ 6 = £2 . 9 . 6¼ ſterl.

## QUESTION CCIX.

| Days. | Work. | Day. | Work. | | |
|---|---|---|---|---|---|
| If 12 | 1 | 1 facit | $\frac{1}{12}$ = .0833333 &c. | = A+B+C |
| 14 | 1 | 1 | $\frac{1}{14}$ = .0714285 | = B+C+D |
| 15 | 1 | 1 | $\frac{1}{15}$ = .0666666 | = C+D+A |
| 18 | 1 | 1 | $\frac{1}{18}$ = .0555555 | = D+A+B |

Divide by combined Nº of Men    3 ) .2769841

| | | |
|---|---|---|
| + .0923280 | = A+B+C+D |
| — .0714285 | = B+C+D |
| .0208995 | = A only. |
| — .0666666 | = A +C+D |
| .0256614 | = B |
| — .0555555 | = A+B    D |
| .0367725 | = C |
| — .0833333 | = A+B+C |
| .0089947 | = D |

| Work. | Day. | Work. | Days. | |
|---|---|---|---|---|
| Then if .0923280 | 1 | 1 facit | 10.83 | = All. |
| .0208995 | 1 | 1 | 47.848 | = A. |
| .0256614 | 1 | 1 | 38.931 | = B. |
| .0367725 | 1 | 1 | 27.194 | = C. |
| .0089947 | 1 | 1 | 111.176 | = D. |

## QUESTION CCXI.

| s. d. Flem. | d. ſter. | d. Flem. | d. ſter. | |
|---|---|---|---|---|
| If 34 . 4 | 240 | 52 facit | 30$\frac{110}{212}$ |

| Rees. | d. | Rees. | d. |
|---|---|---|---|
| Then if 400 | 30$\frac{110}{212}$ | 1000 facit | 75$\frac{75}{101}$ |

## QUESTION CCXII.

$$7 \left\{ \begin{matrix} 9 \\ 8 \\ 6 \\ 5 \end{matrix} \right. \quad \begin{matrix} 2 \\ 1 \\ 1 \\ 2 \\ \hline 6 \end{matrix}$$

Cwt. lb.
1½ = 168

Then

Then if 6 —— 168 —— 2 facit 56 at 9 = 504 Proof.
      6 —— 168 = 1    28   8 = 224
      6 —— 168 = 1    28   6 = 168
      6 —— 168 —— 2    56   5 = 280

           168   2|0 ) 117|6
                £ 58 . 16

And 168 *l*. at 7*s*. = 2|0 ) 117|6 *s*.
         £ 58 . 16

## QUESTION CCXIII.

100 Reams at 10*s*. = £50     1600 Pamphlets at 6*d*. = £40
                                 12 . 10
       ¼ 12 . 10
                                 £27 . 10

      100 Reams at 8*s*. = £40 . —
        deduct   27 . 10

         £ 12 . 10 in B's favour.

## QUESTION CCXIV.

$\frac{2}{3}+\frac{1}{5} = \frac{10\times3}{15}$    402.
                 7

Then if 10 —— 2800 —— 3 facit 840 ÷ 5 = 168 = A.
And if 10 —— 2800 —— 2 facit 560 ÷ 8 = 70 = B.

## QUESTION CCXV.

$\frac{20-12}{20}$ = $\frac{8}{20}$ = $\frac{2}{5}$ or 5 to 2 against the Hare.

   *Seconds.*     *Feet.*     *Seconds.*    *Feet.*
Then if 3600 —— 63360 —— 34 facit $598\frac{4}{10}$
            Add for 5 Rods $82\frac{5}{10}$

           Feet   $680\frac{9}{10}$ = Ground run
       Then multiply by     5    before Dog's
                                   outfet.

         Divide by   2 ) $3404\frac{5}{10}$

        Feet   $1702\frac{6}{4}$ = Ground run
                         by the Dog.

   *M.*     *Feet.*      *Sec.*      *Feet.*      *Sec.*
Again fay if 20 or 105600 —— 3600 —— $10702\frac{1}{4}$ facit $58\frac{1}{32}$.

                                   QUES-

## Question CCXVI.

oz.    s.  d.      lb. oz.      £    s.  d.

If 1 ——— 7 . 2 ——— 140 . 11 facit 605 . 18 . 10

Then $\frac{1}{7}$ of £605 . 18 . 10 = £86 . 11 . $9\frac{1}{7}$ and £605 . 18 . 10 —
£86 . 11 . $3\frac{1}{7}$ = £519 . 7 . $6\frac{6}{7}$.

lb. of Tea.   s.  d.    Cwt. qr. lb.    £   s.

Then say, if 1 ——— 11 . 2 ——— 7 . 2 . 18 facit 479 . 1
and subtract £479 . 1 from £519 . 7 . $6\frac{6}{7}$ there remains £40 . 6 . $6\frac{6}{7}$
= Discount allowed. Now A gains 10d. $\oplus$ Ounce on his Plate,
therefore his whole Gain is £70 . 9 . 2, from this take the Discount
for $\frac{1}{7}$ of the Money, viz. £40 . 6 . $6\frac{6}{7}$ and there remains £30 . 2 .
$8\frac{1}{7}$ = A's neat Gain. Now B gains 20d. $\oplus$ lb. on his $85\frac{8}{10}$lb. of
Tea = £71 . 10, from this take A's Gain and the Remainder
£41 . 7 . $4\frac{6}{7}$ is the Advantage B has by the Bargain.

## Question CCXIX.

Hours from 10 o'Clock to 6 = 8 and at 2 Miles an Hour = 16
Miles, then from 130 take 16 remain 114 Miles, then $\frac{2}{5}$ of 114 =
$45\frac{3}{5}$ Miles, and this + 16 = $61\frac{3}{5}$ Miles from Exeter.

## Question CCXX.

Min.    Work.    Min.    Work.

If 44 ——— 1 ——— 1 facit $\frac{1}{44}$ } the Sum of these = $\frac{104}{2640}$.

If 60 ——— 1 ——— 1     $\frac{1}{60}$

Min.    Work.    Min.

Then if 30 ——— 1 ——— 1 facit $\frac{1}{30}$, and $\frac{104}{2640} - \frac{1}{30} = \frac{480}{79200}$
of the Work, then say

Work.    Min.    Work.

If $\frac{480}{79200}$ ——— 1 ——— $\frac{1}{3}$ facit $\frac{79200}{480}$ = 2 Hours 45 Minutes.

## Question CCXXI.

$\frac{100}{8} = 12\frac{1}{2}$ Miles, then $12\frac{1}{2} - 2\frac{1}{2} = 10$, and this $\div 2 = 5$
Miles an Hour travelled by B, whence $12\frac{1}{2} - 5 = 7\frac{1}{2}$ Miles travelled by A.

## Question CCXXIII.

Min.    Gall.    Min.

If 9 ——— 14 ——— 1 facit = $1\frac{5}{9}$ Gallon.

31 ——— 40 ——— 1     = $1\frac{9}{31}$ Gallon.

Then $\frac{14}{9} - \frac{40}{31} = \frac{74}{279}$ Gallon.

Min.    Gall.    Ho.  Min.    Gall.

Then if 1 ——— $\frac{74}{279}$ ——— 3 = 180 facit $47\frac{207}{279}$ of Water in the
Cistern at 5 o'Clock. Now the Tub holds 147 Gallons.

$47\frac{207}{279}$ in Tub at 5
———    o'Clock.

$99\frac{72}{279}$ Lost out of
———    the Tub.

Gal.    Min.    Gal.    Min. Sec.

Then if 14 ——— 9 ——— $99\frac{72}{279}$ facit 63 . 48, add this to 5
o'Clock and the Answer is 6 Hours 3 Minutes 48 Seconds.

Ques-

## Question CCXXIV.

M. M. M.          M. Ho. M.
$7\frac{1}{2} + 2\frac{1}{2} = 10$ in one Hour, then if $10 \longrightarrow 1 \longrightarrow 34$ facit $3\frac{2}{16}$
Then $7\frac{1}{2} \times 3\frac{2}{16} = 25\frac{1}{2}$ and $2\frac{1}{2} \times 3\frac{2}{16} = 8\frac{1}{2}$ Miles Anſwer.
For $25\frac{1}{2}$ Miles $+ 8\frac{1}{2}$ Miles $= 34$ Miles as before.

## Question CCXXV.

35 Feet $=$ Depth, 12 Feet $=$ A's ſet off, and $35 - 12 = 23$, then 23 Feet $- 100$ Inches $= 8\frac{1}{3} = 14\frac{2}{3}$ Feet.   Then ſay,

Inch.    Hour.    Feet.
If $\frac{11}{16} \longrightarrow 1 \longrightarrow 14\frac{2}{3}$ facit $\frac{2116}{13}$ Hour, and

Hour.    Feet.    Hour.    Inch.
If $\frac{2116}{13} \longrightarrow 26\frac{2}{3} \longrightarrow 1$ facit $1\frac{11}{13}$ inſtead of $1\frac{9}{11}$.

**N. B.** In a former Edition the Deſcent of A is $\frac{11}{16}$ Inch $\wp$ Hour, and then the Anſwer comes out $2\frac{4}{11}$ Inches.

## Question CCXXVII.

Sec.    Gal.    Sec.    Gal.
If 60 $\longrightarrow 3 \longrightarrow 1$ facit $\frac{1}{20}$ $\Big\}$ then $\frac{1}{20} + \frac{1}{25} = \frac{9}{100}$.
   75 $\longrightarrow 3 \longrightarrow 1$         $\frac{1}{25}$

Gal.    Sec.    Gal.    Min. Sec.
And if $\frac{9}{100} \longrightarrow 1 \longrightarrow 103$ facit 19 . $4\frac{4}{9}$ Anſwer.

## Question CCXXX.

A's Ground $= 182200$ Yards, B's $= 186200$, the common Difference is 4000 Yards, whence the reſt may be had by common Addition of 4000.   Now their Sums $= 2002000$.   Then ſay,

Yards.    £    Yards.    £    s.
If 2002000 $\longrightarrow 300 \longrightarrow 182200$ facit 27 . $6 + \frac{108}{2002} = $A's Mon.
                                       27 . $18 + \frac{108}{2002} = $B's.
Now the common Difference of their reſpective Shares being 12 *l.* the reſt may be eaſily had, and their Sum total amounts to £ 300. Then 182200 Yards $= 103$ Miles 4 Furlongs 40 Yards $=$ A's Journey, and B's $= 105$ Miles 6 Furlongs 80 Yards, now this common Difference being 2 Miles 2 Furlongs 40 Yards, the reſt may be eaſily obtained.     M.    F.
       Their Sum total is   1137 . 4
Subtract the Diſtance of York   720 . 0 $=$ twice and back.
                                  _____
                                  417 . 4

## Question CCXXXII.

Inches 13.5 cubed $= 2460.375$ and 7.5 cubed $= 421.875$ their Difference 2038.5   Then if $64 \longrightarrow 9 \longrightarrow 2038.5$ facit 286 *lb.* nearly.

## Question CCXXXIII.

7970 cubed $\div$ 2170 cubed $= 49.5446$.

## QUESTION CCXXXIV.

Say if $1\frac{1}{1}$ —— 2 —— 1 facit $\frac{2}{11}$ m.    Then $\frac{2}{11} - 1\frac{3}{17} = \frac{1}{187}$ Min.

And if 17 —— 3 —— 1 facit $\frac{3}{17}$

Then if 1 —— $\frac{1}{187}$ m.    $1\frac{1}{1}$ facit $\frac{11}{187}$ Mi.   Then again,

If $\frac{11}{187}$ of the Time —— 1 Round, how many in the whole time $= 1$ T.

Thus, As $\frac{11}{187} : \frac{1}{1} :: \frac{1}{1} : \frac{187}{11} = 17$ Times Round.

## QUESTION CCXXXV.

If 40 *Inches* —— 104 *Feet* —— 36 *Inches* facit 93.6 *Feet*.

And if 93.6 —— 13 —— 73 facit 10 .. 8 $\frac{1}{2}$.

## QUESTION CCXXXVI.

If 70 *Inches* —— 1064 *lb*. —— 2 *Inches* facit 30 $\frac{4}{16}$ *lb*.

## QUESTION CCXXXVII.

100 *In.* $= 7\frac{1}{2}$ *In.* $= 92\frac{1}{2}$ *Inches*. Then say, if $7\frac{1}{2}$ *In.* —— $1\frac{1}{2}$ *Cwt.* —— $92\frac{1}{2}$ *In.* facit 2072 *lb*.

## QUESTION CCXXXVIII.

To 448 *lb*. $=$ Weight of Passengers and Baggage

Add   70   $=$ Weight of the Vehicle

     518

Then say, if 11 *Feet* —— 518 *lb*. —— 30 *In.* facit $117\frac{9}{11}$ *lb*.

And again, if 11 —— 518 —— 24 facit $94\frac{2}{11}$

## QUESTION CCXXXIX.

From 100 *In.* take $7\frac{1}{2}$ *In.* remain $92\frac{1}{2}$ *Inches*. Then the Ratio will be as $92\frac{1}{2}$ is to $7\frac{1}{2}$ reduced $= \frac{10}{15} = \frac{3}{37}$ or as 37 to 3.

## QUESTION CCXL.

From 9 *Feet* take 6 *Feet* remains 3, and this $\times$ by 9 *In.* $= 27$ *Inches*.

## QUESTION CCXLI.

$62\frac{1}{2}$ *lb*. $\times \frac{9}{2} = 281\frac{1}{4}$ *lb*.

## QUESTION CCXLII.

*lb.*                      *lb.*

$1 . 5 \times 12$ *Inches* $= 18$ *lb*. and $1 .. 5 \times 28$ *Inches* $= 42$ *lb*.

Then 42 *lb*. — 18 *lb*. $= 24$ *lb*.

B 4                      QUES-

### Question CCXLIII.

$$\frac{81\ \square\ (Mill.)}{2} = 3280.5 \text{ then } \square\ \sqrt{3280.5} \text{ \&c.} = 57275650\ Miles.$$

### Question CCXLIV.

$$115\ \square = 13225 \text{ Degrees.}$$

### Question CCXLV.

$$\frac{81\ \square}{424\ \square} = \tfrac{1}{27} \text{ of the Earth's Light.}$$

### Question CCXLVI.

$$\frac{32\ \square}{777\ \square} = \text{the Proportion } 1024 \text{ to } 603729$$

### Question CCXLVII.

$$112 \times \overline{10\ \square}\ (lb.) = 11.2 \text{ then } \square\ \sqrt{11.2} = 3.3466 \text{ femidiameters}$$
from the Earth's Centre.

### Question CCXLVIII.

$$\frac{3985\ \square \times 16}{3985 + 50\ \square} = 15.9\ (oz.\ drs.)\ \frac{11312575}{16281225}$$

### Question CCXLIX.

$$\frac{\overline{7970}^{\,3} \times 100}{\overline{2170}^{\,3} \times 123\frac{1}{4}} = 40\,\tfrac{117}{1080} \text{ Times more Mattter contained in the}$$
Earth than in the Moon.

### Question CCL.

At the New Moon the enlightened Hemifphere will be more diftant from the Earth than its mean Diftance by the Moon's Semidiameter.

### Question CCLI.

$$4.63 - 1.5688 = 30611 \times 1728 = \text{Cub. In.} \times 1\tfrac{1}{2}\ Foot.$$
$$2592 = 7931.52\,oz. = 4\,Cwt.\ 1\,qr.\ 19\,lb.$$

### Question CCLV.

$$16 \times 6\ \square\ (Feet) = 576 \text{ and } 16 \times \text{to } \square = 1600 \text{ their Difference is } 1024$$

### Question CCLVI.

$$\frac{16 \times \overline{19.5\ \square}\ (Feet)}{6} = 1014.$$

Que

## Question CCLVII.

As 16 : 1 □ :: 400 : 25 its $\sqrt{}$ is 5 Seconds.

## Question CCLVIII.

$$\text{As } 16 : 1 \square :: 3923 \times 5000 : \frac{19615000}{16} = \sqrt{1225937} = 1107 = 18.27\frac{488}{2207}$$

Min. Sec.

## Question CCLXIII.

First, Sec. 60 □ = 3600. Then say ℞ Quest. CCLIX.

In.  Sec.  In.  Sec.  Vib.  M.  Vib. M.  Se.

As 39.2 : 3600 :: 18 : 88.5  Then as 88.5 : 1 :: 8 : $\frac{1}{11} = 5$ ferè then ℞ Quest. CCLVII. 5 Sec. = 400 Feet, the Heighth of Salisbury Steeple.

N. B. *The Questions in* Recreation XVIII. *respecting Annuities, may be more readily answered by a Table of Logarithms, or by my* COMPLETE ANNUITANT.

## Question CCLXXIX.

$\frac{2}{3}$ of $\frac{1000000}{1} = 66666\frac{2}{3}$.

## Question CCLXXXI.

By the Rule of Three Indirect, say,

lb.  Feet  lb.
If 20 —— 100 —— 8 facit $\frac{100 \times 20}{8} = 250$ Feet.

## Question CCLXXXII.

lb.  I.  lb.
If 60 —— 8 —— 100 facit $\frac{40}{3}$ or 3 to 40.

## Question CCLXXXIII.

$\frac{3}{48} = \frac{1}{8} = 6$ to 1.

## Question CCLXXXIV.

2 Hours = 120 Min. facit $\frac{120}{40} = 1$ to 3.

## Question CCLXXXV.

$30 \times 12 = 360$, and $360 \times \frac{60}{12} = 1800$ Feet, subtract 60 Inches $= 5$ Feet, remain 1795 Feet.

## Question CCLXXXVI.

$5 \times 5 = 25$, now 25 is the $\frac{1}{2}$ of 50, therefore their Ratio is 2 to 1.

QUES-

## QUESTION CCLXXXVII.

If $1 \overset{\text{C.Inch}}{\longrightarrow} 10 \overset{\text{oz.}}{\longrightarrow} 9 \overset{\text{C.In.}}{}$ facit 90 Ounces in Air.

If $1 \overset{\text{C.In.}}{\longrightarrow} 256 \overset{\text{gra.}}{\longrightarrow} 9 \overset{\text{C.In.}}{\longrightarrow} \overset{\text{oz. dwts.}}{}$ facit 4.16 then from 90 take 4.16 Remains 85 oz. 4 dwts.

## QUESTION CCXCI.

If $10.36 \overset{\text{oz.Gold}}{\longrightarrow} 1 \overset{\text{C.I.}}{\longrightarrow} 63 \overset{\text{oz.}}{}$ facit 6.081 $\overset{\text{C.I.}}{}$

If $5.85 \overset{\text{oz.}}{}$ of Silv. $\longrightarrow 1 \overset{\text{C.I.}}{\longrightarrow} 63$ facit 10.77 Cub. In.

Then say $\psi$ Alligation $\begin{array}{c} \text{C.I.} \\ 8 \quad 2245 \end{array}$ $\begin{array}{|c|} 6.081 \\ 10.77 \end{array}$ $\begin{array}{|c|} \overset{\text{C.I.}}{} \\ 2.5455 \text{ Gold} \\ 2.1435 \text{ Silver} \\ \hline 4.6890 \end{array}$

Then if $4.689 \overset{\text{C.I.}}{\longrightarrow} 63 \overset{\text{oz.}}{\longrightarrow} 2.4555 \overset{\text{C.I.}}{}$ facit 34.$\frac{1}{10}$ Ounces.

And if $4.689 \longrightarrow 63 \longrightarrow 2.1435$ facit $28\frac{1}{10}$ Oz. of Silver.

## QUESTION CCXCIII.

$3.5 \overset{\text{oz.}}{=}$ Weight of the Glass Bottle.

By $\dfrac{12}{42}$. and $\dfrac{42}{1.36} = 30.88235$ Cubic Inches in the Bottle.

$231 \cdots = $ Ditto in the Brandy.

$\overline{261.88235} = $ Ditto in both.

Then $261.88235 \times$ by $5427 = 142.1236 = $ Weight of Salt Water occupied by the Bottle and Brandy. Then $.48926 = $ Weight of a Cubic Inch of Brandy $\times 231 = $ Cubic Inches in Gallon produce $113.02$ ferè $\overset{\text{oz.}}{=}$ Weight of Brandy, add to this the Weight of the Bottle facit $155.02 \overset{\text{oz.}}{=}$ Weight of both. Then from this take the Weight of the Salt Water leaves $12.896 \overset{\text{oz.}}{}$ the Answer, supposing the Bottle full.

## QUESTION CCXCV.

$216 = $ Gallons in a Tun, this $\times$ by $1300$ Tuns, produce $280800$ Gallons; this Product $\times 282$ Cub. Inches facit $79185600$ Cubic Inches, and this $\times$ by $5949$ facit $47107513,44$ Ounces $=$ $26287 . 2 . 19 . 9.$ $\overset{\text{C. gr. lb. oz.}}{}$

QUES-

## QUESTION CCCXIX.

## QUESTION CCCXX.

## QUESTION CCCXXI.

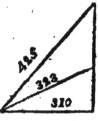

## QUESTION CCCXXII.

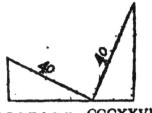

## QUESTION CCCXXVII.

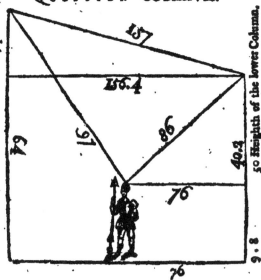

QUESTION CCCXXIII.

$$\sqrt{\frac{125}{3}\bigg|^{2} - \frac{125}{4}\bigg|^{2}} = 36.07 = \text{the Perpendicular, then } 41.666 =$$

one of the Sides or Base $\times$ by $\frac{1}{2}$ the Perpendicular $18.035$ gives $752$ nearly,

QUESTION CCCXXIV.

If $18 \text{——} 1 \text{——} 24000$ facit $1333\frac{1}{3}$ Feet $=$ Area. Then here are the Base and Area of an Isocelas Triangle given to find the other Sides; now $\dfrac{1333\frac{1}{3}}{44} = 30.303 = $ Perpendicular

$\therefore \sqrt{44|^{2}+30.303|^{2}} = 53.4$ &c. either of the Sides; then $53.4$ &c. $\times 2 = 106.85 = $ the Sum of the Two equal Sides.

QUESTION CCCXXVIII.

$$A \qquad B$$

The Area of $A\ 4\frac{1}{2}$ to $8 = 9$ to $16$. Then $A+C : B$ as $17$ to $8 = 36$ to $16$. Whence $A = 9$, $B = 16$ and $C = 25$; then the Sum of the Sides $= 50$, and the $\sqrt{9} = 3 = A$, $\sqrt{16} = 4 = B$, and the $\sqrt{25} = 5 = C$. Whence the Area of the Triangle may be easily found $= 6$ Poles, and these $\times 272\frac{1}{4} = $ the $\square$ Feet in a Pole; and then $\times$ Depth 6 Inches and this last Product $\times 1728$ Cubic Inches, and $\div 231$ solid Inches, and then reduced by 63

$$Hhds. \quad Gall.$$

Gallons, facit $1163 . 47\frac{1}{2}$.

QUESTION CCCXXXIV.

$42 + 14.5 = 56 . \times \frac{22}{7} = 177.7$ and $177.7 \times 145 = 2576.65$

$$In. \quad Feet \qquad Feet \qquad\qquad\qquad s. \quad d.$$

and this $\div 144 = 17.89$, and $17.89$ at $8d.$ $\mathcal{H}$ Foot, facit $11.11$.

QUESTION CCCXXXV.

$3.25\square \times .7854 = 8.29$ &c. Then $\sqrt{8}.29 = 2.88$ and the $\sqrt{2}.88 = 1.7$ then $5 \square \div 1.7 = 14.69$ Inches.

QUESTION CCCXXXVI.

The Hole through which the Spindle past was 5 Inches Square, which call, $A\ B\ C\ D$, then to find the Diagonal say,

$\sqrt{B C|^{2} + C D|^{2}} = \sqrt{B D|^{2}} = 7.071$. Then $36\square = 1296$.

Then deduct for the Spindle 50, and remains 1246. Then say

$$s. \qquad Sq. In. \qquad s.$$

by the Rule of Three, If $20 \text{——} 1246 \text{——} 13$ facit $809.9$. Then $809.9 + 50 = 859.9$ and the $\sqrt{859}.9 = 29.324$ Inches

$$s. \qquad In. \qquad s. \qquad In.$$

for $B$. Then for $C$ say, If $20 \text{——} 1246 \text{——} 5$ facit $311.5$ then $+ 50 = 361.5$ Inches; then $\sqrt{361}.5 = 19.013 = C$.

*Observation on* QUESTION CCCXXXVII.

According to the indubitable Principles of Geometry, there can only be one Square inscribed in a Circle, and one Square circumscribing it, hence there is no greatest and least.

## QUESTION CCCXL.

The greater Diameter being 20 Feet, and this multiplied by 3.1416, the Circumference of that Circle, whose Diameter is 1, facit 62.832 Feet.

## QUESTION CCCXLI.

63 Feet = 21 Yards, its $\frac{1}{2}$ = 10.5 Yards, this × by 30 = the Semidiameter of the Circle, facit 315 Yards.

## In QUESTION CCCXLIV.

As 4:7 $\square$ :: 11.46 : $\dfrac{49 \times 40}{4}$ = : $\sqrt{\dfrac{49 \times 40}{4}}$ = 22.136 Inches.

## QUESTION CCCXLVII.

*Inch*
1.25 $\square$ = 1.5625 and this × 20 = 31.25 Feet.
.875 $\square$ = .765625       × 50 = 38.28125 Feet.

Then say, If 31.25 *Feet* —— 1120 *lb.* —— 38.28125 *Feet* facit £ 20.

## QUESTION CCCL.

*Feet*                *Feet*                          *Cub. Inches*
64. × .03125 = 2.009375, and this × 1728 = 3472.2

*C. Inch*  *oz.*          *C. Inches*              *oz.*
Then if 1 —— $4\frac{3}{11}$ —— 3472.2 facit 15151.5.   Then if 34944 *oz.* —— £21 —— 15151.5 *oz.* facit £ 9.2.1.

## QUESTION CCCLIV.

*Feet*   *Feet*   *Feet*        *Feet*
112.5 × 32 = 3600, and this × 5.5 = 19800 solid Feet.

*Feet* *Feet*       *Feet*        *Feet In.*
Then deduct for the Gang-way 112.5 × 5.5 × 4.5 = 2784.4$\frac{1}{4}$.

*Feet In.*
remain 17015.7$\frac{3}{4}$. Then find the solid Content of a Bale of 

*Feet In.*                      *Feet In.*         *Feet In.*
Goods. Thus 3.4 by 3 Feet deep, and 2.4 broad = 23.4 

*Feet In.*   *Feet In.*
solid. Then 17015.7$\frac{3}{4}$ ÷ 23.4 = 729$\frac{1}{4}$ Bales nearly.

QUES-

### QUESTION CCCLV.

| lb. | Feet | lb. | Feet | | Feet | Feet |
|---|---|---|---|---|---|---|

Say, if $16 - 1\square - 2184$ facit $136.5$, then $4.25 \times 8 = 34$ Feet, and $136.5 \div 34 = 4.014706 =$ Depth. Then from this take .0625, remain 3.952206 this $\dfrac{\times 34 \times 1728 \text{ solid Inches will}}{231 \times 63}$

*Hbds. Gall.*
give 16 . 40.

### QUESTION CCCLXI.

Remark, it must be cut off perpendicular to the Axis.

### QUESTION CCCLXII.

$1.25$ cubed $\times .7854 = 1.2272$ and $\dfrac{231 \text{ Cubic Inch.}}{8 \text{ Pints}} = 28.875$

*Inches*
and this $\div 1.2272 = 23.5294$.

### QUESTION CCCLXV.

True Proportion, as .6168 to .7854, or as 1 to 1.273.

### QUESTION CCCLXVII.

*Miles*
2170 cubed, and this Product $\times$ by Cubic Inches in a Mile, and this last Product $\times .5236$ (being $\frac{2}{3}$ of .7854) and this last Product $\div 17203.2$ (the Cubic Inches in a Quarter) gives the Answer 791070349484701.44000 Quarters. Then to find what Quantity of Yard-wide Stuff will make her a Jacket, the Rectangle of the Number of Yards in her Diameter and Circumference give .45824284391424.

### QUESTION CCCLXVIII.

Is performed much after the same manner, only remember to add 120 for the Height of the Atmosphere to the Earth's Diameter, then proceed with Care and Patience.

### QUESTION CCCLXX.

Or use this Analogy, as the Difference of the Diameters 18 is to 42 the Depth :: 72 Great. Diam. : $\dfrac{42 \times 72}{18} = 168$ the whole Altitude. *N. B.* This Rule is general for every strait-sided Solid, whose Ends are parallel and similar.

### QUESTION CCCLXXV.

Find the Area of the Diameter 21, thus $21\square \times .7854 = 346.3614$ this $\times$ the Length 31 $= 10737.2034$, and this last Product $\times 1728$ the Cubic Inches in a Foot, and $\div 231$ Quotes 80319 Gallons $=$
*Tuns Gall.*
318 . 183 &c.

## *F I N I S.*

www.ingramcontent.com/pod-product-compliance
Lightning Source LLC
Chambersburg PA
CBHW080411060326
40689CB00019B/4205